VARIETIES OF
MONASTIC EXPERIENCE
IN BYZANTIUM, 800–1453

MEDIEVAL INSTITUTE
UNIVERSITY OF NOTRE DAME

The Conway Lectures in Medieval Studies 2014

The Medieval Institute gratefully acknowledges the generosity of Robert M. Conway and his support for the lecture series and the publications resulting from it.

PREVIOUS TITLES PUBLISHED IN THIS SERIES:

Paul Strohm
Politique: Languages of Statecraft between Chaucer and Shakespeare (2005)

Ulrich Horst, O.P.
The Dominicans and the Pope: Papal Teaching Authority in the Medieval and Early Modern Thomist Tradition (2006)

Rosamond McKitterick
Perceptions of the Past in the Early Middle Ages (2006)

Jonathan Riley-Smith
Templars and Hospitallers as Professed Religious in the Holy Land (2010)

A. C. Spearing
Medieval Autographies: The "I" of the Text (2012)

Barbara Newman
Medieval Crossover: Reading the Secular against the Sacred (2013)

John Marenbon
Abelard in Four Dimensions: A Twelfth-Century Philosopher in His Context and Ours (2013)

Sylvia Huot
Outsiders: The Humanity and Inhumanity of Giants in Medieval French Prose Romance (2016)

William J. Courtenay
Rituals for the Dead: Religion and Community in the Medieval University of Paris (2019)

ALICE-MARY TALBOT

VARIETIES OF MONASTIC EXPERIENCE IN BYZANTIUM, 800–1453

UNIVERSITY OF NOTRE DAME PRESS

NOTRE DAME, INDIANA

Copyright © 2019 by the University of Notre Dame Press
Notre Dame, Indiana 46556
www.undpress.nd.edu
All Rights Reserved

Published in the United States of America

Library of Congress Cataloging-in-Publication Data

Names: Talbot, Alice-Mary Maffry, author.
Title: Varieties of monastic experience in Byzantium, 800–1453 / Alice-Mary Talbot.
Description: Notre Dame : University of Notre Dame Press, 2019. | Series: The Conway Lectures in medieval studies, 2014 | Includes bibliographical references and index. |
Identifiers: LCCN 2019002371 (print) | LCCN 2019006928 (ebook) | ISBN 9780268105648 (pdf) | ISBN 9780268105631 (epub) | ISBN 9780268105617 (hardback : alk. paper) | ISBN 0268105618 (hardback : alk. paper) | ISBN 9780268105624 (pbk. : alk. paper) | ISBN 0268105626 (pbk. : alk. paper)
Subjects: LCSH: Monastic and religious life—Byzantine Empire. | Byzantine Empire—Church history.
Classification: LCC BX2435 (ebook) | LCC BX2435 .T35 2019 (print) | DDC 271/.81909495—dc23
LC record available at https://lccn.loc.gov/2019002371

∞ This paper meets the requirements of ANSI/NISO Z39.48-1992
(Permanence of Paper).

CONTENTS

List of Illustrations   vii
Preface   ix
Abbreviations   xiii

Introduction   1

ONE   Monks and Male Monastic Communities   15

TWO   Nuns and Nunneries   53

THREE   Hermits and Holy Mountains   101

FOUR   Alternative Modes of Monasticism   133

Conclusion   189

Glossary   199
Notes   201
Bibliography   257
Index   283

LIST OF ILLUSTRATIONS

FIGURE 1
Theodore of Stoudios, eleventh-century mosaic, Nea Moni, Chios (photo: Image Collection and Fieldwork Archives, Dumbarton Oaks, Trustees for Harvard University, Washington, DC)   17

FIGURE 2
Katholikon at the Great Lavra, Mount Athos (photo: Robert Ousterhout, Image Collection and Fieldwork Archives, Dumbarton Oaks, Trustees for Harvard University, Washington, DC)   25

FIGURE 3
Athanasios of Athos, fresco from Protaton, Mount Athos (photo: Miodrag Marković, Image Collection and Fieldwork Archives, Dumbarton Oaks, Trustees for Harvard University, Washington, DC)   27

FIGURE 4
Church of the Lips convent, Fenari Isa Camii (photo: Image Collection and Fieldwork Archives, Dumbarton Oaks, Trustees for Harvard University, Washington, DC)   57

FIGURE 5
Lincoln College Typikon (Lincoln College gr. 35), fol. 12^r: group portrait of nuns from convent of Sure Hope (photo: By permission of the Rector and Fellows of Lincoln College, Oxford)   61

FIGURE 6
Lincoln College Typikon (Lincoln College gr. 35), fol. 11ʳ:
Theodora Synadene with her daughter Euphrosyne
(photo: By permission of the Rector and Fellows
of Lincoln College, Oxford)   62

FIGURE 7
Portrait of Maximos the Hutburner from *vita* by Ioannikios
Kochylas, Vatopedi 470, fol. 1ʳ (photo: Patriarchal Institute
of Patristic Studies, Mone Vlatadon, Thessalonike)   110

FIGURE 8
The hermitages of Saints Gregory and Anthony,
close to *skete* of St. Nicholas of Badova. Meteora, Greece.
(photo: Hercules Milas / Alamy Stock Photo)   114

FIGURE 9
Cell of Neophytos the Recluse at his monastery near Paphos
(photo: Image Collection and Fieldwork Archives, Dumbarton
Oaks, Trustees for Harvard University, Washington, DC)   141

FIGURE 10
Luke the Stylite from Menologion of Basil II (Vaticanus gr. 1613),
p. 238 (photo: ©Biblioteca Apostolica Vaticana)   151

PREFACE

The theme of this book is the variety of monastic experiences in Byzantium, the many ways in which pious men and women renounced the secular world in order to devote their lives to prayer and the service of Christ. The most basic division between monastics was their choice of the communal life in a cenobitic monastery or a solitary existence as a hermit (eremitic). Many monks espoused both forms of monasticism sequentially during the course of their careers, and there was much discussion in monastic circles about which form of spiritual life was superior. A monastic founder of the early fifteenth century, the patriarch Matthew I (1397–1402, 1403–10), commented, "There are many paths of piety for athletes, since our heavenly Father also has 'many mansions,' or rather, since there are many paths, there are also many mansions."[1]

This book is not intended to be an overall survey of the history of Byzantine monasticism. I have more modest aims here: a typological overview that outlines the varied forms that the Byzantine monastic experience could take, and an examination of the special phenomenon of the Byzantine holy mountain, inhabited by both cenobitic monks and hermits. I emphasize the lifestyle experienced in various monastic environments rather than the differences in structure, organization, and patronage among imperial, patriarchal, and private monasteries (though I do mention this). I also discuss differences between urban and rural monasticism, and between male and female monasteries, and describe unusual institutions, such as double and idiorrhythmic monasteries, and monastic houses restricted to eunuchs. Finally, I investigate those who chose alternative lifestyles: wandering monks, transvestite nuns, holy fools, recluses, stylites, and the shadowy figures of quasi-autonomous monks and nuns who lived in a city or village outside the confines of a monastery and the authority of a superior, sometimes in their own or others' homes. I cover the ninth to fifteenth centuries and with rare exceptions focus on the heartlands of the middle and late Byzantine Empire, Greece and Anatolia, with occasional forays into Italo-Greek monasticism.

It is somewhat surprising that no book-length synthetic overview of Byzantine monasticism exists in any language. So far, Peter Hatlie has been the only scholar brave enough to attempt to meet this need. In 2007, he published *The Monks and Monasteries of Constantinople, ca. 350–850*, but it is limited in geographical scope to the imperial capital and covers only the first half of the history of the empire. He has announced a sequel, *Byzantine Monasticism, ca. 850–1450*, which promises to expand its geographical coverage beyond Constantinople. The time is now ripe for such a publication, since many of the primary sources on monasticism have been made accessible in recent decades through exemplary editions and translations. I am referring, for example, to the splendid series of the Archives de l'Athos, which is publishing the surviving documents from twenty Athonite monasteries—to date twenty-two volumes have appeared—and to the five-volume collection of monastic foundation rules in translation published by Dumbarton Oaks in 2000, *Byzantine Monastic Foundation Documents*. Also essential are the reference works prepared by the Assumptionist Fathers in Paris, such as Raymond Janin's monumental tomes on the monasteries and churches of Constantinople and the provinces, and the *Regestes* of the patriarchal acts edited by Venance Grumel, Vitalien Laurent, and Jean Darrouzès. The other indispensable sources for this study are the numerous saints' lives published over many years in Brussels by the Bollandists in the *Acta Sanctorum*, *Analecta Bollandiana*, and volumes of the Subsidia Hagiographica. These have been supplemented in recent years by a spate of English translations of Byzantine hagiographical texts in different series.

I have long had an interest in Byzantine monasticism, especially in convents for nuns, and in the tensions between the communal regimen of the cenobitic monastery and the solitary life of the hermit; as a result, much of my scholarship has involved the editing and translation of texts relating to monastic rules and the lives of monks and nuns. Thus, in 2011 when I was invited by the late and lamented Olivia Remie Constable to deliver the 2014 Conway Lectures at the University of Notre Dame, I thought the time was right to focus on the forms of Byzantine monasticism that prevailed during the second half of the Byzantine Empire, approximately 800–1453. The three lectures I delivered—on cenobitic monks, nuns, and hermits—have been revised and expanded and make up the first three chapters of this book, to which I have added a fourth chapter on alternative forms of monasticism. I also include an introduction that briefly sketches out the origins and history of monastic institutions in the Byzantine world. Because I hope that a book published in the Conway Lecture Series will attract an audience of Western medievalists and of Byzantinists, wherever possible I have referenced primary sources available in English translation, but have also included citations of the original Greek texts in the footnotes. For texts available only in Greek, I have provided my own translations.

Sadly, by the time I visited Notre Dame in the fall of 2014, Remie had suffered an untimely death, but I was warmly hosted by John van Engen, who took over her duties as director of the Medieval Institute and ensured that my stay on campus was enjoyable and stimulating. I am also grateful to Roberta Baranowski, associate director of the Medieval Institute, who took care of all the practical arrangements, and, among others, to Thomas Noble, Alexis Torrance, Susan Sheridan, and Charles Yost, all of whom warmly welcomed me to the university.

In the preparation of this book I have greatly benefited from insights into contemporary Orthodox monasticism on Mount Athos provided by Father Maximos Constas of Simonopetra and Father Damaskenos of Xenophontos (Jaakko Olkinuora), and I thank them for the information they have so kindly provided. I am particularly grateful to Nathanael Aschenbrenner, a Tyler fellow at Dumbarton Oaks from 2015 to 2017, who generously offered to review a first draft of this work and made many insightful suggestions for improvement. I should also like to thank the anonymous peer reviewers and my editor at the University of Notre Dame Press, Stephen Little, and copyeditor Scott Barker. Konstantina Karterouli, postdoctoral fellow in Byzantine art history at Dumbarton Oaks' Image Collections and Fieldwork Archives, provided generous assistance in identifying appropriate photos for this book and furnished digital images. Robert Ousterhout and Miodrag Marković graciously provided permission for me to reproduce their photographs.

Finally, I should like to acknowledge my debt to the late Alexander Kazhdan, my mentor, colleague, and friend for almost twenty years at Dumbarton Oaks until his death in 1997. During our long years of association and collaboration, I learned much from him about Byzantine hagiography, and I was introduced to his theories on the role of individualism in Byzantine society. His ideas have greatly influenced the direction of my research into Byzantine monasticism, and I should like to dedicate this book to his memory.

ABBREVIATIONS

AASS = *Acta Sanctorum*, 71 vols. (Paris: Victor Palme, 1863–1940)

BHG = *Bibliotheca hagiographica graeca*, 3rd ed., ed. François Halkin (Brussels: Société des Bollandistes, 1957)

BMFD = *Byzantine Monastic Foundation Documents*, ed. John P. Thomas and Angela C. Hero, 5 vols. (Washington, DC: Dumbarton Oaks, 2000)

CIC = *Corpus iuris civilis*, ed. Paul Krueger, Theodor Mommsen, et al., 3 vols. (Berlin: Weidmann, 1928–1929)

CPG = *Corpus paroemiographorum Graecorum*, ed. Ernst L. von Leutsch and Friedrich G. Schneidewin, 2 vols. (Göttingen: Vandenhoeck et Ruprecht, 1839–1851, reprint, Hildesheim: G. Olms, 1965)

Janin, *Constantinople byzantine* = Raymond Janin, *Constantinople byzantine: Développement urbain et répertoire topographique* (Paris: Institut français d'études byzantines, 1964)

Janin, *Eglises CP* = Raymond Janin, *La géographie ecclésiastique de l'empire byzantin. I. Le siège de Constantinople et le patriarcat oecuménique. III. Les églises et les monastères* (Paris: Institut français d'études byzantines, 1969)

Janin, *Grands centres* = Raymond Janin, *Les églises et les monastères des grands centres byzantins* (Paris: Institut français d'études byzantines, 1975)

LbG = *Lexikon zur byzantinischen Gräzität, besonders des 9.–12. Jahrhunderts*, ed. Erich Trapp et al., 8 fasc. (Vienna: Verlag der Österreichischen Akademie der Wissenschaften, 1994–2017)

MM = *Acta et diplomata graeca medii aevi sacra et profana*, ed. Franz Miklosich and Joseph Müller, 6 vols. (Vienna: C. Gerold, 1860–1890)

ODB = *Oxford Dictionary of Byzantium*, ed. Alexander P. Kazhdan et al., 3 vols. (New York: Oxford University Press, 1991)

PG = *Patrologiae cursus completus, series Graeca*, ed. Jacques-Paul Migne, 161 vols. (Paris: Migne, 1857–1866)

PGL = *A Patristic Greek Lexicon*, ed. G. W. H. Lampe (Oxford: Clarendon, 1961)

PLP = *Prosopographisches Lexikon der Palaiologenzeit*, ed. Erich Trapp, 12 vols. (Vienna: Verlag der Österreichischen Akademie der Wissenschaften, 1976–1996)

PmbZ = *Prosopographie der mittelbyzantinischen Zeit*, ed. Ralph-Johannes Lilie et al., series 1, 6 vols., series 2, 9 vols. (Berlin: De Gruyter, 1998–2013)

RegPatr = *Les regestes des actes du Patriarcat de Constantinople*, ed. Venance Grumel, Vitalien Laurent, and Jean Darrouzès, 7 fasc. (Istanbul: Socii Assumptionistae Chalcedonenses; Paris: Institut français d'études byzantines, 1932–1991)

RPK = *Das Register des Patriarchats von Konstantinopel*, ed. Herbert Hunger, Otto Kresten, et al. (Vienna: Verlag der Österreichischen Akademie der Wissenschaften, 1981–)

SynaxCP = *Synaxarium ecclesiae Constantinopolitanae: Propylaeum ad Acta Sanctorum Novembris*, ed. Hippolyte Delehaye (Brussels: Société des Bollandistes, 1902)

INTRODUCTION

Monasticism was an essential feature of Byzantine civilization throughout the eleven centuries of its empire, centered in the new Christian capital of Constantinople, founded in 330 by Emperor Constantine I (r. 306–37). Monasteries were established to provide a community where especially devout Byzantines might seclude themselves from the secular world to pray for their own salvation and that of their fellow Christians. Monks served as spiritual fathers to local laypeople who attended the liturgy at the monastery and who, if they became institutional benefactors, might be buried in the main church and commemorated in annual services on the anniversary of their death. Monastic institutions played a prominent role in cities, where they carried out social services in addition to their spiritual function, and in the countryside, where their vast estates were a key element in the agricultural economy of the empire. Some Byzantines took vows as teenagers and spent almost their entire lives in the cloister, while others retired to monasteries in the final phases of life, most often after the death of a spouse. Some monasteries were small and poor, others very large and well-endowed, able to support artistic and intellectual activities, such as icon painting, copying of manuscripts, and the composition of hymns, saints' lives, and theological treatises.

2 MONASTIC EXPERIENCE IN BYZANTIUM

THE ORIGINS OF MONASTICISM

The term "monasticism" is derived from the Greek word *monazein*, meaning "to live alone." Christian monasticism began in the eastern Mediterranean in the late third century, in the deserts of Egypt where devout believers, such as St. Anthony the Great (ca. 251–356) and Paul the First Hermit (d. ca. 341), withdrew from the world to lead a life of solitary prayer and asceticism, often termed "eremitism" from the Greek word *eremos*, meaning "desert, wilderness," or "anchoritism," from the Greek word *anachoresis*, meaning "withdrawal, retirement from the world." As these hermits attracted disciples, cenobitic monasteries for men and women were established, from the fourth century on, with a superior to whom the monks and nuns owed absolute obedience. The term "cenobitic" derives from the Greek words *koinos bios*, meaning "common/communal life," and it refers to monks and nuns who lived in a community under the leadership of an abbot rather than as solitaries. In Upper Egypt was founded the Pachomian federation of both male and female monasteries, with a rule attributed to the Coptic monastic leader Pachomios, who died in 346. In the late fourth and first half of the fifth century appeared the dominant figure of Abbot Shenoute (ca. 350–466), who expanded the White Monastery near Sohag into an enormous complex housing more than 2,000 monks and 1,800 nuns.

Meanwhile, Basil of Caesarea (ca. 329–79), one of the so-called Cappadocian fathers, was promoting cenobitic monasticism in Anatolia, in present-day Turkey; in the 360s or 370s he composed two sets of general rules, preserved in a longer and shorter version.[1] Also in the fourth century, monasteries began to be founded in Palestine, where the archaeological remains of numerous urban and rural complexes have been surveyed or excavated; a number of the sites have been identified as convents.[2] Monasticism was somewhat slower to establish itself in Syria, which was to become celebrated for the extreme asceticism of the stylites, or pillar saints, who lived atop columns.[3] One of the most well-known stylites was Symeon

Stylite the Elder, who stood on his column at Qal'at Sem'ān, not far from Antioch, for many years until his death in 459.

Yet another type of foundation with Egyptian origins developed in Greater Syria, the *lavra*, which combined features of eremitic and cenobitic life. An example is the famed *lavra* of St. Sabas (Mar Saba) near Jerusalem, founded in the late fifth century.[4] *Lavrai* typically had a group of dispersed monastic cells, often caves in a nearby cliff face, associated with a central complex housing a church, refectory, common hall, and outbuildings. Lavriot monks resided in their individual scattered cells during the week but owed obedience to a common superior. They would return to the *lavra* on weekends to attend the liturgy, dine in the refectory, and pick up food provisions and raw materials for handwork for the coming week.

Monasticism also began to spread to Constantinople in the second half of the fourth century, and numerous institutions had been founded by the mid-fifth century.[5] Gilbert Dagron has estimated that by the time of the Council of Chalcedon in 451 there were 10,000 to 15,000 monks in the region of the capital.[6] A century later, under the rule of Justinian I (r. 527–65), there were almost seventy monasteries in the city itself, and many more in its suburbs, thirty-nine, for example, in Chalcedon on the Asian shore of the Bosporos.[7] The foundation of monasteries in mainland Greece and the southern Balkans occurred much more slowly.

The fifth century also saw the appearance of the first holy mountains in Anatolia.[8] Such mountains were particularly attractive to hermits, but they also featured one or more cenobitic monasteries.[9] Mount St. Auxentios, on a hill southeast of Chalcedon, took its name from a Syrian monk named Auxentios (d. ca. 470), who spent the last twenty years of his life as a hermit in a cave on the mountain. It later attracted other solitaries, and a nunnery was founded there around 460, followed much later by the monastery of St. Stephen the Younger, a monk allegedly martyred for his support of icon veneration in 765.[10] Bithynian Mount Olympos, near Prousa (to be distinguished from its more famous namesake in Thessaly), also attracted hermits in late antiquity. At least one monastery is attested in the region in the fifth century, but it was most active as a monastic center during the eighth to tenth centuries; its monks were celebrated for their opposition to iconoclasm, that is, the rejection of image veneration.[11] Other holy mountains appeared in Anatolia in the eighth century (Latros, near Miletos), tenth century (Kyminas, in Bithynia), and eleventh century (Galesion, near Ephesos), while Athos in Macedonia was first settled by hermits in the ninth century; cenobitic monasteries began to appear there in the tenth century.[12]

In late antiquity, monasticism spread to Western Europe through the agency of such intermediaries as John Cassian (d. after 432), a monk of Scythian origin who received his monastic training in Palestine and Egypt and then moved west in the early fifth century to found two monasteries in Provence. His writings in Latin introduced into Western Europe accounts of monastic life in the eastern Mediterranean world. St. Benedict of Nursia (480–543/47), founder of numerous Italian monasteries, including Monte Cassino, south of Rome, composed his extremely influential rule in the mid-sixth century.[13] At first, Benedict's rule was just one of several competing monastic rules in the West, but during the Carolingian period it gained ascendancy and became the dominant form of regulation in early medieval Europe.

Around the sixth century, monasticism in the Byzantine East and medieval West began to diverge in significant ways. In every cenobitic monastery, where the monks lived in community, there were certain fundamental principles in both East and West: the authority of the superior to whom each monk owed absolute obedience; the necessity for observance of the regulations in the monastic rule; a lifestyle based on communal prayer in the church and communal meals in the refectory; the division of the monks into two groups: the choir monks and those in charge of household duties.

The most important distinction to emerge between Eastern and Western monasticism was the absence in Byzantium of separate monastic orders, such as one finds in the medieval West, the Benedictines, for example, and the Cistercians, Dominicans, and Franciscans, who appeared later in the high Middle Ages. With few exceptions, each Byzantine monastery was an individual and separate entity, with its own rule, or *typikon*, that prescribed the regulations for the organization and administration of that specific monastic foundation. This meant there could be a wide variety in the procedures for the election of a superior, for instance, or the length of the novitiate or dietary restrictions on fast days. In the earlier scholarly literature, however, as recently as 1960, there were still misleading references to the "Basilian Order" of monks in Byzantium, under the misguided impression that the so-called *Ascetic Rules* of Basil, the fourth-century Church father and bishop of Caesarea, laid the foundations for a single monastic order in the East.[14] John Thomas's careful comparison of the Longer and Shorter Rules of Basil with medieval Byzantine *typika* demonstrates that Basil's rules were certainly influential for certain fundamental aspects of monastic life in middle and late Byzantium, but that later monastery founders often disregarded many of Basil's precepts.[15]

BYZANTINE MONASTICISM FROM THE NINTH TO FIFTEENTH CENTURIES

I focus this study on the second half of the Byzantine Empire, the ninth century through the first half of the fifteenth century (800–1453), for several reasons. First of all, the first quarter of the ninth century was a turning point in the history of Byzantine monasticism, a period of intense monastic reform under the leadership of Theodore, superior of the Stoudios monastery in Constantinople. Theodore sought to restore a more rigorous form of cenobitism, emphasizing manual labor and self-sufficiency. The monastic regulations he formulated were to prove a basic model for subsequent monastic establishments. The year 1453 marked the fall of Constantinople to the Ottoman Turks and the effective end of the Byzantine Empire. Although many rural monasteries, especially on Mount Athos, continued to function during the Ottoman occupation of the Balkans, most urban monasteries failed to survive. A few monasteries in the capital remained active following the conquest, but many were closed or destroyed, and today the only remains are their churches, or *katholika*, now turned into museums or mosques. As for geographical range, I focus on the core territory of medieval Byzantium, that is, Greece, western Anatolia, and the capital, Constantinople, with occasional allusions to Italo-Greek monasticism in southern Italy.

The years 800–1453 are better documented than earlier centuries with regard to monastic history because almost all the surviving monastic foundation documents date from this period, as do the archival acts from Mount Athos. No foundation document prior to the seventh century survives for an individual Byzantine monastery.[16] The rules devised by earlier monastic founders may have been passed down orally from one generation of monks to another in the early centuries of Byzantine monasticism, but not until the ninth century did it become the norm for the regulations to be set down in a codified form called a *typikon*. The earliest such texts to be preserved are two very short rules: an early seventh-century testament for a monastery near Thebes in Egypt, and a late eighth-century *typikon* for a monastery on the island of Pantelleria near Sicily.[17] In the ninth century, a short but seminal document appeared, the so-called Testament of Theodore of Stoudios. This is actually a compilation of excerpts from previous testaments and other compositions of Theodore, most probably drafted by his successor Naukratios shortly after his death in 826, outlining Theodore's vision of the organization of a monastery restored on strict cenobitic principles;[18] a few years later, sometime after 842, a more fully developed *typikon* was composed.[19] The rules Theodore devised for Stoudios were to influence monastic organization and routines for many years to come. A subsequent series of Greek monastic foundation documents (more than sixty are preserved overall), which continues up to the fifteenth century, illuminates the diversity of regimens in cenobitic houses. These texts also enable scholars to place on a firmer basis the study of Byzantine monasticism during the second half of the empire and to draw on sources beyond the hagiographies of monastic founders.

Among the many distinctions between monasteries illuminated by the texts of *typika* was the nature of their foundation, patronage, and governance: imperial, patriarchal, private, and independent or self-governing. Imperial monasteries were founded by an emperor or member of the imperial family and can be traced back to the sixth century.[20] The *typika* for imperial foundations attest to some of the basic characteristics of this type of monastery: they were well-endowed and offered the opportunity of a comfortable life in seclusion for relatives of the imperial donor. Sometimes they might be led by a holy man, such as Athanasios at the Great Lavra on Mount Athos, who was given much autonomy in his administration.[21] Patriarchal monasteries were founded by the patriarch, were independent of the local bishop, and provided revenues for the patriarchate.[22] Most monasteries were in fact private foundations, often established by wealthy individuals to provide a place for their burial and the assurance of prayers for their salvation and commemorative services by monks or nuns.[23] These institutions were most often supported by the generous endowment of landed properties. A fourth type of monastery, independent or self-governing, first appeared in the tenth century. The superior and steward of such a monastery managed its properties and endowment without interference from the donor.[24] The *typika* of these monasteries stressed self-governance, that is, the selection of the superior by the community without any intervention by the patron.

There were significant differences in the sizes of Byzantine monasteries. The minimum number of monks according to canon law was three, and many monasteries in fact were small, with only a few monks. Others were of moderate size, with twenty-four or thirty monks or nuns, while a few, especially in Constantinople or on Mount Athos, might have a hundred or even several hundred inhabitants.[25]

The overall number of monasteries in Byzantium in any given century is impossible to determine for lack of sufficient evidence. Some scholars have ventured an attempt nonetheless, but the figures they propose must be treated with caution. Peter Charanis, for example, tallied about 240 monasteries from the Byzantine centuries that are known by name, and he argued that there must have been countless others, perhaps as many as 7,000.[26] A few years later, Anthony Bryer compiled a census of 700 recorded monasteries within the twelfth-century borders of the empire.[27] Raymond Janin's survey listed 325 monasteries in and around Constantinople over the eleven centuries of the empire's existence.[28]

Although the size and endowments of monasteries varied widely, many monastic institutions accumulated vast landed properties, through gifts from pious patrons or through deliberate consolidation of neighboring estates by purchase or exchange. Such properties also included significant urban holdings, such as houses and workshops that provided rental income, or other revenue sources, such as salt pans and mines. Monastic administrators had to be skilled financial managers, and their daily concerns were far removed from those of their brethren, who chose a life of solitary withdrawal into the wilderness for spiritual contemplation.

Monastic life, in its various forms, continued to attract Byzantine men and women until the very end of the empire; in fact, as the empire declined, lost territory, and faced significant economic challenges, many monasteries retained their wealth and power, and monks played a prominent role in intellectual life and in the Church hierarchy, especially as patriarchs.

SOURCES ON MONASTICISM

A rich variety of sources is available to the historian of middle and late Byzantine monasticism, that is, from the ninth to fifteenth centuries.[29] At the head of the list should come monastic foundation documents, an assortment of texts that includes founders' testaments and rules; the latter are often referred to as *typika*, a generic term for the regulations governing daily life and liturgical observances in a monastery. The so-called *ktetorika typika* contain rules established by the founders (*ktetores*) or early abbots for all aspects of monastic routine; they sometimes include sections on the prescribed liturgy and daily offices, but the liturgical prescriptions can also be preserved in a separate *typikon*.[30] Sixty-one of the founders' *typika* (six of them for nunneries) survive from the period under discussion, and in the year 2000 they were conveniently assembled by a Dumbarton Oaks project in five volumes of translations and commentary. This publication, also available online on the Dumbarton Oaks website, is without doubt the most important single published source on Byzantine monasticism.[31] The six *typika* for nunneries are particularly valuable for our understanding of female religious life, since relatively few *vitae* of saintly nuns have been preserved.

A few of the *typika* written by monastic founders contain precious autobiographical information in their prologues. These first-hand accounts of the motivation for establishing a new monastic complex, as in Theodora Synadene's *typikon* for the Constantinopolitan convent of Sure Hope, or of the author's introduction to monastic life as a two-year-old, as in Ioacheim of Zichna's *typikon* for the monastery of St. John Prodromos on Mount Menoikeion, offer unusual personal insights into the Byzantine monastic experience.[32]

Nonetheless, a few caveats are in order for users of *typika* as historical evidence. First of all, one must remember that they represent only a small percentage of such documents that were originally issued and that the majority of *typika* have not been preserved. Thus there may have been even greater variation in monastic practices than is already attested in the existing documents. Second, these rules on such topics as length of novitiate, dietary regimen, monastic garments, access to bathing facilities, care of the sick, and the like are normative texts that represent an ideal of the expectations envisaged by the founder; the very existence of the rules implies that the types of behavior that were prohibited did occur, in even the best-managed monastery. Third, as detailed analysis of the *typikon* for the eleventh-century Constantinopolitan monastery of Theotokos Evergetis has demonstrated, these documents were not fixed and immutable but might change and evolve over the years; thus the preserved version of a *typikon* represents the state of the text at one point in time and might have already been modified or be changed subsequently.[33] Moreover, many monastic rules copied large sections from earlier *typika*, especially those of the Stoudios and Evergetis monasteries, and the reader needs to be aware of where a *typikon* is following an earlier model.[34]

Another kind of text, the saint's life (*vita*), nicely complements the *typika* as a source of information on monasticism.[35] Byzantine holy men and women were preponderantly monastics, and their *vitae* provide insights into the experiences of individual novices, monks, and nuns: the forms of temptation they faced; the rivalries, tensions, and clashes of personality to be expected within a closed community, shut in by high walls; the monks' and nuns' spiritual exercises and ascetic feats. In contrast to the ideals enjoined by monastic rules, *vitae* more often present the realities of the hardships endured by the residents of monastic communities or hermitages. Obviously, these hagiographic texts, written to edify the faithful and provide models of spiritual life, must be used with care, and they no doubt exaggerate the asceticism of the monks, nuns, and solitaries they describe, but they also contain much of value to round out our picture of everyday existence in a monastery or isolated cave. For our understanding of the lifestyle of hermits, *vitae* are in fact usually the only available source. One must always keep in mind, however, that the *vitae* describe the regimens of exemplary holy men and women, famed for their asceticism and spirituality, rather than those of the many unheralded, ordinary monks and nuns who were the norm.

Another problem with the use of hagiography as a source for the reconstruction of the careers and daily life of Byzantine monks and nuns is the frequent use of *topoi* (commonplaces) in the lives of saints, such as the description of a holy child who refused to play games with other children and gave his food away to the poor.[36]

The reader must also be aware that some *vitae* copied large sections from earlier texts without any overt indication of the borrowing, and in some cases new critical editions are needed to highlight passages that derive from earlier authors. Examples are the *vita* of Nikon the Metanoeite, which copies miracle stories from the *vita* of Luke of Steiris,[37] and the fourteenth-century *vita* of patriarch Athanasios of Constantinople (1289–93, 1303–9), about 20 percent of which is derived from earlier compositions, such as the orations of Gregory of Nazianzos (fourth century) and Niketas Choniates (early thirteenth century).[38] Other *vitae* were inspired by the *vitae* of earlier saints and show marked similarities (but also dissimilarities) with their models. Examples are the *vita* of Theoktiste of Lesbos, which draws heavily on the *vita* of Mary of Egypt, and the *vita* of Mary the Younger, which Stavroula Constantinou has recently argued is modeled on the *vita* of Makrina.[39]

At the same time, it must be recognized that many saints' lives seem to present much trustworthy information, especially when written by people close to the saintly individual. I have tried to avoid using *vitae* of personalities who may be fictional or anachronistic, such as the heroes of the tenth-century *vitae* of Andrew the Fool, Basil the Younger, and Niphon, but I have relied for the most part on biographies of well-known historical figures, such as patriarchs, bishops, and abbots of monasteries, written by their disciples within a generation of the holy man's death. Some of these saints, such as Theodore of Stoudios and Athanasios of Athos, are also documented in other sources, such as the *typika* for their monasteries and their own writings, and the data presented in the *vita* can be corroborated. Three versions of the *vita* of Theodore survive, and two *vitae* of Athanasios of Athos, so that discrepancies in biographical information can be easily spotted. Some *vitae* of late Byzantine saints, such as Athanasios I, patriarch of Constantinople, and Gregory Palamas, archbishop of Thessalonike (1347–59), include copies of historical documents that add credibility to the hagiographical account.[40] I would also argue that a reader of hagiographic literature can have confidence in information about everyday life that is incidental and does not serve to enhance the image of the holy man or woman. If a hagiographer tells us, for example, that a hermit foraged for arbutus fruits or wild chickpeas or that his bedcovering was made of woven reeds, this is likely to be a credible detail.

The Dumbarton Oaks Hagiography Database has greatly facilitated research on many topics related to monasticism, such as age of tonsure, diet, clothing, handwork, sleeping arrangements, and the like. It is a relational database compiled at Dumbarton Oaks in the 1990s, based on information found in saints' lives of the eighth to tenth centuries, and is accessible through the Dumbarton Oaks website.[41] Also useful is the database on Palaiologan hagiography prepared by Eleonora Kountoura-Galake under the auspices of the National Research Foundation of Greece.[42]

A third kind of source, Byzantine monastic archives, is very limited in nature compared with such documents in the medieval West, probably because of the destruction of so many monasteries during the long centuries of Ottoman occupation. Such archival materials are best represented by the 1,200 surviving documents from Mount Athos, where the twenty major monasteries have continued to function since the Middle Ages.[43] Their archives deal primarily with real estate transactions, such as the donation and sale of lands by private individuals to Athonite institutions. These documents tell us much about the properties held by monasteries on the Holy Mountain (Mount Athos) and elsewhere, especially disputes over their boundaries, but very little about life within the walls of the monasteries. Regrettably, no archives are preserved from a Byzantine convent. I have therefore had little recourse to archival materials for this study.

A fourth type of textual evidence is found in the acts of the patriarchate of Constantinople and the permanent standing synod of bishops (*synodos endemousa*), particularly for the Palaiologan period (1261–1453).[44] These acts contain synodal decisions in cases involving bishops, clergy, monks, and nuns. More rarely, the synod issued rulings to laypeople on such matters as betrothal, marriage, dowries, adultery, and inheritance that came under canon law. For the purposes of this study, most useful are decisions with regard to individual monks and nuns who have been wronged in some way, adjudications of charges against monks or nuns who have misbehaved, or petitions from monastic representatives with regard to disputes over monastic property.[45] The documents provide information about aberrant behavior within monasteries, details on vineyards, gardens, and orchards belonging to Constantinopolitan monasteries, and clues about the existence of autonomous monks and nuns apparently unaffiliated with a monastic institution, and these have proved to be an essential source for the discussion in chapter 4. These texts, most of which are firmly dated, are particularly numerous for the late Byzantine period, especially the years just before and after 1400. Although as sworn court testimony they would seem to be reliable, witnesses often presented differing accounts of a dispute, and the truth is sometimes difficult to discern. Moreover, only a small number of these acts are available in a critical edition.

A fifth type of evidence, the archeological and architectural analysis of surviving monastic structures, provides little assistance for scholars interested in the institutional development of Byzantine monasticism. Typically, monastic complexes of the Byzantine era have either totally disappeared (for example, the Evergetis monastery outside the walls of Constantinople), or only the church has survived (for instance, the Chora and Pantokrator monasteries within the walls of Constantinople), or, in a few instances, they continue to function to this day (for example, the monasteries on Mount Athos). In the second case, we know nothing of any of the monastic buildings except for the main church (*katholikon*). In the third case, the overall ground plan and walls may be preserved, but many of the buildings have been so heavily remodeled or restored over the centuries that it is difficult to reconstruct the original form of the structures.[46] In Istanbul not a single Byzantine monastic building survives except for the churches that were once the heart of monastic complexes. Among the twenty monasteries of Mount Athos, only five original Byzantine churches still stand today; most of the present-day churches, refectories, and outbuildings are post-Byzantine or heavily restored. Although they may stand in their original Byzantine location, the walls and fresco decoration are of later date.[47]

There is a similar paucity of evidence from the archaeological excavation of Byzantine monasteries in Greece and Anatolia. In contrast to the rich finds for early monasteries in Egypt and Greater Syria, until recently there has been relatively little excavation at monasteries of middle and late Byzantium, and publication has focused on the main church and refectory, not the ancillary buildings.[48] For Greece, that picture is beginning to change with the work of archaeologists such as Charalambos Bakirtzis, Stavros Mamaloukos, and Michael Kappas. Yet archaeological excavation can provide important new information, as on Mount Papikion in Thrace, a Byzantine holy mountain only rarely mentioned in textual sources, where the remains of sixty monasteries have recently been identified.[49] For Cappadocian monasticism in Anatolia, archaeology is the only source, since textual documentation is virtually nonexistent.[50]

CHAPTER 1

MONKS AND MALE MONASTIC COMMUNITIES

CENOBITIC MONASTERIES

Male cenobitic communities were by far the most common form of monastic institution in Byzantium. This chapter will describe the administrative structure and daily routine of typical cenobitic monasteries by examining two model establishments: the Stoudios monastery in the urban center of Constantinople, and the Great Lavra on the holy mountain of Athos. Both Stoudios and the Great Lavra were large and wealthy institutions, but they had marked dissimilarities because of their very different locations, one in the midst of a bustling metropolis, the other on an isolated peninsula.

We are well informed about these two famous monasteries because both complexes are still in existence today—even though Stoudios is in ruins—and the monastic rules of both institutions and the *vitae* of their founders have also been preserved. Theodore, the abbot responsible for Stoudios's revival in the early ninth century, was also a prolific writer whose voluminous correspondence and catechetical teachings survive and provide valuable sources of information about the monastery, its monks, and its history.[1] Three versions of his *vita* are also preserved.[2] As for information on the foundation and formative years of the Great Lavra, there are two versions of the *vita* of Athanasios of Athos, his rule (originally composed in 963, the year of the Great Lavra's foundation), his *typikon* (dated 973–75), and his testament (written after 993, a few years before his death).[3]

St. Theodore and the Monastery of Stoudios

The celebrated Stoudios monastery was originally founded in the Psamathia region of southwestern Constantinople in the mid-fifth century and revived by Theodore of Stoudios around the year 800 after a period of decline.[4] St. Theodore (fig. 1) was a pivotal figure in the history of Byzantine monasticism and a noted defender of image veneration during the lengthy iconoclastic controversy that divided Byzantium in the eighth and first half of the ninth centuries. Born in 759, he became a monk at age twenty-one at the family monastery of Sakkoudion in the region of Bithynian Mount Olympos, and he was subsequently its superior.[5]

At just about the same time as the ninth-century Carolingian monastic reform movement in Western Europe, Theodore arrived in the Byzantine capital and led the reform and revival of the Stoudios monastery. I have chosen 800 as the starting date for the period covered in this book because it was precisely at the very end of the eighth century, in 798 or 799, that Empress Irene (r. 797–802), a supporter of icon veneration (iconodule), invited Theodore, a staunch defender of images, to become superior of the Stoudios monastery in Constantinople. Irene's reign and her support for the iconodule Theodore came during a brief lull (787–815) in the period of rule by a series of iconoclastic emperors who sought to abolish image veneration in the empire. At this time the monastery was in severe decline because of previous imperial persecution of iconodule monks, but under Theodore's new leadership the monastic population grew within a few years from a low of about ten monks to around three or four hundred.[6]

The remains of the monastery today are in a sorry state, consisting only of the ruined structure of a cistern and the church. The latter, the oldest surviving church building in Istanbul, has suffered

FIGURE 1 Theodore of Stoudios, eleventh-century mosaic, Nea Moni, Chios (photo: Image Collection and Fieldwork Archives, Dumbarton Oaks, Trustees for Harvard University, Washington, DC)

over the years from fire and earthquake, and it now faces the threat of being rebuilt as a mosque. Originally, however, the large fifth-century basilica was divided into three aisles by two rows of green marble monolithic columns. There was a gallery level and an apse with chancel barrier, altar, and crypt. The floor is now badly damaged, but a half century ago it still retained handsome stone mosaic (*opus sectile*) panels of animals, installed at a later date, probably the mid-eleventh century. The church also originally had a narthex, preceded by a colonnaded atrium open to the skies.[7]

Although Theodore is now remembered in close connection with the monastery, ironically he was to spend only about ten years in residence at Stoudios, since from 809 onward he lived mostly in exile away from the capital, persecuted at first because of his opposition to the patriarch Nikephoros I (806–15) and later because of his stance in support of icons after the revival in 815 of iconoclastic policy. Yet even in exile his concern for the monastery did not cease; he maintained extensive correspondence with members of his dispersed iconodule monastic community and issued a series of testaments laying out his vision for the future regulation of the monastery. Even as Theodore lay on his deathbed in 826, on the island of Prinkipo in the Sea of Marmara, he summoned his faithful steward, Naukratios, to inquire if there was anything he had neglected to do with regard to his beloved monastery.[8]

After his death, Naukratios succeeded him as abbot and drew up what purported to be Theodore's final "testament" containing his confession of faith and brief regulatory injunctions for the superior and brethren of Stoudios.[9] Following the decisive defeat of iconoclasm in 842 and the restoration of an imperial policy of image veneration, the Stoudite monks returned from exile to their monastery, and Theodore's body (miraculously uncorrupted, according to hagiographic tradition) was transferred to its final resting place at Stoudios.

Sometime thereafter, probably in the second half of the ninth century, a monastic rule was written for the monastery. This is the earliest *typikon* to survive from the middle Byzantine period; its author is unknown, but it was probably an abbot of Stoudios, who based his written version on oral tradition handed down from Theodore. The *typikon* was longer than the earlier so-called testament of Theodore and focused primarily on liturgical and dietary rules. It was intended (and this is unusual) to regulate not just Stoudios but four rural monasteries in Bithynia, the "Stoudite federation," including Sakkoudion, where Theodore had been tonsured and both he and his uncle Platon had been superior.[10] Thus the Stoudite rule not only represents the earliest *typikon* of the period, but it also contrasted with the normal Byzantine practice that each monastery was an independent institution with its own individual rule.

The Stoudite *typikon* is much more limited in scope than later *typika*—it focused on liturgical observance and dietary regimen, and it condensed into one document rules that later on would be covered separately, and more expansively, in a liturgical *typikon* and a founder's *typikon*. Thus we must look to other sources, such as the three *vitae* about Theodore, the testament of 826, his letters, catechetical writings, and regulations for the punishment of disciplinary infractions, to round out a picture of the ideals of Stoudite monasticism as envisaged by Theodore and the realities of daily life at his federation of monasteries.[11]

The anonymous author of the Stoudite *typikon* boasted that his rule, also used by the monasteries of the Stoudite federation, was superior to that of other monasteries: "Although there are many and various traditions from prior times holding sway in the holy monasteries and although different monasteries are administered and governed by different rules . . . , there is *one* of all these—the one in force among us—which is the best and most excellent, avoiding both excesses and deficiencies. This rule we have received from our great father and confessor Theodore."[12] In fact, it was to have substantial influence on subsequent *typika* for more than two centuries, until it was supplanted by the Evergetis *typikon* in the eleventh century. For example, the Stoudite *typikon* provided a model for Athanasios's tenth-century rules for the Great Lavra on Athos.

One of Theodore's main goals was to reassert the primacy of cenobitism and the value of the communal lifestyle as opposed to that of the solitary monk. Part of his reform program was also "intended to return monasteries to the economic self-sufficiency more common in monasteries of late antiquity."[13] To this end he banned personal and agricultural slaves in order to encourage manual labor by the monks themselves,[14] such as farming in the rural monasteries, artisanal crafts, and the copying of manuscripts in the urban complex of Stoudios, where one could find a remarkable array of specialized craftsmen. These included weavers, tailors, and shoemakers; carpenters and builders; basket-weavers and metalsmiths; makers of candles, parchment, keys, saddles, fishnets, and knives. The products they manufactured seem to have been primarily for the use of the monastery.[15] He also banned the presence of female domestic animals.[16] It has been argued that this prohibition was not out of moral concerns about the dangers of bestiality, as we see elsewhere, but rather from a desire to encourage manual labor and avoid the practice of cattle-breeding and the commercialization of his rural monasteries.[17] He enjoined avoiding as much as possible any contact whatsoever with women. Theodore also emphasized absolute submission to the will of the superior, and he developed an elaborate hierarchy of monastic officials to run the extensive operations of the monastery. These included a steward, who served as a manager of facilities and rural estates, with the help of a deputy; a cellarer, the keeper of stores; a librarian; a gatekeeper, responsible for keeping monks inside the walls and unwanted visitors outside; a head infirmarian, and his assistants; a head calligrapher, who ran the scriptorium; and church officials, such as a precentor (*kanonarches*) and choir monitor (*taxiarches*).

A major liturgical reform instituted by Theodore may have been in part motivated by his desire to provide his monks more time to carry out manual labor. Theodore's innovation was the introduction at Stoudios of the Jerusalem *typikon* of St. Sabas as the basis for liturgical rites to replace the centuries-old practice of continuous twenty-four-hour services observed by his predecessors, the "sleepless monks" (*akoimetoi*). The Stoudite *typikon* provided for the daily observance of seven canonical hours: a combined midnight office and matins (*orthros*), offices for the first, third, sixth and ninth hours, vespers (*lychnikos*, lit. "lamplighting," or *hesperinos*), and compline (*apodeipnon*), the last service of the day, literally the "after-supper prayer." Besides spending long hours in church, Stoudite monks were expected to perform manual labor, all the while reciting the Psalter; during break periods they would read or nap. Theodore placed great emphasis on the reading of books, especially on Sundays, when the monks were not expected to work; they obtained their reading materials from a librarian and had to return them before the vespers service.[18]

The monks were provided with two sets of warm clothing, undergarments, and wool tunics, plus an outer garment, two cowls (*koukoullion*), and two scapulars (*epomion, epomis*); they also had two kinds of boots.[19] A remarkable, indeed unique, feature of Stoudite monasticism was the weekly exchange of undergarments among the monks. The exchange was made without regard to the disparate sizes of the monks, or the relative cleanliness and state of repair of the garments. This practice was designed to instill a sense of community and humility in the brotherhood, a literal communal sharing of garments.[20]

The sleeping arrangements at Stoudios in the early ninth century are unclear. We do not know for sure whether Stoudite monks slept in a common dormitory, as would be customary in a medieval Benedictine or Cistercian abbey,[21] or in individual cells. Texts from Theodore's *Great Catechesis* and his *Epitimia* inform us that the monks slept in a *koitarion*, but the word seems to have several different meanings, ranging from "bed" to "cubicle" to "sleeping chamber." It may be that younger monks were assigned to a common sleeping chamber, while their older brethren had their own cells.[22] By the late tenth century, when Symeon (the future "new theologian") entered Stoudios, individual cells were definitely the norm for all monks; since no vacant cell was available to accommodate the young novice, he was assigned to the cell of his mentor, the elder Symeon Eulabes, and slept in the space under the staircase. Also, the youthful Symeon was enjoined not to "go around from cell to cell."[23] The beds were straw pallets covered with a mat of goat hair, and each monk was issued two fleece woolen blankets.[24] Bathing was evidently limited to sick monks, who had to go to a facility outside the monastery grounds.[25]

Normally, two meals a day were served in the refectory, with bread plus vegetables and legumes cooked in olive oil as the staple foods at midday, supplemented by fish, cheese, and eggs; fruit was considered a delicacy.[26] Each monk was allotted daily about one pound of bread, weighed out by a special official.[27] The basic beverage was wine, consumed in large quantities, as much as six measures a day, but probably diluted with hot water. In the evening a light supper was provided of bread and leftovers from the midday meal.[28] During the Great Lent only one meal was served on weekdays, consisting of boiled legumes without oil, pickled cabbage, olives, and fruit; no dairy items, eggs, or seafood were permitted, and wine was replaced with a hot drink (*eukraton*) flavored with cumin, pepper, and anise. On Lenten weekends, two meals were served daily with wine.[29] Throughout the year, one of the monks read aloud at the midday meal from spiritual treatises or saints' lives.[30]

Information from the so-called testament of Theodore and the Stoudite *typikon* can be supplemented with a text of prescribed punishments for infractions of monastic rules called the *Epitimia* (*Penances*). Although its authorship has come into question, most scholars now believe that the first section was drafted by Theodore himself.[31] The *typikon* itself mentions confinement in a cell as punishment, while forbidding the use of flogging;[32] the list of penalties prescribes other punishments, primarily prostrations or genuflections (*metanoiai*), but also a form of temporary excommunication (*aphorismos*) in which the offender was briefly refused communion. Other penalties included being forced to stand in humiliation in the refectory at mealtime and the imposition of a strict fast called *xerophagia*, literally "dry eating," a dietary regimen limited to bread, fruit, vegetables (either uncooked or cooked in water rather than oil), and nuts.[33]

From this list of penalties we learn more about the mistakes and accidents that occurred during the duties (*diakoniai*) to which monks were assigned. The cellarer, for instance, was ordered to perform five or more prostrations for spilling wine, oil, vinegar, or dried legumes, and 100 to 300 prostrations for breaking a ceramic pot; the number of prostrations depended on the amount spilled in the breakage. Alternatively the careless monk was made to stand in the refectory at mealtime, holding the pieces of broken ceramic in his hands.[34] The cook would be punished for not adding salt and oil to the pot at the proper time, for letting the soup boil over, or for breaking a pot.[35] The baker had to perform three prostrations if he added the wrong amount of wood to the fire or did not bake the bread properly.[36]

Expectations were also spelled out for officials assigned to the church. The lamp tender was responsible for lighting the lamps, cleaning them, and trimming their wicks; he also had to polish metal lamps so they did not rust. If he broke a lamp, he had to pay for its replacement.[37] The precentor (*kanonarches*) was assigned to striking the wooden or metal sounding board (*semandron*) to summon the monks to services or to the refectory, and he was responsible for setting out the service books.[38] The choir monitor (*taxiarches*) was supposed to keep good order in the choir, make sure the choir brothers lined up properly, discipline monks who fell asleep during services, and pursue monks who ran away.[39]

We also learn from this source about the duties of the gatekeeper, guestmaster, infirmarian, and teacher of children, and about various craftsmen who worked in the monastery. The shoemaker was punished for breaking a leatherworking tool, the tailor for breaking a needle or scissors, the carpenter for cutting wood to the wrong length, the weaver for careless manufacture of cloth.[40]

Other penalties were for agricultural workers, who may have been employed either at Stoudios itself, which had an attached vineyard,[41] or at one of the affiliated rural monasteries. Thus the gardener was punished if he did not plant seeds on time, water the plants sufficiently, and plant an adequate variety of vegetables to feed the monks. The stablemen were expected to give the animals food and water at the right time, lay down fresh straw for their bedding, and brush their coats. They were penalized for overworking or overloading the animals or beating them. The ploughman had to make ten prostrations if he struck an ox in anger or cursed it.[42] This series of injunctions reveals a sympathetic side of Theodore's nature, concerned about the well-being of the animals that served his monastery.

Noteworthy in the list of punishments are the chapters relating to intellectual and scholarly life in the Stoudios monastery. Evidently, from the time of Theodore, this monastery, which was to develop an unparalleled reputation for its scriptorium and library, placed great emphasis on the book arts and the life of the mind. The chapter on the librarian stresses that he is to take proper care of the books in his charge and ensure that the monks to whom they were loaned are also careful in handling them. Monks were not to complain about the book they were assigned; if they grumbled, they were denied access to the book that day. If a monk did not return a book on time but hid it in his sleeping cell/cubicle (*koitarion*), he had to endure the public humiliation of standing in the refectory during mealtime.[43]

Further prescriptions on the copying of manuscripts (chapters 53–60) suggest a well-organized scriptorium with a head calligrapher (*protokalligraphos*), who was to act as supervisor and make sure the parchment and writing implements were in good condition.[44] There were punishments for carelessness with regard to the spelling of diphthongs and the insertion of accents and punctuation marks.[45] Scribes had to perform prostrations for breaking a pen in a fit of anger, for using too much glue, and for writing a phrase from memory instead of copying from the exemplar manuscript.[46] In fact, the Stoudios monastery did have a celebrated scriptorium where a new minuscule script (as opposed to the earlier uncials, or majuscules) may have been developed in the early ninth century.[47] The earliest surviving Byzantine manuscript written in a minuscule hand, the Uspenskij gospel book (St. Petersburg Public Library, gr. 219), was copied in 835 by the scribe Nicholas the Stoudite;[48] the new script, which evolved from cursive, was to quickly supplant uncial or capital letters, and scribes were kept busy transcribing old manuscripts into the new letter forms. In minuscule manuscripts, words were separated from each other, and the script saved space (and expensive parchment) by being more compact, was more legible for the reader, and was more efficient for the scribe.

The rules established by Theodore and his successors created a distinctive monastic institution, highly regulated and administered by an elaborate hierarchy of staff. Stoudios placed great emphasis on manual labor, especially the artisanal crafts, and to this end forbade the use of slaves and abandoned previous traditions of perpetual liturgical services. It also encouraged the intellectual life and adherence to cenobitic ideals, as in the extreme example of mandated sharing of undergarments we saw earlier. The monastic community revived by Theodore at Stoudios was to survive until the end of the Byzantine Empire; by the fourteenth century, after a period of decline in the thirteenth century during the Latin occupation of the capital, it again held first place among the monasteries of Constantinople. Although its rule was not adopted by other monasteries outside the Stoudite federation, the large corpus of Theodore's writings, especially his *Catecheses*, continued to have immense influence on Byzantine monasticism.

St. Athanasios of Athos and the Great Lavra

The Stoudios monastery was an urban institution par excellence, but it also had affiliated rural monasteries. For my second case study, I discuss the Great Lavra (fig. 2), a monastery founded in the mid-tenth century on the holy mountain of Athos in a virtual wilderness, far from the hustle and bustle of a city. However, its rule was influenced by that of the Stoudios.

Athos, the preeminent Byzantine holy or monastic mountain during the middle and late Byzantine centuries, is the northernmost

FIGURE 2   Katholikon at the Great Lavra, Mount Athos (photo: Robert Ousterhout, Image Collection and Fieldwork Archives, Dumbarton Oaks, Trustees for Harvard University, Washington, DC)

promontory of the Chalkidike peninsula that juts out into the northern Aegean Sea like three fingers. The Athonite "finger" is twenty-eight miles long, and quite narrow, with a width of three to six miles. It is connected to the mainland by a narrow isthmus one mile wide. Almost completely surrounded by the sea, it is the most isolated of all the Byzantine holy mountains, and the furthest from a major population center, located about sixty-two miles east of Thessalonike, the second city of the empire.[49]

The Athonite peninsula has a geology and climate distinct from that of its two sister promontories on account of its domination by the 6,600-foot peak of Athos and its foothills, which break up the landscape into a series of deep gorges. The mountain itself rises almost directly out of the Aegean and is characterized by a variety of climatic zones, from relatively mild Mediterranean along the coastline to climates more typical of the Balkan mountain ranges at higher altitudes, and an alpine zone at the peak. In many places along the coast the rocky cliffs plunge right into the sea, and there are few natural harbors.[50] The craggy landscape, with little flat terrain, combined with the lack of good ports, is not conducive to human habitation, and as a consequence the Athonite promontory was only very lightly populated in classical antiquity. The few ancient settlements were abandoned by the third century of the Christian era,[51] and the peninsula remained uninhabited for about 500 years. By the early ninth century, when a few hermits began to settle on Athos, it had returned to the state of a primeval wilderness, and in the absence of sheep and goats who liked to browse on tree saplings was no doubt more heavily forested than today.

Such was the condition of the peninsula when Athanasios, the future founder of the Great Lavra, first arrived in the mid-tenth century (fig. 3). He was born to an aristocratic family in Trebizond on the south coast of the Black Sea around 925–30. Orphaned as a young child, he was raised by a nun and received his elementary schooling in Trebizond. Subsequently, he went to Constantinople to pursue his secondary education.[52] He excelled as a student and soon became a highly regarded and popular teacher in his own right. At

FIGURE 3   Athanasios of Athos, fresco from Protaton, Mount Athos (photo: Miodrag Marković, Image Collection and Fieldwork Archives, Dumbarton Oaks, Trustees for Harvard University, Washington, DC)

the same time he followed an ascetic regimen (abstemious in food and drink) and slept in a chair. He gave away almost all his clothes to the poor, and he began thinking about a monastic vocation as an anchorite, a solitary hermit. One of his patrons, a general who was also a relative by marriage, once took him along on a naval patrol in the Aegean Sea. It was at this time that Athanasios first glimpsed Mount Athos, from the island of Lemnos, and conceived a longing to take up his abode there and abandon his life in the capital.[53]

Upon his return to Constantinople, he met Michael Maleinos, abbot of the *lavra* on Mount Kyminas, a holy mountain in Bithynia, and conveyed to him his desire to take the monastic habit.[54] Since a *lavra* was a type of monastery where most of the monks lived as solitaries in *kellia* (cells) outside the monastic complex, coming to the *lavra* only for weekend services and to secure food provisions, Athanasios felt this would be an appropriate place to begin his monastic career. Unlike Theodore of Stoudios, who was always a staunch advocate of cenobitism, Athanasios was at first attracted by the eremitic life that characterized holy mountains.

He left for Kyminas and was immediately tonsured by Michael without the usual waiting period and novitiate. Michael denied his request to move right away to a solitary cell, however, and insisted that he stay in the monastery to learn obedience and carry out various monastic duties. The abbot also placed strict limits on his self-mortification, seeking to "restrain his will." Only after four years did Michael allow Athanasios to move to a cell one mile distant from the *lavra*, but even here the abbot closely supervised the rigor of his ascetic exercises, "again separating him from his own will."[55]

As Athanasios became celebrated for his ascetic regimen, despite the abbot's restraints, there were rumors that he was being groomed to succeed the elderly Michael as abbot. Upset at this unwelcome threat to his solitary lifestyle, Athanasios decided to leave for Athos around 957. His *vita* gives the impression that at the time of his arrival on the peninsula, it was inhabited primarily by hermits and there was no developed agriculture; the *vita* alludes to only one cenobitic monastery (Xeropotamou) and the *lavra* of Karyes, which had been very recently founded.⁵⁶ This is a misleading image, however, for fifty-six monastic superiors and monks signed the *typikon* of John Tzimiskes just fifteen years later, in 972, and one scholar has calculated that forty-six monasteries were in existence by the end of the tenth century.⁵⁷ No doubt the hagiographer deliberately omitted references to other existing monasteries in order to emphasize Athanasios's role as a pioneer founder on Athos.⁵⁸ Athonite monks and hermits of the mid-tenth century did face constant danger from Arab pirates, for Athanasios arrived on Athos just before the Byzantine reconquest of Arab-occupied Crete in 961, a victory that made the Aegean a much safer place. But the pirates would not have raided the peninsula unless there were established monasteries to pillage.

Athanasios first attached himself to an elderly hermit who lived near the monastery of Zygos, just outside the boundary of Athos, and took care of his basic needs. Later on he moved to a *kellion* three miles from the *lavra* of Karyes; here he copied manuscripts to earn sufficient money to purchase bread. As he attracted attention and visitors, however, he decided to seek even greater isolation and built a hut at the tip of the peninsula, at a remote spot called Melana, "extremely desolate, and a long way from the abodes of the other ascetics."⁵⁹ After some months he fell victim to severe depression, attacked by the demons of *akedia*, a kind of mental torpor or despondency that often tormented solitary monks. He came to loathe his hermitage and was tempted to abandon it. But he summoned the strength to make a vow that he would persevere in his isolated hut for a full year, and if at the end of that time he was still despondent, he would return to Karyes. On his 365th day of solitude, just as he resolved to give up and leave, "a heavenly light poured over him and flashed all around and made him luminous."⁶⁰ After this experience of transfiguration, his attitude totally changed, and he came to love the site of Melana as much as he had previously despised it.

This was to be the location of Athanasios's new foundation, the Great Lavra. But first it is necessary to backtrack a bit to explain why Athanasios, who was seemingly a solitary at heart, decided to establish a cenobitic monastery and how he secured the funds for this major construction project. In Constantinople, in the early 950s, even before he became a monk, Athanasios had become acquainted with the future emperor Nikephoros II Phokas (r. 963–69) and his brother Leo, who were at that time prominent generals from an aristocratic family. The Phokas brothers were related to Michael Maleinos, and they renewed acquaintance with Athanasios at the *lavra* of Kyminas, where Athanasios, despite his youth, became their spiritual father. At this time, Nikephoros revealed to Athanasios his desire to eventually retire from his military career and become a monk.

In 961, Nikephoros Phokas sailed to Crete with an expedition to drive out the Arabs, who had occupied the island for almost 150 years. He sent a message to Athos, summoning Athanasios to his side. When Athanasios arrived in Crete, Nikephoros disclosed his plan to retire (he was about forty-eight years old at that time), and he asked his spiritual father to build on Athos a modest complex of five cells and a church where he could join Athanasios and three other monks in a life of contemplation and withdrawal. He anticipated the subordination of these *kellia* to a *lavra*, where the five solitaries could go on Sunday "to partake of the divine sacraments and eat together with the brethren and the superior."[61] It is clear that at this time Nikephoros did not envisage Athanasios as the superior but rather as his companion in the contemplative life. Athanasios initially refused to accept the funds that Nikephoros offered him, and he would not agree to carry out the project. But after Athanasios returned to Athos, Nikephoros, who was not a man to take no for an answer, sent an emissary with six pounds of gold coins for the construction project, in the same year, 961, that he successfully drove the Arabs from Crete.[62]

Unlike Theodore of Stoudios, who came to a monastery that needed only revival, Athanasios had to build his monastery, and his *vita* gives an unusually detailed description of the process. After receiving the funds from Nikephoros, Athanasios was persuaded to change his mind and hired workmen to build the new *lavra*. He gave priority to the construction of a *kellion* for Nikephoros and then turned his attention to the erection of a church dedicated to the Virgin at the precise site of his hermitage at Melana. His *vita* reports that Athanasios himself seized a spade and took part in the labor, setting a good example for the workmen. We are told that many of the laborers decided to take monastic vows and remain at the *lavra*. Next came the construction of cells for the brethren around the church and the refectory with twenty-one built-in marble tables that still survive to this day, each accommodating twelve diners. The size and number of dining tables suggest that Athanasios was planning from the beginning for a community of about 250 monks. He also built a hospital, a hostel for visitors, and a bathhouse. His greatest challenge was a water supply for the complex, because the site itself offered no adequate source. After a long search he found water sources eight miles distant from the *lavra*, and he had to build a pipe in a trench to supply the complex. The pipes brought water to every part of the *lavra*, to the fountain in the courtyard, the cells, and to a water mill that in turn provided water for the laundry, for the irrigation of fruit trees, the vegetable garden, and vineyards.[63]

The scope of this project boggles the mind when one remembers that up to this point Athanasios had been living in some sort of simple hut as a hermit. The name Athanasios gave to his monastery, the Great Lavra (in Greek, *Megiste Lavra*, literally, "the biggest lavra") was well deserved; for it was larger than any monastery existing on Athos at the time, and indeed its size would never be surpassed by any subsequent monastic complex on the Holy Mountain.[64] The scale of the construction was possible only thanks to the largess of Nikephoros Phokas, the pious general whose generous donation facilitated the hiring of workmen and materials; his patronage would provide a model for later monastic foundations on the Holy Mountain. But in 963, the same year that the monastery was established, an unexpected event occurred: Emperor Romanos II (r. 959–63) died suddenly at the age of twenty-four, leaving two minor sons as heirs, and Nikephoros Phokas took advantage of the power vacuum to seize the throne. Overnight the new *lavra* had lost its prospective distinguished resident, for whom a special *kellion* had been built, but it now had a patron who was none other than the emperor himself; the *lavra* seemed destined to become an imperial monastery instead of a private foundation. Athanasios was devastated at this development, perhaps dismayed by the change in character of the monastery, by its projected scale, or by its future control by the emperor in Constantinople. In an apparent fit of pique, he temporarily abandoned the fledgling foundation and headed for Cyprus, ostensibly on pilgrimage to the Holy Land, but unsafe conditions in Palestine soon led him to cut his journey short and return to Athos.

The following year, 964, Athanasios met with Nikephoros Phokas in Constantinople and successfully negotiated the future relationship between the new foundation and the new emperor. Phokas issued an imperial edict with a gold seal affixed (chrysobull), which stipulated the donation of three relics to the Great Lavra (including a fragment of the True Cross and the head of Basil of Caesarea) to be placed under the altar in the main church (*katholikon*) and deemed essential for the consecration of the church.[65] Another chrysobull ensured the monastery's independence of imperial authority, stating that the superior was without exception to be an internal candidate chosen by the monks of the Great Lavra.[66] At the same time, the emperor promised an annual cash payment of 244 gold pieces, sufficient to support eighty monks.[67] It is noteworthy that one of these chrysobulls of 964 designated Athos as the "holy-named mountain,"[68] and ten years later the *typikon* of Athanasios, of 973–75, twice refers to Athos as the Holy Mountain.[69]

Athanasios also had his way with regard to another essential point. The Great Lavra, originally intended to support five solitary monks, including Nikephoros, had been transformed during its construction period into a cenobitic monastery, and the rule drafted by Athanasios at the time of the foundation was closely modeled on that of the Stoudios monastery in Constantinople, in all regards the epitome of a *koinobion*. John Thomas has demonstrated how closely Athanasios's rule follows the *typikon* of Stoudios with regard to liturgical celebration and monastic offices, the discipline and dietary regimen to be observed in the refectory, and the distribution of clothing. In Athanasios's rule of 963, the year of the monastery's foundation, twenty-three of the thirty-seven chapters contained citations from the *typikon* for Stoudios, the other fourteen chapters were original. For example, the provisions for diet in chapter 22 of Athanasios's rule for the Great Lavra are virtually identical to chapter 29 of the rule at the Stoudios:

> **It should be known that from Eastertide until All Saints we eat two cooked dishes—garden vegetables and legumes** and season them both *with* three *litrai* of olive *oil*. On feasts of the Lord, unless there is also a relish dish, we add one more [*litra*], since another cooked dish is added, of course. On these days *we also eat fish*, if available, *cheese, and eggs. We drink three* [*measures of wine*]. In the evening *when the signal is struck, the brothers* who so wish *come out to eat their bread as well as any food that may have been left over from the morning. For the* **community has no food prepared especially for the evening;** [they also drink] **two servings of wine.**[70]

Likewise in his *typikon* written ten years later, Athanasios cited parts of eighteen chapters from the so-called testament of Theodore, but most of the Athonite *typikon* was original. Curiously, Athanasios nowhere acknowledged his borrowings from the Stoudite rule.[71]

The regulations for clothing are also very similar at the two monasteries, but there is no provision at the Great Lavra for exchange of garments:

> **It should be known that each brother ought to have two undergarments**, *two outer garments, one woolen garment*, one *cowl*, two monastic cloaks, *a shorter one for work and another more copious one which according to custom must be used in church*, a heavy cloak, **shoes, boots**, and his bed clothing.[72]

The transformation of the Great Lavra into a cenobitic monastery (although it retained its original name of *lavra*) was a startling development. Up to 963, Athanasios himself had almost always espoused the solitary life, either as the kelliot of a *lavra*, on Kyminas and at Karyes, or as a hermit's disciple at Zygos, or as a completely isolated hermit, at Melana. So his change of course is puzzling, and we can only speculate on his reasons. It may be, for example, that as Athanasios undertook the construction of a large monastic complex, with substantial funding, he realized that he needed to adopt the Stoudite model, which had proven so successful.[73] Yet at the same time he retained an element of the lavriot system with the designation of five monks as kelliots.

Athanasios lived on for another forty years as superior of the Great Lavra and devoted himself from this point on to the optimal organization and expansion of his new foundation. To supplement his original rule, he issued an additional regulatory document, the aforementioned *typikon* of circa 973–75, which reveals that within ten years of its establishment the Great Lavra had expanded from 80 to 120 monks. Among the provisions copied from Stoudite regulations were the prohibition of female animals and personal possessions, and an emphasis on inexpensive monastic garb.[74]

Athanasios's *vita* relates that he was not one to sit in his cell and issue orders but always an active participant in the daily functioning of the monastery, even engaging in heavy manual labor. He used to harness himself to a yoke, for example, to pull heavy wagons like a draft animal.[75] Once, when he was assisting with the transport of lumber for the construction of the harbor, a heavy wooden beam careered out of control, struck Athanasios, and broke his leg and ankle so badly that he was bedridden for three years. He did not waste this period of enforced leisure, however, but copied manuscripts assiduously to keep busy.[76] In the infirmary he headed the staff and would personally clean festering wounds and apply bandages; in the refectory he helped to prepare and distribute the food; he also gathered firewood and carried water.[77]

As depicted in his *vita*, Athanasios was a man of common sense who realized that the monks who performed heavy labor needed greater amounts of sustenance, so his rule ensured that carpenters, shipwrights, metalworkers, muleteers, and laborers in the vineyard should receive extra rations of food and wine. He also provided an extra measure of wine to bakers on the days that they performed the arduous task of kneading bread for the growing numbers of monks.[78] He had an inventive mind and devised an ox-driven contraption to knead large amounts of bread dough.[79] He also installed a bronze hook on the church door to serve as a lost and found receptacle: "If a monk should happen to lose a needle or a pen or a knife or a towel or any such item, they were to watch that he did not go around the cells looking for it . . . , but went to the church and looked on the door of the nave, to find the lost item."[80]

Despite Athanasios's condemnation of commercial ventures in his *typikon* of 973–75 and his *vita*'s idealization, indeed exaggeration, of the simple lifestyle that existed on Athos before the mid-tenth century, the development of economic activity at the Great Lavra was astoundingly rapid. The Great Lavra was located on a slope just above the seacoast, and within a few decades the monastery built its own harbor and warehouses where cargo could be unloaded. It owned boats for short voyages and ships that carried its monks on business to Constantinople, Smyrna, and the nearby Strymon River, an economic corridor into Bulgaria. Its shipwrights not only built vessels for the monastery but repaired passing ships that had been damaged by storms as they negotiated the treacherous waters off Athos.[81] As it gained wealth and dominance, the Great Lavra began to acquire smaller satellite monasteries together with their properties, both on the Athonite peninsula and further afield; one of them, Mylopotamos, housed a school for novices and had a vineyard.[82] The Great Lavra pastured flocks of sheep, Angora goats, and various beasts of burden and draft animals on the nearby island of Neoi, apparently thus circumventing Athanasios's prohibition of sheep and goats on the Holy Mountain.[83] The monastery had a smithy with a bellows, a trained coppersmith, a calligrapher, a physician, fishermen who used nets to catch fish, a mason, and workers in the fields and vineyards.[84] The Stoudite influence is clear.

On the one hand, Athanasios's *vita* reports that his establishment of a cenobitic monastery was so successful that all the elders (*gerontes*) on the Holy Mountain abandoned their contemplative and eremitic lifestyle to come live at the Great Lavra;[85] on the other hand, he is also said to have attracted hermits from even greater distances. Nikephoros the Naked, the companion of St. Phantinos, arrived at the Great Lavra wearing tattered rags and insisted on continuing his customary regimen of one meal a day, consisting of bran husks soaked in water. Athanasios permitted this for a while, but then persuaded the ascetic to wear normal monastic garb and to take his meals regularly in the refectory as a sign of obedience.[86] But surely the story of the wholesale abandonment of hermitages on Athos is an exaggeration, for the same *vita* of Athanasios tells us of the grumbling of many local hermits who were upset at the innovations that Athanasios was introducing. Their conservative reaction was supposedly inspired by the devil, who whispered in their ears that "Athanasios is lording it over the Mountain and destroying the ancient rules and customs. For he has erected luxurious buildings and has constructed churches and harbors, and channeled streams of water and bought teams of oxen and has already transformed the Mountain into a worldly place."[87]

As a result, a group of monks complained to Emperor John I Tzimiskes (who had succeeded Phokas as emperor in 969) that Athanasios "is transgressing our ancient rules and transforming the old customs of the Mountain." Summoned by Tzimiskes to Constantinople, Athanasios not only persuaded him that the elders' charges were unfounded, but the emperor granted the Great Lavra an additional subsidy of 244 gold pieces a year.[88] The document issued by Tzimiskes around 971, called the *Tragos* ("billy goat") on account of its thick goatskin parchment, sought to calm the dissension on Athos by proclaiming in its preface that both parties in the dispute were "absolutely guiltless."[89] It was in essence a *typikon* or regulatory document for the entire Athonite community and sought to preserve a balance between the newly emerging cenobitic monasteries and the solitaries and small groups of *kelliotai* sanctioned by long tradition.

By the time of Athanasios's death around 1001, the Great Lavra was a thriving enterprise. The number of monks had expanded to 120, so many that the main church needed to be enlarged. During the construction, Athanasios was engaged as always in close supervision of the progress of the work, and one day he ascended the scaffolding with six of the monks for an inspection tour—the scaffolding collapsed, killing Athanasios and all six monks, an unusual accidental death for a Byzantine holy man, most of whom died peacefully in their beds.[90] His blood continued to flow after his death, a sign of his sanctity, and his tomb soon became a site of pilgrimage and miraculous healing.

Although the Stoudite *typikon* served as a model for the Great Lavra, there were significant differences in the monastic experience of a monk in Constantinople and his counterpart on Mount Athos. Urban monks were constantly exposed to the temptations of the city, and they interacted much more often with laypeople, including women; there was more pressure for their institutions to offer charitable services, such as distribution of alms and food to the poor, and to include institutions such as old age homes and orphanages. City monks were less likely to engage in agricultural labor, although fields and vineyards are well attested at the monasteries of Constantinople. A monk on the Holy Mountain led a much more isolated life, but as monasteries developed on Athos, there was an increasing flow of visitors and pilgrims. A monk of the Great Lavra would never set eyes on a woman after taking his vows, unless he traveled outside the bounds of the Holy Mountain on monastery business. If he wanted, he could easily leave the monastery for the wilderness and embark on the more arduous and spiritual life of a hermit. However, from the tenth century on, as the Athonite monasteries became the owners of vast landed estates outside the peninsula, at least some of the monks had to serve as businessmen, concerned about property titles, harvests, the acquisition of merchant vessels, the importation of foodstuffs and other necessities, and the transportation of surplus crops to markets for sale. To the greatest extent possible, a monastery on Athos tried to be a self-sufficient entity, since it was so isolated from marketplaces.

The Monastery of Theotokos Evergetis

These two major monasteries of the middle Byzantine period, in the imperial capital and on a remote holy mountain, provided sound models for other foundations of the ninth, tenth, and eleventh centuries. Before concluding this discussion of cenobitic monasteries, however, I should add a few words about a third important foundation of the period: the eleventh-century Evergetis monastery located just outside the walls of Constantinople.[91] In contrast to the Stoudios and Great Lavra monasteries, nothing survives of this monastic complex; in fact, we do not even know its precise location, except that it was outside the city, about two miles west of the Theodosian Wall.[92] The Evergetis also is mentioned only rarely in the historical sources; its founder's *typikon*, however, was to have great influence in later centuries on a number of monastic foundations, which could be described as following the Evergetian tradition.[93] Just as with the Stoudite rules, its *typikon* was intended to promote monastic reform, emphasizing institutional independence and self-governance, and the superiority of the cenobitic life, seeking to abolish privilege and inequalities and to closely regulate financial management. The Evergetis *typikon* placed great stress on the sacraments, mandating daily celebration of the liturgy and urging the monks to take communion frequently. It placed less emphasis than Stoudios on the monks' performance of manual labor.[94] Many of the Evergetis *typikon*'s provisions were adopted wholesale by subsequent *typika* or used in subtly modified form, often without acknowledgment of the source. To use the formulation of John Thomas, "It was through the borrowing of its *typikon* rather than through the development of any kind of monastic order that

Evergetis saw its institutions and customs introduced into many of the most influential monasteries of later Byzantium."[95] The influence of the Evergetis *typikon* parallels earlier developments in institutional monasticism, as when monasteries such as the Great Lavra made selective appropriation from the Stoudite model in establishing their rule.

IDIORRHYTHMIC MONASTERIES

The Greek word *idiorrhythmia* can be translated literally as "one's own individual rhythm." With regard to monasticism, the term means a form of monastic life in which monks (and, much more rarely, nuns) lived in the same institution but followed an individualistic regimen, focused on one's cell rather than the monastic community as a whole. Thus idiorrhythmic monks might have personal possessions and could earn money from their handwork to purchase their own clothing and food. Such monks did not take their meals in the communal refectory, but in their cells, and they might be permitted to eat meat. They might not even attend church services regularly, but instead engaged in private prayer. Such monasteries were sometimes administered by an oligarchic council (*synaxis*) of top officials rather than by a superior elected for life to whom absolute obedience was expected.[96]

The idiorrhythmic regimen has some elements in common with eremitism, which also rejected obedience to a superior and communal meals and stressed private prayer in a cell rather than church services, but hermits normally led a very ascetic life, with frugal diet and a minimum of possessions. In fact, the pejorative label of idiorrhythmic was occasionally applied to hermits, as in a thirteenth-century Athonite document describing two solitaries (*idiotai*) motivated by their own inclinations (*idiois logismois*), who wanted to build hermitages "not for the sake of practicing spiritual contemplation (*hesychia*), but in order to live as they wished in self-indulgence and *idiorrhythmia*."[97] In general *idiorrhythmia* was viewed by the Byzantines and now by modern scholars of monasticism as a more comfortable lifestyle than the rigorous regimen imposed by cenobitism and eremitism, and it has been condemned as a sign of decadence in a monastery. The term *idiorrhythmia* usually has a negative connotation, as opposing cenobitic ideals, and this form of monasticism was criticized in several founders' *typika* and Athonite acts. The twelfth-century *typikon* for the monastery of Areia, for example, stated bluntly that "the idiorhythmic and uncounseled life is perilous."[98]

Elements of the idiorrhythmic lifestyle began to appear in the middle Byzantine period, as in Calabria, on Mount Galesion in Anatolia, at St. Sabas (Mar Saba) in the Judean Desert, and at the monastery of Roidion in northern Syria. One of the earliest allusions to this individualistic form of monastic practice is found in the *vita* of Neilos of Rossano, a tenth-century monk of Calabria. At the time of Arab raids around 976, most monks at his monastery near Rossano fled to the safety of the fortress, but three stayed behind, "following their own individual regimen."[99] To turn to the eleventh century, the *vita* of Lazaros of Galesion provides valuable information on idiorrhythmic practices in both Palestine and Anatolia. Before settling on Mount Galesion as a stylite and monastic founder, Lazaros was for a time a monk at the *lavra* of St. Sabas When he insisted on spending the forty days of Lent wandering in the desert (as was customary for many Sabaite monks) despite the abbot's refusal to grant him permission, the abbot expelled him from the *lavra* upon his return, accusing him of "being an idiorrhythmic and someone who would rather follow his own wishes than those of his superior."[100] Subsequently, when Lazaros returned to Anatolia and became superior at the monastery of the Resurrection on Galesion, he himself was faced with the problem of disobedient monks who did not come to the refectory on a major feast day but took their meals in their cells, a typical mark of the idiorrhythmic regime.[101] He scolded these rebellious monks from his column, but we do not learn what ensued. At the north Syrian monastery and hospice of Roidion, which had adopted *idiorrhythmia* in the early twelfth century, the monastic reformer Nikon of the Black Mountain tried to impose a *typikon* that would begin to restore the monastery to cenobitism, but he was forced to make a number of concessions to the recalcitrant monks.[102] He reminded the monks that possession of private property was forbidden, but he acknowledged that monks could entertain guests in their cells, "on account of its not being a cenobitic community, but each brother separately takes care of his own [cell]."[103]

In the late Byzantine period, as idiorrhythmic practices became more prevalent, so did criticism of this new tendency in monastic practice. Thus, the rule of 1247 for the Skoteine monastery, near Philadelphia in western Anatolia, specifically enjoined that its monks should maintain a strictly cenobitic regimen:

> Nobody is to be off by himself [ἰδιάζοντα], or live by himself [ἰδιοβιοῦντα] or acquire things for himself. But together they are all to dine at one and the same table and to share the same food.... There is no doubt that living by oneself cuts one off from the others. By so being cut off one is preoccupied with oneself and left to one's own devices [ἰδιορυθμεῖ], and this is totally incompatible with common life. One thinks about and is concerned about one's own good rather than that of another.[104]

Likewise at the Charsianeites monastery in Constantinople, which was founded in the fourteenth century and zealously maintained the cenobitic tradition, admission was refused to idiorrhythmic *kelliotai* lest they be a source of "infection" to the community and persuade others to follow in their footsteps.[105] Monks already resident in the monastery who preferred a "self-regulating regime" should withdraw from the monastery.[106] The patriarch Matthew I (r. 1397–1410), the author of the Charsianeites *typikon*, even forbade the monks to receive letters, "for this is a sign of an idiorrhythmic discipline."[107]

The idiorrhythmic regimen became most prevalent on Mount Athos, where in the mid-fourteenth century this monastic lifestyle was adopted by a number of formerly cenobitic monasteries.[108] At Docheiariou, for instance, when Gregory Isbes was tonsured there at a mature age, around 1355, he retained his personal fortune, including a vineyard and 157 *hyperpyra* in cash.[109] An example of tensions over attempts to introduce *idiorrhythmia* can be seen at the Koutloumousiou monastery in the 1370s, when its superior, Chariton, wrote three separate testaments that dealt in part with Vlach monks from wealthy and noble families who wanted to follow an idiorrhythmic regime. Chariton was forced to permit this concession in order to gain financial support from the voivode of Wallachia: "I exempt and permit the Vlachs who shall come from a lordly station and who provide the monastery with sufficient funds for their comfort . . . to regulate their manner of life as each is able from his own resources."[110] Yet even here in 1387 one can see signs of resistance to private property in the case of an abbot and a monk who had received life interest in a *kellion* with chapel and vineyard; they both decided, however, that it was improper for them to hold personal title to real estate, and they turned it over to the monastery.[111] Koutloumousiou did not return to a cenobitic status until the mid-nineteenth century.

In 1394 and again in 1396, the patriarch Anthony IV (r. 1389–90, 1391–97) exhorted the Athonite monks of Pantokrator to continue to adhere to cenobitic rules, a clear sign that their observance was being neglected; he specifically forbade the acquisition of private property.[112] His contemporary, Manuel II Palaiologos (r. 1391–1425), however, in his general *typikon* for all the Athonite monasteries, written in 1406, recognized the reality that a monk might grow restive with the cenobitic regime and "remain in his cell without the consent of his own superior, embracing the idiorhythmic life on the pretext of seeking solitude."[113]

During the many centuries of Ottoman rule over the Holy Mountain there was a marked decline in cenobitism, and many of the major monasteries, even the Great Lavra, became idiorrhythmic. During this period, monks were not bound by vows of poverty or obedience, and they could have servants and private apartments.[114]

But with the renewal of monasticism on Athos in the second half of the twentieth century, and a great increase in the number of monks, cenobitism has been revived; by 1992, all monasteries were again following the communal form of monastic life hallowed by tradition, but an idiorrhythmic regimen continues in the *sketes* (dependencies of the monasteries) with small numbers of kelliots.[115]

EUNUCHS IN MONASTERIES AND MONASTERIES FOR EUNUCHS

Eunuchs, relatively rare in medieval Western Europe, were more common in Byzantium, but few in overall numbers. They are attested in many aspects of Byzantine society, especially at the imperial court but also in the army and in the Church.[116] In the middle Byzantine period, most eunuchs had been castrated as youths by their families in the expectation that they would thus attain high positions and attendant remuneration, especially at court where a number of offices, such as chamberlain, were reserved for eunuchs.[117] They were highly valued at court because their physical imperfection rendered them ineligible to be emperor and incapable of fathering children and establishing a potential rival dynasty. Eunuchs could become monks, priests, bishops, and even patriarch; a noted example was Ignatios (patriarch, 847–58, 867–77). The son of Emperor Michael I (811–13), he was castrated after his father was deposed from the throne and forced to take monastic vows. He became superior of three monasteries that he established on the Princes' Islands near Constantinople, and he later served two terms on the patriarchal throne.

There was a wide range of attitudes among Byzantine monastic leaders about whether it was a good idea to permit eunuchs to join a monastery as tonsured monks. At many monasteries there was an outright prohibition of castrated monks, who were viewed as a potential source of disruption to the community and, when lumped together with boys and beardless youths, as posing a sexual temptation. At other monasteries they were admitted without any apparent prejudice, and sometimes even became superiors.[118] And a very few monasteries were reserved for eunuchs alone. Nunneries welcomed eunuchs into their precincts as priests, doctors, and stewards, precisely because they were regarded as not likely to be a source of temptation for the nuns or to engage in sexual improprieties.

Prohibition of Eunuch Monks

A number of middle Byzantine monasteries explicitly banned the admission of eunuchs to their communities, continuing a tradition that is found in earlier establishments in late antiquity. For example, the mid-tenth-century *typikon* of Emperor John I Tzimiskes for the holy mountain of Athos was very strict about forbidding the tonsuring of eunuchs along with youths and boys.[119] The contemporaneous *typikon* of Athanasios for the Great Lavra also specified that no eunuch was permitted at the monastery, "even if he be an old man."[120] Clearly there were violations of this ordinance, for a mid-eleventh-century *typikon* of Emperor Constantine IX (r. 1042–55) reiterates that any eunuch or youth who had been tonsured in violation of the earlier rulings was to be expelled.[121] In fact, the monastic authorities removed several of these individuals at this time.

The problem reemerged some decades later with the surprising story of Symeon the Sanctified, a eunuch who became superior of the Xenophon monastery and was viewed as its second founder. Despite the renewed ban on beardless youths and eunuchs on the Holy Mountain, Symeon, a eunuch and former imperial official, arrived on Athos during the reign of Nikephoros III Botaneiates (r. 1078–81), accompanied by three unbearded youths, who may also have been eunuchs. He was apparently able to take over the leadership of Xenophon on account of his large donations, which facilitated repairs to the dilapidated monastery. In 1081, however, he and his three companions were expelled and made their way to Thessalonike, where he founded a monastery for eunuchs.[122] By 1089, he was permitted to return to Xenophon, where he evidently remained until his death. This is a flagrant instance of a major donor being permitted to flout the rule forbidding eunuchs on Athos.[123]

We know that the problem of illicit eunuch monks still persisted on Athos in the early fifteenth century when Emperor Manuel II once again declared a ban on youths and eunuchs, specifying that this rule was to prevent women in disguise from sneaking onto the Holy Mountain![124] By this date, however, the overall demand for eunuchs had declined, and there were in fact very few eunuch monks,[125] so the rule was probably directed primarily against beardless youths.

We see similar prohibitions in the eleventh-century *typikon* of Gregory Pakourianos for his monastery at Bačkovo in Bulgaria and in Christodoulos's almost contemporary rule for his monastery on the island of Patmos; the latter specified that this ban was necessary to avoid any form of sexual temptation for the monks.[126] At the Kosmosoteira monastery in Thrace, established in the mid-twelfth century, its founder Isaak Komnenos also banned eunuchs, whom he viewed as a "cause of turmoil to natural habits and to morals," that is, a cause of sexual temptation; he was willing to make an exception, however, if the eunuch had a prominent position and was wealthy.[127]

Acceptance of Eunuch Monks

At other monasteries, eunuchs were admitted without any discrimination. At least two eunuchs from Paphlagonia served as superior of the St. Mamas monastery in Constantinople: Symeon the New Theologian, and his disciple and immediate successor, Arsenios.[128] It has only been recognized relatively recently that Symeon, who had taken his vows at the Stoudios monastery, was a eunuch; as a youth he had held the court position of imperial escort (*spatharokoubikoularios*), normally reserved for eunuchs.[129] When the youthful Symeon entered the Stoudios monastery as a novice, he was instructed by his spiritual father, Symeon Eulabes, to sleep under a stairwell in Eulabes's cell and perform menial tasks for him.[130] One wonders if perhaps Eulabes had ulterior motives, since the Stoudite rule specifically prohibited the superior from having an adolescent disciple in his cell "out of affection."[131]

A certain Nikephoros, castrated as a young child, became bishop of Miletos in the second half of the tenth century. He was also admitted to the monastery of St. Paul on Latros without any difficulties when he renounced his pastoral duties.[132] His hagiographer launches into a disquisition about Nikephoros's successful control of his sexual appetites, and he comments that one should not believe that sexual desire was cut out along with the genitals and that continence was thus easier for Nikephoros as a eunuch: "For those who are experts on nature say that the sexual urge for intercourse is more extreme and fierce in eunuchs than in those whose bodies have not suffered castration."[133]

Monasteries Restricted to Eunuchs

Finally, a few monasteries were restricted to eunuchs;[134] as Greenfield has suggested, this may have been on account of the unease we have seen about the presence of eunuchs in monastic institutions.[135] Around 900, Emperor Leo VI (r. 886–912) established the monastery of St. Lazaros in Constantinople near the palace and reserved it for the use of eunuchs. It is doubtful, however, if this restriction continued down through the centuries, since no later account refers to eunuch monks there.[136] Also located in Constantinople was the monastery of Christ Panoiktirmon, whose rule survives. Founded by Michael Attaleiates in the late eleventh century, it was very small, limited to five to seven eunuch monks, evidently of aristocratic background since they were provided with servants and allowances. Attaleiates's motive in limiting this monastery to eunuchs was his conviction that they were less subject to sexual temptation; he wanted these monks to be "free from passions" because the monastery was situated in the middle of the imperial city, close to the marketplace with all its potential distractions. Even here, however, Attaleiates stipulated that exceptions to the rule could be made, and a bearded monk could be admitted if he were one of Attaleiates's relatives, or if he were of good character, over fifty years of age, and brought with him an endowment of real estate.[137]

In contrast to the urban monastery of Christ Panoiktirmon, the monastery of Christ the Savior on Mount Galesion, near Ephesos, was isolated on a barren mountainside. This was one of three monasteries founded on the holy mountain by Lazaros the stylite in the mid-eleventh century. Apparently, eunuch monks had originally been integrated into the two other Galesiot monastic communities of the Theotokos and the Resurrection, but problems arose, probably because of the temptations to homosexual behavior posed by the eunuchs. Hence Lazaros decreed that all the eunuchs on Mount Galesion should be forced to live together in a community of twelve brethren at the monastery of Christ the Savior.[138]

The sources provide virtually no information about relations between eunuchs and whole men in monasteries where they were integrated, and we know almost nothing about how or whether the spiritual life of eunuchs might have differed from that of other monks. Certainly, there were opposing views of eunuch monks, seen by some as beardless and effeminate sources of homoerotic temptation, by others as earthly angels, reflecting the representation of angels as eunuchs in dream and waking visions. One of the most helpful sources on attitudes toward eunuch monks is found in the famous work of Theophylact, archbishop of Ohrid in the late eleventh and early twelfth centuries, *In Defense of Eunuchs*.[139] In this work, addressed to his eunuch brother Demetrios Hephaistos, Theophylact presents the argument that eunuchs make better monks than ascetics do because they are necessarily chaste and cannot ejaculate sperm.[140] He also offers the rejoinder that eunuchs did not deserve such praise because they did not have to struggle to preserve their chastity, but had no choice but to remain celibate. Thus the ascetic who practices voluntary chastity is superior to the eunuch.[141]

Some eunuch monks were invited to fill staff positions at nunneries as priests, confessors, physicians, and stewards. Because of their close contact with nuns, they had to be above suspicion; castrated men were deemed to pose less of a risk.[142]

COMPARISON OF CENOBITIC MONASTICISM IN BYZANTIUM AND THE MEDIEVAL WEST

Scholars have paid surprisingly little attention to the divergent monastic practices that emerged as the worlds of Byzantium and Western medieval Europe grew apart. The best comparative analysis of which I am aware is the masterful preface by Giles Constable to the collection of Byzantine monastic foundation documents in translation to which I have alluded so frequently.[143]

In contrast to the Benedictine rule, which stressed the necessity for monastic stability, in Byzantine monasteries there was a noteworthy lack of emphasis on *stabilitas loci*, that is, a monk's obligation to remain for life in the monastery where he took the habit. Byzantine monks were free to leave their monasteries to go on pilgrimage or to transfer to another institution, or to move away from a cenobitic monastery to a hermitage in the wilderness.[144]

As Constable has emphasized, by the high Middle Ages in the West, a substantial number of monks were ordained as priests and could celebrate Mass, whereas in Byzantium this was less common. One set of statistics from *typika* suggests that perhaps only one-fifth of the residents of a Byzantine monastery were priests or deacons, whereas data from a different source, a prosopographical dictionary of the late Byzantine period, indicates that almost half of known Byzantine monks were ordained as hieromonks (*hieromonachoi*), that is, priest-monks.[145]

The average age for entry of novices tended to be higher in the East than in the West, where it was more common for children to be given to monasteries as oblates. In Byzantium many monastic *typika* restricted the age of admission to the high teens or even early twenties, and the novitiate also tended to be longer.[146]

The reluctance to admit adolescents to monasteries before they grew a beard may help to explain another basic difference between Western and Eastern monasteries, namely, the relative paucity of monastic schools in Byzantium. John Thomas has argued that this lack of emphasis on formal schooling in a monastic environment demonstrates a less prominent "commitment to literacy and sense of educational mission ... in medieval Byzantine monasteries."[147] Schools are very seldom mentioned in the *typika* and hagiographic texts, and they were not designed for the education of lay children but usually reserved for children or adolescents who intended to remain in the monastery and take vows. The few documented Byzantine monastic schools were also at times physically separated from the monastery, so that the students would not be a distraction or temptation for the monks. Thus, Athanasios of Athos, in order to segregate the young novices from the older monks, founded one school (*phrontisterion*) at the satellite monastery (*metochion*) of Mylopotamos, and another on the island of Neoi near the Great Lavra.[148] In the West, on the other hand, monastic schools were more common and provided educational opportunities not only for future monks but also for lay boys destined for careers outside the monastery.[149]

Rules on personal poverty also diverged in East and West; in the medieval West, divestment of one's personal property was the rule, whereas in Byzantium practice varied widely between monasteries. Some *typika* were very strict in requiring new monks to get rid of all their possessions before they could be admitted, whereas others were much more lenient on this point.[150] At Evergetis, for example, following the Stoudite tradition, monks were forbidden to have even a piece of fruit or small coin in their cells without seeking permission from the abbot.[151] At the contemporary monastery of the Resurrection on Mount Galesion, however, the superior Lazaros found it difficult to dissuade his monks from keeping icons and votive lamps in their cells.[152] And, as we have seen, in the very late Byzantine period an idiorrhythmic, or individualized, form of monasticism began to appear, especially on Mount Athos, which permitted the retention of possessions and the earning of money.

Byzantine monks almost always lived in private cells, usually alone, but sometimes in pairs, in contrast to the West where communal dormitories were common practice in certain monastic orders, such as the Benedictines and Cistercians.[153] In the earlier days of Byzantine monasticism, in sixth-century Constantinople,

Emperor Justinian had decreed that monks should sleep in a common dormitory so that they could keep an eye on each other.[154] But this strict rule fell into abeyance, with only a few exceptions, as on Mount Latros in western Anatolia where there was a dormitory at the male monastery of Stylos.[155]

There also seem to have been differences in the dietary regimen: the Polish scholar Maria Dembińska has argued, on the basis of quite limited evidence, that in general the dietary regimen in the East was stricter and provided fewer calories than that for Western medieval monasteries.[156] In the East, complete abstinence from meat seems to have been so much the norm that only a few Byzantine foundation documents even mention the topic.[157] In contrast the Benedictine rule permitted the consumption of poultry, and gravely ill monks were allowed to eat the meat of quadrupeds.[158]

Yet another noteworthy point of distinction is the presence of eunuchs in Byzantine monasteries, a phenomenon rare in the West.[159] Some Eastern monasteries, in fact, housed only eunuchs, while in nunneries eunuchs were often the only men trusted to serve as priests, confessors, stewards, and physicians.[160] In the East, eunuchs (and adolescents, where permitted) were the only beardless men allowed in male monasteries, whereas in the West Latin monks and clerics normally wore short hair and shaved, but, in the words of Giles Constable, "not too closely or too often."[161] In fact, as Linda Safran has observed, "in the twelfth century, a European monk was permitted to shave only fourteen, seven or six times per year, according to the Cluniacs, Cistercians and Carthusians, respectively, so few monks were truly beardless, if indeed these regulations were enforced."[162]

Finally, let me return to the fundamental distinction between East and West: there were no separate monastic orders in Byzantium. Perusal of the sixty-one translated Byzantine foundation documents demonstrates the great variety in regulations for individual monasteries, and one can see a whole spectrum of positions on such issues as the age of tonsure and the proper way to elect an abbot. Hans-Georg Beck has argued that this diversity can be explained by the individualism that was characteristic of Byzantine society.[163] Yet this should not obscure the reality that certain monasteries provided influential models for their successors and affiliates. For instance, there were linkages among some monasteries, such as those of the Stoudite federation, which were loyal to a common religious leader, Theodore, and shared a common rule; between the Great Lavra on Athos and Stoudios, which inspired parts of Athanasios's rule; and between the Evergetis monastery and later foundations that selected parts of its *typikon* for incorporation into their own foundation rules. One of the major contributions of John Thomas's edition of the translated Byzantine monastic foundation documents was his painstaking recording of intertextual borrowings between these texts. In my view, further inquiry into the relationships between monasteries with similar *typika* would prove fruitful for future scholarship.

It was also common for large monasteries to have smaller satellite monasteries as dependencies (*metochia*); thus, the superior of the imperial monastery of Pantokrator in Constantinople controlled six smaller monasteries, each of which had a steward to manage its financial affairs.[164] It seems likely that, as with the Stoudite federation, the dependencies of other monasteries followed the same *typikon* as their mother house. Current fieldwork in Greece is investigating the architectural and artistic relationships between the monastery of Hosios Loukas in Phokis and its *metochia*, and has found similarities in church types and decoration. When this research is further developed, it could provide fascinating corroboration of networks of monasteries in Byzantium.[165]

Finally, as Rosemary Morris has noted, on Mount Athos, apart from the rules for the Great Lavra, "there are no formal Greek typika for individual Athonite houses ... this would suggest that the regulations laid down in the Typikon of John Tzimiskes ... and later in that of Constantine Monomachos, formed a basic set of regulations to which all the Athonite monasteries were expected to adhere."[166] She has also suggested that perhaps there were "territorial *typika*" that might serve as a rule for all the monasteries on a holy mountain. At Mount Galesion, however, we know that Lazaros had somewhat different rules for his two earlier foundations, the Savior and the Theotokos, which were strictly cenobitic, in contrast to his final Galesiot establishment, the Resurrection, where private property was permitted in the cell.[167] Moreover, one of the monasteries, that of Christ the Savior, was restricted to eunuchs.

One can conclude, therefore, that although there were no monastic "orders" in Byzantium, there were relationships and affiliations between certain monasteries, those which followed a similar *typikon*, smaller dependencies of a larger monastery, and regional groupings, such as were to be found on a holy mountain.

CHAPTER 2

NUNS AND NUNNERIES

In this chapter I discuss the female monastic experience in Byzantium and deal almost exclusively with cenobitic convents, for a simple reason: in contrast to their male counterparts, most Byzantine nuns were cloistered in a community. They did not live as solitaries, belong to small groups of hermits on holy mountains as *kelliotai*, or move back and forth between cenobitic life and the wilderness, but they almost always remained within the convent walls after taking their monastic vows.[1] The twelfth-century canonist Theodore Balsamon applauded this difference between the sexes, praising nuns for their more faithful adherence to the ideals of cenobitism and unfavorably comparing Byzantine monks with their brethren in the medieval West, who dined together and slept in a communal dormitory: in his view, "only in [Byzantine] female monasteries are a common dietary regimen and sleeping arrangements observed." He argued that the cenobitic lifestyle was both necessary and appropriate for nuns, following the argument of canon 47 of the Council of Carthage (419), which maintained that women who had left their fathers' homes needed the mutual protection of communal living and should not live by themselves.[2]

SOURCES FOR NUNS AND NUNNERIES
BETWEEN 800 AND 1453

Anyone familiar with the resources for the study of female monasticism in the medieval West, such as saints' lives, foundation charters, archival documents, episcopal visitation records, texts authored by nuns, archaeological data, and the like, would be shocked at the paucity of materials for research on Byzantine nuns. I should note that my own original inspiration for researching female religious in Byzantium, forty-five years ago, was reading Eileen Power's book *Medieval English Nunneries* (1922);[3] regrettably there is nothing in the Byzantine world comparable to the bishops' registers she so deftly mined. The richest data on Byzantine nunneries is to be found in the six surviving *typika*, or foundation documents, all composed between the twelfth and fourteenth centuries. Some of them are quite long and detailed, and they tell us a great deal about the organization of nunneries and rules for enclosure, meals in the refectory, attendance at church services, and the like, but they must be treated with caution as normative documents, which present an ideal for female monastic life.[4]

Thus, data from the foundation rules must be weighed against information from hagiography, which often presents telling insights into details of everyday life in a Byzantine convent. Yet female monastic saints were much rarer than their male counterparts in Byzantium, and from the period 800–1500 there survive only a handful of *vitae* of sanctified nuns who lived in cenobitic convents. The three *vitae* with most useful information on convent life are those of Athanasia of Aegina, Theodora of Thessalonike, and Irene of Chrysobalanton.[5]

Also useful at filling in some of the lacunae in our knowledge are the records of provincial ecclesiastical courts and the synod in Constantinople. A few documents found in monastic archives mention nuns, but it should be noted that no documents at all are preserved from Byzantine nunneries except for the foundation rules we just mentioned.

It is also important to remember that most of the above sources, such as the *vitae*, synodal records, and monastic archives, were written by men; five of the *typika* for convents were ostensibly authored by their female founders (the sixth is by Neilos Damilas), but the *typikon* for Lips, supposedly drafted by Empress Theodora Palaiologina, was actually composed by a ghostwriter.[6] Irene Doukaina's *typikon* for the Kecharitomene convent is based indirectly (via another *typikon*) on the rule for the male monastery of the Theotokos Evergetis.[7] The *typikon* of Theodora Synadene for the nunnery of Sure Hope is based on an Evergetian model, but its autobiographical introduction, concern for her daughter's lifestyle as a tonsured nun, and detailed instructions for the commemoration of deceased relatives strongly suggest that Theodora herself may have dictated large portions of the document to a notary.

THREE BYZANTINE NUNS

Let me now introduce three Byzantine nuns: one was from a pious family in ninth-century Thessalonike, devoted to service of the Church, and two were founders of convents in Constantinople in the late Byzantine period. Inconveniently for my readers, they were all named Theodora, but I will do my best to distinguish them for you.

St. Theodora of Thessalonike and the Convent of St. Stephen

The *vita* of St. Theodora of Thessalonike (812–92) has preserved a vivid description of the nunnery of St. Stephen in Thessalonike where she lived for more than fifty years.[8] The original buildings of the nunnery have disappeared, but the convent, now dedicated to St. Theodora, continues to function: a modern church and living quarters occupy the site at present. This first Theodora, a refugee from Arab attacks on the island of Aegina in the early ninth century, settled in Thessalonike where she suffered the loss of two of her three children. After Theodora and her husband dedicated their sole surviving child, a six-year-old girl, to monastic life, Theodora was widowed at age twenty-five and entered the convent of St. Stephen, where one of her female relatives, Anna, served as abbess. Here, too, family ties were maintained: Anna's sister was also a nun at the convent, and Theodora soon moved her young daughter, Theopiste, to St. Stephen's to join her. Eventually Theopiste would succeed Anna as abbess.

Despite her comfortable background, the future saint eagerly embraced the hardships of monastic life. Although strict asceticism was not normally expected of nuns, Theodora would sometimes go a week without drinking water and scarcely touch her food in the refectory.[9] She also willingly assumed all sorts of menial duties out of humility: in the words of her hagiographer, "she performed by herself almost all the work of the convent, grinding grain, making bread with her own hands, and cooking, work which she had never done before. And in addition to this, she used to carry out another responsibility, going to the marketplace . . . for the abundance of goods for sale; and she used to walk through the marketplace carrying a huge load of wood . . . on her shoulders."[10]

She and her daughter also wove cloth on a loom.[11] Theodora slept on a rush mat and sheepskin in a communal dormitory (*koiton*) equipped with a fireplace, which also doubled as a dining room in wintertime when the refectory was too chilly to use.[12] When the elderly abbess Anna fell and dislocated her hip, it was Theodora who took on nursing duties for her bedridden relative, bringing her food, turning her in bed to avoid bedsores, and bathing her. When Theodora herself grew old, she continued to work as long as she could, carrying a small pitcher to the well to fetch her own water, spinning coarse flax and wool, and making bags.[13]

Empress Theodora Palaiologina and the Convent of Lips

Byzantine women from noble and imperial families sometimes demonstrated their piety by founding convents that were intended to serve as refuges for female members of the family or as a family

FIGURE 4   Church of the Lips convent, Fenari Isa Camii (photo: Image Collection and Fieldwork Archives, Dumbarton Oaks, Trustees for Harvard University, Washington, DC)

mausoleum. The dowager empress Theodora Palaiologina, widow of Emperor Michael VIII (r. 1259–82), is best known for her establishment of the Constantinopolitan nunnery of Lips in the late thirteenth century.[14] The empress's primary focus was the restoration as a convent of an older tenth-century male monastery that had fallen into disrepair, but she also added a second church and a narthex, both intended to serve as a mausoleum for members of her family.[15] Located in the center of Constantinople, near the Lykos River, the double church survives to this day as a mosque called Fenari Isa Camii (fig. 4).

The surviving copy of her *typikon*, a deluxe manuscript of the fourteenth century, is now in fragmentary condition because of the excision of some of the decorative headpieces, but most of it is preserved.[16] The newly established convent was designed to house fifty nuns: thirty choir sisters and twenty nuns charged with housekeeping duties, such as a sacristan, cellarer, and gatekeeper. As was to be expected, the main avowed purpose of the institution was the performance of the canonical offices in praise of the Lord and the Virgin, the appropriate celebration of feast days, and prayers for the salvation of mankind. The dowager empress clearly also intended, however, to establish an imperial nunnery that would accommodate herself and her female relatives who chose to take the veil, normally after they were widowed or in old age. The rule grants extraordinary privileges to these women, if they should choose not to abide by the regulations laid down for ordinary nuns. Thus, in contravention of cenobitic practice, her daughters, nieces, and granddaughters were not required to eat at communal tables in the refectory, but they could take meals in their private quarters, attended by personal servants. Each of her daughters was granted the food provisions of four nuns and was entitled to three personal attendants, either from her own secular household or nuns assigned to these duties. These female relatives were, however, expected to attend church services.[17] In contrast, the ordinary nuns were charged to respect the principle of equality, not to request special food, or complain about the seating order in the refectory.[18] The omission of any reference to "handwork" by the nuns may suggest that weaving and other textile arts were not required of nuns in this privileged convent.

Another motivating factor for Empress Theodora's foundation was to provide a mausoleum for members of the Palaiologan dynasty, such as the Komnenoi had established for themselves at the Pantokrator monastery in the twelfth century. When Theodora formulated the foundation document, she noted that one daughter was already buried at Lips, and she made provision for additional tombs for herself, her mother, and her surviving children, including her son, Emperor Andronikos II (1282–1328).[19] Unfortunately, her husband, Michael VIII, who had died in 1282, could not be interred in the family mausoleum, because in 1274 he had supported the Union of the Churches at the Council of Lyon, and hence was deemed a schismatic. Theodora's foundation may thus have been inspired in part by a desire to atone for her marriage to a Unionist husband and her own brief acceptance of Catholicism.[20] Dorothy Abrahamse has remarked on the number of imperial mausoleums established at convents, such as Gastria, Euphemia in Petrion, Myrelaion, and Lips, as follows: "The attachment of mausolea to women's communities must have rendered their functions in the care and remembrance of the dead particularly important."[21]

Yet another purpose was the commemoration of deceased members of the imperial family. At each of the four prescribed weekly liturgies, four loaves of bread were to be consecrated in memory of Theodora's relatives: one for her own ancestors, a second for her son, the emperor, and his wife; a third for her other children; and a fourth for herself and her mother. In addition, every Saturday small Eucharistic loaves in the shape of a cross were to be offered up in memory of her deceased ancestors and children and all her relatives who would die thereafter.[22] The nuns were to ensure that candles were kept burning in perpetuity over Theodora's tomb and those of her children.[23]

Empress Theodora's final aim was the provision of charitable services to less fortunate members of society. Her distribution at the gatehouse of alms and bread to the poor seems to have been minimal, limited to the feast day of John the Baptist, the patron saint of the nunnery.[24] She did, however, build a twelve-bed hospice (*xenon*) at her new foundation, apparently intended for the long-term care of women who were elderly or disabled. Provision was made for bedding and clothing for the patients, plus food, wine, and firewood. Theodora also designated a priest to conduct services for the ailing women, perform the last rites, and accompany their funeral processions.[25]

Thus, multiple motives prompted Empress Theodora to restore and enlarge the convent of Lips: her desire to atone for her husband's embrace of the Union of Lyon, her wish to create a dynastic mausoleum for the Palaiologan family and provide for their commemoration, her yearning to provide a place of spiritual refuge for herself and her female relatives and descendants, and a pious urge to furnish a charitable institution to care for laywomen in their old age.

Theodora Synadene and the Convent of Sure Hope

A second *typikon* for a Constantinopolitan convent presents the rule for the aristocratic nunnery of the Virgin of Sure Hope (*Bebaia Elpis*), founded in the late thirteenth century by Theodora Synadene, niece of Emperor Michael VIII and the young widow of a prominent general.[26] The buildings of the convent, located in the south central region of the city on the slope above the Heptaskalon harbor on the Sea of Marmara, have long since disappeared, but the foundation rule is preserved in a deluxe edition at Oxford University, the Lincoln College Typikon.[27] The first twelve folios of the manuscript contain beautiful miniatures of the foundress and her family, her parents, husband, children, four granddaughters, and their husbands. The sumptuous dress of these members of the aristocracy demonstrates the wealth of the Synadenos family and contrasts markedly with the plain habits of the nuns who are depicted in a separate group portrait (fig. 5).

Theodora Synadene states in the prologue to her *typikon* that she decided to dedicate a nunnery to the Virgin of Sure Hope for several reasons: to provide a safe refuge for women who had chosen to withdraw from the world, as an act of thanksgiving for all the blessings she had received in life, and as a haven for herself, since as a widow she had decided to take the veil as the nun Theodoule. She brought with her into the cloister her beloved daughter Euphrosyne, "dedicated to God since infancy," whom she expected also to become a nun (fig. 6). Theodora made special provisions for her daughter's comfort, however, because of her frail health and "many serious illnesses."[28] Noble women who entered this convent also received unusual privileges, such as dietary concessions, more frequent baths, and entitlement to the assistance of a servant.[29]

The thirty choir sisters were required to attend all church offices. The housekeeping nuns were excused from attendance if they were busy with their domestic responsibilities, but if they were free they were expected to come to church whenever possible. At the same time they were enjoined not to bring with them

FIGURE 5 Lincoln College Typikon (Lincoln College gr. 35), fol. 12ʳ: group portrait of nuns from convent of Sure Hope (photo: By permission of the Rector and Fellows of Lincoln College, Oxford)

FIGURE 6   Lincoln College Typikon (Lincoln College gr. 35), fol. 11ʳ: Theodora Synadene with her daughter Euphrosyne (photo: By permission of the Rector and Fellows of Lincoln College, Oxford)

their handwork (perhaps spinning) but to concentrate on the hymns and prayers.[30]

A prominent feature of the *typikon* for the convent of Sure Hope is its detailed description of the commemorative services to be held on the death anniversaries of both male and female members of Theodora Synadene's family, most of whom were also benefactors of the convent. In exchange for donations, such as an icon of the Virgin of Sure Hope (now at the Vatopedi monastery on Mount Athos), her deceased relatives were to be honored with special liturgies and illumination of the church, and extra food for the nuns.[31]

COMMON THEMES

Widowhood

All three Theodoras were widowed when they entered monastic life, at least one of them (Theodora of Thessalonike) still in her twenties. This was a quite common phenomenon in Byzantium: although some girls chose to take the veil as teenaged virgins, out of a true vocation, many women entered convents later in life, often after losing their husbands. Widowhood usually brought about momentous changes in a woman's life that might lead her to seek the social and financial security of retirement to a convent. Remarriage was discouraged in Byzantium, and some widows might find themselves without family support; the tenth-century Italo-Greek monk Neilos of Calabria urged the townsmen of Rossano to maintain a nunnery so that their widowed spouses could seek refuge there and not be forced into a second marriage.[32] For some widows, monastic tonsure was a question of financial necessity, as in the case of a certain Zoe from Thessaly, who found herself in dire straits, not only widowed but with no siblings or children to look after her, and so strapped for cash that she had no money for food. In 1271 she made an arrangement with a nearby nunnery that in exchange for her sale to the convent for a nominal sum (five gold pieces) of some fields, vineyards, and a fig tree she would be tonsured as a nun and be supported for the rest of her life. Upon her death, the convent would see to her proper burial and commemoration.[33] For wealthy women, such as Empress Theodora Palaiologina and the noblewoman Theodora Synadene, widowhood provided the opportunity to recover control of their dowries and use them for pious purposes, such as the foundation of convents, where they could also find companionship and a secure home for their old age. They were also assured of decent burial and annual commemorations on the anniversary of their death. For Theodora of Thessalonike, a refugee who had lost a husband and two of her three children, a convent where two of her relatives were already nuns provided a welcome haven.

Involuntary Vocations

Two of our Theodoras, Theodora Synadene and Theodora of Thessalonike, were mothers who dedicated their daughters to the service of God at a young age, long before the age of consent. Theodora Synadene brought with her to the convent of Sure Hope her young daughter, Euphrosyne, whom she describes as her "only daughter, the ... light of my eyes, my sweetest love, the flame of my heart, my breath and life, the hope of my old age, my refreshment, my comfort, my consolation."[34] She had vowed to make Euphrosyne a bride of Christ, and it is unlikely that Euphrosyne had any voice in this decision. Despite Euphrosyne's frail constitution, she survived her mother and continued Theodora's role as a foundress of the convent, increasing the number of nuns from thirty to fifty and adding some regulations to the *typikon*.

Likewise, Theodora of Thessalonike brought her daughter Theopiste to a convent at age six; since Theodora's two younger children had died as infants or toddlers, she decided to offer her oldest child to God as "first fruits" in the hope that he would spare the girl's life.[35] Theopiste had no choice in the matter and spent her entire life as a nun, ending up as abbess of the convent. At the same nunnery, a toddler, named Theopiste after the abbess, was dedicated to monastic life by her father, Theodotos, at the age of one year after her miraculous recovery from a serious illness; supposedly the girl lived happily ever after in the convent.[36]

Many other girls and women ended up in a convent against their will or because they had no other recourse: orphans, the daughters and wives of deposed emperors, girls disfigured by smallpox and deemed unmarriageable, the mentally ill, wives of priests who were promoted to the rank of bishop.[37] For many such women the convent proved to be a welcome refuge, but a few could not tolerate the strict routine and left, if they could. They might run away or be expelled for disobedience or bad behavior.[38]

Family Ties

A third theme that echoes through these three biographies of nuns is the importance of family ties.[39] Although there are numerous Byzantine examples of an uncle and nephew residing in the same monastery, women religious seem to have felt more keenly the desire to be surrounded by family members, even in spiritual retirement. On the one hand, visitation of relatives was officially discouraged, and in theory nuns were to treat family members in the same institution just like any other nuns, as spiritual mothers, sisters, or daughters. A famous story from the *vita* of Theodora of Thessalonike demonstrates, however, how difficult it was to ignore the bonds of kinship. The widowed Theodora had arranged for her young daughter, Theopiste, her sole surviving child, to come live in the same nunnery with her. She could not forget her maternal ties, however, and was unusually solicitous of the girl's well-being, worried about whether she was getting enough food to eat and complaining about her tattered garments. When the abbess became aware of Theodora's attachment to her daughter, she imposed a terrible punishment: the two were to live together in the same cell, grinding grain and weaving at the loom, without ever exchanging a word with each other. This punishment lasted for fifteen years, until Theodora fell ill and the abbess released mother and daughter from this penance.[40]

In reality, many Byzantine convents, particularly the aristocratic and imperial foundations, seem to have been family-centered institutions to a greater degree than male monasteries. We have already noted that Theodora's convent in Thessalonike housed at least four members of her extended family. She sought admission to a convent where a relative served as abbess and where her daughter would eventually become the mother superior and promote her mother's cult. Foundresses, such as Irene Doukaina at Kecharitomene, Theodora Palaiologina at Lips, and Theodora Synadene at Sure Hope, made provision for their daughters, nieces, and granddaughters to enter their convents, usually with special privileges.[41] They also were very concerned about commemorative services for their departed relatives, both male and female, and in some cases made arrangements for their burials in the main church.[42] The Lips convent was restored in large part to provide a mausoleum for the Palaiologan family. Theodora Synadene was concerned that her daughter should have a monastic vocation and stressed the commemoration by the nuns of deceased family members. Both her daughter-in-law and granddaughter had taken vows by the time of their death, and her great-granddaughter was tonsured at an early age.[43] Although in theory Theodora Synadene had retired from the world, her two sons lived right across the street from the convent gate, and her sister had her own convent adjacent to that of the nunnery of Sure Hope.[44] The family portraits that form the frontispieces to the Lincoln College Typikon leave no doubt as to the role of the convent of Sure Hope as a family institution, and indeed we know that patronage of the convent in the female line continued down to at least the fourth generation after Theodora Synadene.

Inequality of Nuns

A fourth theme that emerges in the descriptions of Byzantine nunneries is the significant differences in lifestyle between privileged nuns, on the one hand, and the choir sisters and working nuns, on the other. The *typika* of some aristocratic and imperial foundations granted concessions to nuns who were used to luxuries in their secular lives, while absolute equality was the norm for ordinary nuns. The *typikon* for the twelfth-century Kecharitomene nunnery, founded in the capital by Empress Irene Doukaina, even provides her relatives with separate apartments; this was particularly desirable since Kecharitomene was one of the few attested nunneries with a communal dormitory (*koitoniskos*) rather than individual sleeping cells. If the nuns became too numerous, an overflow could be permitted into an adjoining room. Ailing nuns were allowed to move to individual cells.[45] The privileged nuns were also permitted to eat in their cells instead of in the refectory and to have more food than the ordinary nuns. Even burial might be separate: at Kecharitomene, the founder's female relatives who had been tonsured were buried in the exonarthex of the convent church, while the other nuns were laid to rest in a cemetery outside the monastic precincts.[46] Similar privileges were extended at the convent of Lips to female relatives of its imperial foundress, Theodora Palaiologina, who could take meals in their rooms and be attended by personal servants.

Not all wealthy founders, however, replicated external socioeconomic differences within the nunnery. At the aristocratic Constantinopolitan convent of Sure Hope, its founder, Theodora Synadene, insisted on the observance of an egalitarian cenobitic regimen by all the nuns, irrespective of their social background. Every nun was to eat at the common table, and no one was to have any private possessions.[47] Theodora also stressed that all handwork was to be for communal projects, and that no one was allowed to engage in private handwork, "not even to the extent of making a cord of wool [for herself]."[48] In a later addition to the *typikon*, Theodora's daughter Euphrosyne specifically commended the nuns because "you do not have your own dwellings and idiorhythmic occupations, but all follow a common regimen at the convent."[49]

The *typikon* for the early fourteenth-century Philanthropos nunnery in Constantinople also emphasizes "a common refectory ... common kitchen and the same handiwork" as the essence of cenobitic life, prescribes banishment from the church and refectory for wayward nuns, and expulsion from the convent if they do not mend their ways.[50]

The *vita* of Theodora of Thessalonike provides a probably more accurate picture of the daily life of the working nun, wearying days spent in manual labor, such as grinding grain, weaving and spinning, carrying firewood, nursing care of the elderly, and cooking and baking in the kitchen.

Provision of Medical and Social Services

The stipulations in the Lips *typikon* about the twelve-bed hospice attached to the convent are an important reminder of the ways in which urban nunneries, just as monasteries, provided services to the local community.[51] The hospice was not intended to serve the nuns, but ailing laywomen; it seems that it was really a long-term nursing home, since the patients were given yearly allowances of bedding, clothing, food, wine, and firewood. The hospital staff was surprisingly large: three doctors, an assistant, a nurse, a head pharmacist, six attendants, two chief druggists, three servants, a cook, and a laundress. There was also a priest to perform church services and preside over the funeral rites.[52]

On the feast day of the Nativity of John the Baptist, patron saint of the Lips convent, coins, bread, and other food were to be distributed to the poor at the convent gates.[53] At the twelfth-century Kecharitomene nunnery, such special donations of alms and food to the poor occurred much more often: on the feast days of the Nativity of the Virgin, the Nativity of Christ, Epiphany, Holy Thursday, Easter, Ascension, Pentecost, the Holy Apostles, and the Transfiguration. Moreover, there was a daily distribution of bread, grain, and leftovers from the refectory.[54] Additional distributions of grain, coins, and occasionally wine were made on the anniversaries of the deaths of twenty-three of Irene Doukaina's relatives.[55] This meant that the destitute could almost always get some bread and a few copper coins at this convent on a daily basis.

The convent of Sure Hope also provided a daily distribution of food to the poor, such as the leftovers from refectory meals. The *typikon* alludes to the "great poverty" of those who came to the convent gates "driven by starvation and harsh and grievous famine."[56] The nunnery also made distributions of bread and wine to the poor on the feast of the Dormition of the Virgin (the convent's patron saint), on the death anniversaries of the foundress of the nunnery and her relatives, and on the general commemoration day for all the deceased nuns.[57] It should also be noted that when a nun died, for forty days following her death her portion of food was to be given to the poor.[58]

Convents also provided important social services through the admission of women and girls who were in some sort of personal distress. Many of the girls and women who took monastic vows had a true vocation, but for others who found themselves in difficult circumstances the convent was a refuge that provided both physical comforts and spiritual consolation. Some convents were willing to admit a small number of orphaned girls, some of whom ended up as servants, while others received an education and eventually took the habit. Convents also provided a haven for women abused by their husbands, for the mentally ill, and especially for widows of all ages, such as Theodora of Thessalonike. The older widows were assured of nursing care in their declining years, a proper funeral service, and burial.[59]

COMPARISON OF MALE AND FEMALE MONASTERIES

Rules

After this brief overview of three nuns and their convents, one from the middle Byzantine and two from the late Byzantine period, the regime in female monastic institutions should be compared with the male establishments we examined in chapter 1. In many foundation documents, the regulations for female convents and male monasteries were very similar, including most aspects of the monastic habit. Rules for admission of novices, liturgical observance, dietary restrictions, behavior in the refectory, and number of baths per year were basically the same for men and women; the variations in stipulated practice between male and female monasteries were often no greater than those between stricter and more lenient male monasteries. For instance, the twelfth-century imperial nunnery of Kecharitomene in Constantinople derived substantial portions of its monastic rule from the eleventh-century *typikon* for the male Evergetis monastery. We may take as an example the *typikon* chapter about proper procedures for the nuns' procession to the refectory:

> I must now speak about the nuns' eating. Well then, when the holy and **divine** liturgy has been completed they must remain **in the narthex waiting for the summons** to the communal **refectory by the semantron** as is usual. **When the semantron has been struck**, they must go out with the *ekklesiarchissa*, **make obeisance to the superior, and then beginning the customary psalm** in a quiet and fitting voice, ... they must **walk** quietly **to the refectory**, and when they have completed the psalm, **sit down** in an orderly manner **in whatever way the superior arranges** their seats. **Then they should gratefully partake of what is set out without noise** and **disturbance**, while a reading as is usual takes place; **the superior only may speak, if she wishes** to say something, and she must do so quietly.[60]

Irene Doukaina, the author of the Kecharitomene *typikon*, has modeled the text on the Evergetis chapter, needing only to substitute the word "abbess" for "abbot," "she" for "he," "nuns" for "monks," and *ekklesiarchissa* (the church and choir director) for "priest." When it came to provisions for Lenten fasting, the rules for the male Evergetis monastery and female Kecharitomene nunnery were virtually identical:

> **This is the procedure on the ordinary days of the year, but not during the holy fast days and especially during the first and greatest fast, on the first day of the first week of which, that is on Monday, the liturgy should not be celebrated nor**

should care be taken with the table or food. However, on the subsequent days of this week a table should be set, **and whoever chooses should partake of food. This will be composed of legumes soaked in water and perhaps some raw vegetables and fruits**, and you will drink **hot water seasoned with cumin.** However, **on Friday you should eat two dishes of food**, one cooked with olive oil, the other without olive oil, **and drink wine distributed in the larger measure because of the feast of the great martyr St. Theodore, which the superior must celebrate as a duty and give you refreshment on Saturday and feed the community with shellfish.** But if a refreshment were to be provided by some devout person, you will be fed also on fish.

Empress Irene relaxed the rigor of the fast slightly, however: on Saturdays the nuns could eat fish, if it were provided by a pious visitor, rather than the shellfish stipulated in the Evergetis *typikon*.[61]

Physical Structure

Not only were rules for male monasteries and female convents basically similar, but there were also few differences in their physical structures. An archaeologist of today who encounters the ruins of a Byzantine monastery normally cannot determine whether it once housed monks or nuns, if no inscriptions survive; in fact, it may have housed both at different phases in its history, as convents were occasionally converted into male monasteries and vice versa, without any apparent need for alterations.[62] Although the paucity of reliable statistics makes firm conclusions difficult, on the whole the sizes of nunneries and male monasteries seem to have been comparable. A few male monasteries housed several hundred monks, but most ranged from twelve to one hundred; likewise, convents also might have had anywhere from a dozen to a hundred nuns.[63]

The one architectural feature that may have differed on occasion was that some convents housed their nuns in communal dormitories, instead of the cells that were typical of most Byzantine monasteries, both male and female. Such a dormitory was to be found, for example, at the ninth-century nunnery of St. Stephen in Thessalonike, the abode of Theodora of Thessalonike described at the beginning of this chapter, where all the nuns slept together in one room.[64] A single sleeping room was also prescribed for the twelfth-century Kecharitomene nunnery. The stated rationale of the imperial foundress, Irene Doukaina, was that nuns who lived in the same room without any privacy could less easily indulge in indolent behavior.[65] Perhaps unspoken is the empress's conviction that an open dormitory would also deter sexual misbehavior. The twelfth-century canonist Balsamon's comment that "only in female cenobitic monasteries is common diet and habitation observed"[66] suggests that communal dormitories may also have existed at other contemporary nunneries. I have noted only one male monastery with this feature, the tenth-century *lavra* of the Stylos on Mount Latros.[67]

A second difference in the visual appearance of male and female monasteries was with regard to the depiction of female saints, who appear rarely or not at all in the iconographic programs of churches for male institutions. Although very little monumental art survives from Byzantine nunneries, Sharon Gerstel has argued that "they were presumably decorated in a manner that reflected a female population."[68] Thus, at the church of the Blachernitissa monastery near Arta, a nunnery at the time that its narthex was painted (late thirteenth century), the frescoes included a portrayal of the procession of the Hodegetria icon in Constantinople, which featured female pilgrims in the foreground of the composition.[69] Also significant is the evidence from a document pertaining to the fourteenth-century monastery of Maroules in Constantinople. When this nunnery was converted to the use of monks, the frescoes of female saints that adorned the refectory were changed to images of male saints.[70]

The Monastic Habit (*schema*)

The literary and pictorial evidence for the habits worn by monks and nuns is relatively scarce, and not always consistent, but current scholarly research indicates that male and female monastic garb was quite similar, with the exception of head coverings.[71] The basic garment for both men and women was a full-length tunic (*himation* or *chiton*), usually in white or black (the term "black" probably referred to a range of dark colors, including gray and brown). Over the tunic both sexes sometimes wore a scapular (*analabos*, *epomis*); this was a piece of cloth with an opening for the head, worn in front and back over the shoulders. The infrequent mention of this article of clothing suggests, however, that it was not a mandatory element of the habit. The typical outer garment was a cloak (*mandyas*), normally of undyed wool. These garments were often made of coarse materials and worn for long periods of time without replacements, so that they are sometimes described as "ragged" or "tattered." In fact, the Greek word *rakos*, meaning a "ragged or tattered garment," was a standard term for monastic garb. Monks often went bareheaded or wore a hood (*koukoulion*), while nuns always covered their hair with a veil (*maphorion*) or in the late Byzantine era a type of wrapped turban called a *skepe*. Footgear was typically sandals or sturdy leather shoes. There is also evidence from the *vita* of St. Matrona of Perge that monks wore wide leather belts or girdles.[72]

Overall Numbers of Monks, Nuns, and Monastic Communities

Although the physical distinctions between religious communities of men and women were limited, as were distinctions in their monastic garb, there were some essential differences in the numbers, location, staffing, and regulations of nunneries in comparison with male monasteries.[73] The surviving evidence suggests that cenobitic monks may have considerably outnumbered nuns during the middle and late centuries of Byzantium, and that male monasteries were more numerous than their female counterparts. Dorothy Abrahamse has calculated the following ratios between the numbers of female convents and male monasteries founded in Constantinople between the eighth and eleventh centuries, based on Janin's compendium (female on the left, male on right):[74]

8th c. 6:6
9th c. 10:25
10th c. 9:18
11th c. 6:23

These figures suggest a wide range in the ratios, from equal numbers in the eighth century to convents making up only one-fifth of the total number of monasteries in the eleventh century. As with all efforts to tabulate statistics from the Byzantine era, however, one must accept the results with great caution, since Janin's list of monastic establishments in Constantinople obviously reflects references to them in historical sources, and female institutions may well be underrepresented in surviving texts and documents.

My own calculations on numbers of nuns and convents are based on a wider range of sources, which demonstrate a similar striking disparity in the ratios between male and female monastics and monasteries, but still they must also be viewed with suspicion (see table 1).

Most strikingly, the fourteen-volume prosopography for the middle Byzantine period (641–1025) lists a grand total of 3,448 monks and only 250 nuns, that is, nuns represent 0.067 percent of monastics (excluding the superiors).[75] Amazingly similar figures can be calculated for the twelve-volume prosopography for the Palaiologan period (1261–1453), which lists about 3,600 monks and only 250 nuns (also excluding the superiors):[76] just 0.065 percent of the grand total. It is impossible to determine, however, if these discrepancies are the result of actual numerical differences or gender-biased reporting by the sources.

Another indicator is the collection of sixty-one Byzantine monastic foundation documents (*BMFD*); only six of these texts, 10 percent, are for convents. A tally based on Janin's survey of the monasteries of Constantinople from the fourth to fifteenth centuries reveals 77 nunneries and 270 male monasteries, that is, only 22 percent of the recorded institutions were female.[77] For the Palaiologan period, the percentage is higher, thirty convents compared with fifty-five male monasteries, or 35 percent.

TABLE 1. Comparative Statistics on Numbers of Monks and Nuns in Byzantium

Number of listed monks, 641–867	ca. 1,648
Number of listed abbots, 641–867	ca. 480
Number of listed nuns, 641–867	ca. 138
Number of listed abbesses, 641–867	ca. 55
(Source: *Prosopographie der mittelbyzantinischen Zeit*, I)	
Number of listed monks, 867–1025	ca. 1,800
Number of listed abbots, 867–1025	ca. 629
Number of listed nuns, 867–1025	ca. 112
Number of listed abbesses, 867–1025	ca. 16
(Source: *Prosopographie der mittelbyzantinischen Zeit*, II)	
Number of listed monks, 1260–1453	ca. 3,600
Number of listed nuns, 1260–1453	ca. 250
(Source: *Prosopographische Lexikon der Palaiologenzeit*)	
Number of rules for male monasteries, 7th–15th c.	55
Number of rules for convents, 7th–15th c.	6
(Source: *Byzantine Monastic Foundation Documents*)	
Number of male monasteries in Constantinople, 4th–15th c.	270
Number of female convents in Constantinople, 4th–15th c.	77
Number of male monasteries in Constantinople, 13th–15th c.	55
Number of female convents in Constantinople, 13th–15th c.	30
(Source: Janin, *Eglises CP*)	

Outside the capital there seem to have been notably fewer convents. Janin's survey of provincial monasteries, admittedly incomplete, lists 17 convents compared with 225 monasteries, or 7 percent.[78] These figures are untrustworthy, however, since Janin's book deals primarily with holy mountains, where female establishments were rare. Obviously, when dealing with statistics such as these, one must take into account the general underrecording of women in Byzantine sources,[79] since many Byzantine nuns may have been as anonymous as in the group portrait from the Lincoln College Typikon (fig. 5). Recent research on village and rural churches has pointed out inscriptional evidence for a number of donors to these churches, who were termed *monache*, or "nun." None of these nuns, however, are identified as being affiliated with a convent; it may be that they took monastic vows only on their deathbed, belonged to an informal type of house monastery (such as will be discussed further in chapter 4), or were "nun-anchorites who did not belong to an organized monastery."[80]

On the whole, the available evidence suggests that fewer Byzantine women than men entered monastic life and that fewer nunneries than monasteries were founded.

Locations of Monasteries and Nunneries

One reason for this discrepancy in the numbers of monks and nuns may be restrictions on the locations of nunneries, which were primarily founded in cities.[81] This is one of the most notable distinctions between male and female monasteries in Byzantium, for male establishments are also found in the countryside in considerable numbers, especially on holy mountains. Of the six surviving foundation documents for nunneries, five are for Constantinopolitan institutions established by empresses or wealthy noblewomen, the sixth for a rural area of Crete. Other types of evidence suggest a similar pattern: Janin's survey of monasteries outside of Constantinople lists very few convents in the provinces. One reason for this apparent imbalance may be that his incomplete survey focuses heavily on holy mountains, where the presence of nuns was discouraged. Several holy mountains (Athos, Latros, and Meteora) totally forbade the presence of nunneries, while others (Mount St. Auxentios and Mount Galesion) each had a single convent to accommodate the female relatives of monks or hermits resident on or near the holy mountain.[82]

Another factor in the apparent paucity of rural nunneries may have been the founder's fear for the safety of nuns if they were not protected by city walls. The dangers for rural monasteries were real; Arab or Turkish attacks on monastic communities in Asia Minor, Greece, and the Aegean islands were by no means uncommon.[83] One piece of evidence for the special perils of convents is the testimony of Bishop Leo of Argos about the nunnery he founded near Nauplion in the mid-twelfth century. He noted that he had become concerned about the nuns in his new foundation because of the danger from pirates:

> For throughout the year our coastal waters have been swarming with pirates, who plunder everything with total license, and commit any outrage they wish against anyone who falls into their hands. Thus a not ignoble fear has disturbed me, lest this convent, which is vulnerable to attack by pirates because of its proximity to the sea, be destroyed by them, and lest, in addition to the loss of monastic property, the nuns be the victims of rape, which is a special delight for men who once and for all have cast aside their fear of God and embraced the life of a pirate.[84]

Therefore, Leo relocated the nuns to a new convent he constructed farther away from the sea, and he moved thirty-six monks into the former nunnery.

A thirteenth-century bishop, John Apokaukos, metropolitan of Naupaktos in northern Greece, provides explicit evidence for the lack of adequate provision outside of Constantinople for the accommodation of female religious. After the fall of the Byzantine capital to the Fourth Crusade in 1204, he sanctioned the transformation of the male Blachernitissa monastery at Arta in Epiros into a nunnery, on the grounds of a real need for more housing for nuns, an example of medieval affirmative action. Apokaukos argued forcefully for the equality of the sexes, lamenting the neglect of opportunities for female vocations in the provinces: "The [inhabitants] of the provinces and of our region . . . being unaware of the equal honor of these two sexes, and [considering] women unworthy of admission to monasteries and the spiritual livelihood [to be derived] therefrom, provided for the salvation of one sex alone, that of men. And they made no provision for the female sex, either with regard to the construction of female convents, or the enclosure of [women] in such monasteries." The result was that male monasteries "were erected in many locations, but . . . female convents were rare or non-existent, so that nuns were dwelling in the forecourts of churches in dilapidated shacks which had space only for broken-down beds."[85] Consequently, the rulers of Arta moved the Blachernitissa monks to other local institutions and installed in the Blachernitissa both refugee nuns from Constantinople and local women who wished to be tonsured.

As Sharon Gerstel has recently argued, however, evidence from paintings and inscriptions in rural churches suggests the possibility that nuns, especially widows who took vows late in life, may have played a greater role in village society than previously realized. She concludes, "Although the footprints of Byzantine rural nuns are much lighter on the landscape, they are still visible."[86]

Monastic Stability

In contrast to monks, who often resided in several different monasteries over the course of their career, or moved from a cenobitic community to a solitary cell in the wilderness, or might spend years wandering abroad, nuns usually remained for life in the convent where they took their vows. For example, a synodal document reports that when Martha Syriana donned the monastic habit in the mid-fourteenth century at the Constantinopolitan nunnery of Pausolype, "she promised to live in it [the convent] steadfastly until her death."[87] Thus female religious observed much more rigorously the principle of "monastic stability," *stabilitas loci*, enjoined by the canons of the Fourth and Seventh Ecumenical Councils.[88] Although the *typika* make provision for the admission of nuns who transferred from other convents,[89] in practice the biographies of nuns rarely indicate a move from one convent to another. Thus, the ninth-century nun Theodora of Thessalonike, when invited to become abbess elsewhere, refused to leave her nunnery because of her monastic vows, saying, "I have vowed to Him [i.e., the Lord] to remain in the convent until I attain old age and advanced years."[90] Such was her principled stand, even though her transfer to another convent had been explicitly requested by the archimandrite of Thessalonike, the administrator of monasteries in the city. The few documented departures of nuns from their convents were often the result of external duress, such as enemy attack. Thomaïs, for example, godmother of the historian George Sphrantzes, fled from the monastery of St. Theodora in Thessalonike when the city was captured by the Turks in 1387 and sought refuge first on the island of Lemnos and then in Constantinople, where she entered the convent of Kleraina.[91]

Principles of Enclosure and *abaton*

Both male and female monasteries discouraged contact with the outside world by surrounding their complexes with massive walls and limiting the number of entrances. Such an architectural plan facilitated enforcement of two basic principles that attempted to maintain a distinct and separate space for those who took the monastic habit: the rule of enclosure intended to keep monks and nuns inside the cloister walls, and the rule of *abaton* designed to keep unwelcome visitors of the other sex outside the monastic precincts.

On the whole, convents seem to have observed stricter regulations with regard to enclosure, presumably because of their typically urban location and the presumed vulnerability of nuns to sexual temptation.[92] Although in general both male and female monastics were urged to avoid going out of the monastery, the rules for convents are more strict and specific. Two of the convent foundresses state that in theory nuns should never have any desire to see their relatives after taking the habit, but they acknowledge human weakness by making provision for occasional visits. The twelfth-century Kecharitomene *typikon* (in a chapter that notably does not use material from its model, the *typikon* for a male monastery) permitted a nun to leave the convent only to visit a parent who was at death's door; she had to be accompanied by two elderly nuns and return to the convent by evening.[93] A later *typikon* from the Palaiologan era eases the rules for home visits: nuns were allowed to go see their relatives "for the sake of a little relaxation" and not only for the purpose of farewells to dying parents. But they still had to be accompanied by two nuns from the convent, and upon their return to the cloister were cross-examined by the superior about their topics of conversation and whether the nun had been led astray by errant thoughts.[94] The contemporaneous *typikon* for the Lips convent stated that "all the nuns alike should refrain throughout their lives from leaving [the cloister], except in the case of a nun whose virtue is long proven." Nonetheless it did permit brief home visits.[95] The stricter enclosure of female religious may also reflect the norms of contemporary Byzantine society, which assumed that women, especially those of the upper classes, would spend most of their time at home. Just as nuns seem to have placed greater emphasis on the maintenance of family ties within the convent, they did not leave behind the social norm of relative seclusion upon their adoption of the monastic habit.

As so often, however, it must be remembered that the rules for monastic enclosure were an ideal, and there were many practical and valid reasons for nuns to go outside their cloister walls besides visits to relatives. Nonnormative texts, such as homilies, letters, patriarchal acts, and hagiography, attest to some of the circumstances that led nuns to leave their convents for brief periods of time. They were urged, for example, to visit prisoners and the sick.[96] They went to funerals of relatives,[97] to see a father confessor,[98] or on pilgrimage to a local shrine.[99] They might also need to go to the market or to present a petition or testify before the synod.[100] A female steward or superior might be required to inspect monastic properties.[101] Finally, there were ceremonial occasions, such as the installation of the abbess by the emperor or patriarch,[102] or the funerals of nuns if the cemetery lay outside the convent precincts.[103] Compared with monks, however, they led very cloistered lives, and even some abbesses only very rarely left the walls of their convents. Thus, after becoming superior, Irene of Chrysobalanton was described as "never leaving the convent," and indeed went out only twice, for her appointment as abbess and to attend services at the church of the Virgin at Blachernai. She even refused an invitation from the emperor to visit him at the imperial palace.[104] Likewise, Irene-Eulogia Choumnaina, abbess of the convent of Philanthropos Soter, almost never left her nunnery, even to attend her imperial relatives' weddings and funerals, and insisted on her spiritual advisor coming to her rather than her going to him.[105]

The Greek word *abaton* literally means "untrodden" or "inaccessible," and it describes the principle that a male monastery was off limits to women, and vice versa. It was designed to maintain strict segregation of the sexes to avoid worldly distraction and sexual temptation. Some male monasteries imposed the rule very rigidly and refused admission to women under any circumstances; others made exceptions for women wishing to make pilgrimage to relics or healing tombs in the monastic church, to attend commemorative services for relatives, or to take part in services on special feast days. Likewise, nunneries made provision for male visitors to enter the monastic church to pray at relatives' tombs[106] and attend commemorative services; private meetings with nuns who were family members were more closely regulated, usually limited to the gate or gatehouse. Thus at Kecharitomene only women visitors were permitted to enter inside the convent to see their relatives; male visitors had to wait at the gate where the nun, accompanied by an older nun, could speak with her callers.[107]

It was impossible, however, for a nunnery to observe *abaton* as strictly as a male monastery because of the necessity of admitting men on a regular basis to fulfill certain essential functions of monastic life. Since nuns could not be ordained, convents always needed male priests to celebrate the liturgy; they also had to use monks as spiritual fathers to hear confessions, male physicians to attend ailing nuns, and sometimes male stewards to manage the monastic properties. This will be discussed further in the next section.

Convent Staffing

Male Staff

A significant area of divergence in the *typika* of male and female monasteries is found in the chapters relating to certain staff members in nunneries who had to be male and thus contravened the normal rule of *abaton*. The foundresses of nunneries often revealed their anxieties about the presence of male staff, and they did their best to remove any possibility of sexual misconduct. One solution to this problem was the appointment of eunuchs, who were welcomed to female convents as priests, confessors, physicians, and stewards, being viewed as posing less sexual temptation to the nuns. The priests who presided over the liturgy several times a week had to be either of mature years and married, or eunuchs, preferably elderly.[108] Thus at the twelfth-century Constantinopolitan nunnery of Kecharitomene it was stipulated that liturgical services should be provided by two eunuch priests who were ideally, but not necessarily, ordained monks.[109] These priests were expected to live outside the nunnery. The spiritual father of the nuns was normally a monk, either cenobitic or a solitary;[110] at Kecharitomene he was required to be a eunuch, just like the priests.[111] He was charged with hearing the nuns' confessions in the church narthex or, in cold weather, in a convent building.[112] At Lips he was to stay for three days each month and sleep in a room in the hospice; at Sure Hope he was to visit on a daily basis.[113]

Although there were some female physicians in Byzantium, the *typika* for convents specify the summoning of male physicians to treat sick nuns. At Kecharitomene the doctor was to be elderly or a eunuch and was to "live at the convent," perhaps in rooms adjacent to the complex.[114] At Lips he was to come once a week, except during Lent; even then, if a nun fell ill, he could come as often as necessary.[115] It should also be noted that the hospice for laywomen attached to the Lips convent was staffed entirely by men, except for the laundress.[116] It seems surprising that nuns were not used for nursing care at this facility.

Some convents felt it necessary to designate a male steward, who would live off the premises, because a woman was believed to be incapable of holding such an important managerial position, especially since it entailed inspection tours of monastic property outside of the convent. In such cases, as at Kecharitomene, it was often specified that a eunuch should be appointed to avoid the possibility of sexual improprieties.[117] The steward had enormous responsibilities, including facilities maintenance and repair of the convent buildings, oversight of all the convent's immovable properties and revenues from its estates, and the keeping of detailed accounts. The male steward at Lips did not need to be a eunuch; he was to meet with the abbess in the presence of the leading nuns and leave before the midday meal. If the meeting was prolonged, he could take his meal in the hospice and then resume his discussions with the abbess, leaving by nightfall to avoid any suggestion of impropriety.[118] Other men who might need to work within the monastic precincts of a nunnery were gravediggers, gardeners, vinedressers, and singers.

A story in the *vita* of St. Irene of Chrysobalanton illustrates the perils posed by the proximity to the convent of lay workmen: a vinedresser who worked in the convent's vineyard fell madly in love with one of the nuns. He was unable to gain entrance to the nunnery, but one night dreamed that he passed through the gate and had sexual relations with his beloved in her cell. Immediately he was possessed by a demon, and he rolled on the ground uncontrollably, foaming at the mouth. The abbess Irene had him bound with fetters to a column in the convent church where he continued to rave for days on end. Finally, the abbess was able to exorcise the demon through her prayers, and the vinedresser recovered his wits.[119]

Female Staff
The nuns of a convent assumed responsibility for almost all other duties, whether carrying out the daily church services or performing the necessary managerial and housekeeping tasks. The choir sisters (*ekklesiastikai monachai*), who were of necessity literate, were

responsible for the spiritual life of the convent, primarily chanting at the regular monastic offices: "[They] should concern themselves with the divine sanctuary, all of them together unceasingly rendering up to God the divine hymns and holy doxologies prescribed for monastic life, [the services] at midnight, dawn and after sunrise, at the third, sixth and ninth hour, vespers and compline."[120] The superior was chosen from their ranks. The choir sisters formed the majority of the nuns at a given convent; at Lips, for example, thirty nuns out of the total of fifty were assigned to church services, and twenty had housekeeping responsibilities.[121] Nuns took charge of all the other assignments: administration, record-keeping, security, housekeeping, and provision of food and clothing. The numerous positions provided opportunities for women of various talents and personality types to find their niche in the convent hierarchy and to assume responsibilities that would be rarely delegated to women in the secular world.

The convent was headed by the abbess or mother superior, who should be a model and inspiration for the nuns in her charge: "[Her] steadfast and orderly conduct and ... dignified way of life ... [should be] the perfect archetype." She needed to be a teacher, a guide, a manager, a disciplinarian, someone who could delegate responsibility to the most suitable individuals.[122] She could lead certain offices in the church and presided over meals in the refectory. Her spiritual functions were limited, however, to advice and exhortation; she could not hear confession.[123] Above all, she had to ensure that all provisions of the founder's *typikon* were followed.[124]

At two convents at least, and perhaps others, nuns served as the steward. At Sure Hope the woman chosen as steward needed to be mature and experienced in practical affairs. The *typikon* specifically charged her with management of properties external to the convent and of the nunnery itself: "She is also to make inquiries and have accurate information on the revenues and profits and crops of the external estates. Of necessity she is to ask for accounts of each of their managers and bailiffs.... She will determine which estates are being properly managed ... as for those which are not progressing properly, she will demand appropriate improvements, and will make sure that henceforth they do prosper."[125]

The evidence from synodal documents shows that nuns were quite capable of overseeing their properties and intervening with the authorities when necessary.[126] Thus an early fifteenth-century Constantinopolitan abbess, Thomaïs of the Pausolype convent, complained to the synod about a garden the convent had given to the two Spyridon brothers; they were to replant it as a vineyard and at the end of five years share the vintage equally with the nuns. The abbess accused Manuel Spyridon of negligence in cultivation of the vineyard, keeping part of it fallow, not clearing away the stones, and stealing some of the grapes. After an inquiry, the patriarch ruled that the contract of donation was still valid, but Spyridon was sternly warned to keep his side of the bargain.[127]

The foundation rule of the twelfth-century Kecharitomene nunnery clearly sets out the titles and duties of the women who ensured the management and provisioning of the institution: besides the abbess there was a sacristan (*skeuophylakissa*); an *ekklesiarchissa* responsible for the church furnishings and proper lighting;[128] a food buyer; a wine steward (*oinochoe*); a provisioner (*horeiaria*), who supervised the storage of foodstuffs; two treasurers (*docheiarioi*), one for money, the other for the clothing storeroom; a refectorian (*trapezaria*); a disciplinarian (*epistemonarchissa*); two work organizers (*ergodotriai*), who handed out raw materials for handwork, and took back the finished products; and a gatekeeper (*pyloros*).[129] Virtually all of these officials must have been literate and in some cases numerate, since their duties required keeping accounts or working with documents and inventories.[130] Each received a copy of that section of the *typikon* that detailed her responsibilities. Empress Irene acknowledged the contribution each of these nuns made to the institution and recognized that often their duties would keep them from attending church services.

The founder of the convent of Sure Hope, in specifying the type of nun who should hold each leadership position, carefully listed the qualifications for different posts, taking into consideration age, experience, and personality. Thus the gatekeeper should be middle-aged, a woman of good judgment and prudence, dignified, and stable in temperament.[131] The keeper of the clothing storeroom should be gentle, humble, sociable, intelligent, trustworthy, and able to keep precise accounts.[132] The *ekklesiarchissa*, a choir sister who trained and directed the choir and supervised church services, had to be pious, pure in soul, and have a good singing voice. She was also in charge of maintaining good order during services and arranging for proper lighting. Moreover, she needed to be familiar with liturgical routines because she was responsible for selecting hymns and psalms for the different services and for ensuring that nothing was omitted or sung in the wrong sequence. The *typikon* for Kecharitomene instructs the *ekklesiarchissa* to stand in front of the sanctuary and lead the nuns in a disciplined series of fifteen genuflections at morning services; the sisters were to kneel and rise again to their feet in unison. She also was responsible for teaching younger nuns to read and chant.[133]

Many of the female officials' duties resembled those of secular household management: concerns for the provision of adequate food, clothing, and linens, but on a larger scale. Other responsibilities were more specialized, involving the keeping of accounts, registers, and inventories, as well as lists of deceased nuns for commemoration ceremonies and the safekeeping of ecclesiastical furnishings and treasures. Most challenging were the widespread duties of the superior and of the steward in convents where the latter official was a woman. There can be no doubt that leadership positions in convents offered Byzantine women professional opportunities available nowhere else.

Manual Labor and Economic Self-Sufficiency

Compared with the ample descriptions of housekeeping staff in Byzantine convents, there is little information about manual labor, but at most nunneries some kind of work was encouraged as part of the ideal cenobitic life. Even the aristocratic thirteenth-century foundress of the convent of Sure Hope stated that such labor was essential, because hard work mortifies the body, and was for the common good of the nuns.[134] She was referring to the nuns' *ergocheiron*, or "handwork," that is, cloth manufacture, not to hard physical labor in the garden or vineyard. In contrast to a modern Greek nunnery, such as that at Ormylia in the Chalkidike peninsula, where the nuns perform agricultural tasks of all sorts,[135] the physical labor of Byzantine nuns was pretty much limited to food preparation, handwork, cleaning, and laundry.

As we have seen in the *vita* of St. Theodora of Thessalonike, nuns ground grain into flour, baked bread, cooked, wove cloth, and carried firewood.[136] Although care of the elderly by nuns is not specifically mentioned in the *typika*, we know from her *vita* that St. Theodora provided devoted nursing care for the elderly abbess Anna, who had dislocated her hip and become senile.[137] Yet we have also seen that at the hospice of Lips, it was outside male attendants who provided care for the female residents of the old-age home.

The primary activity of nuns was evidently textile production, both linen and wool, but there is surprisingly little specific evidence. The *typika* use the generic term "handwork" to describe the nuns' normal productive activity, and only one passage specifically mentions working in wool.[138] The term "handwork" apparently refers to various processes in cloth manufacture, such as spinning of flax and wool into yarn, weaving of cloth, sewing of garments, and the repair of torn clothing; the *vita* of Theodora of Thessalonike alludes to nuns working at the loom and to her own fabrication of bags out of wool and flax in her old age. At the double monastery directed by Anthousa of Mantineon, the nuns made the habits for the monks at the associated male institution.[139] Likewise, the nuns at the Cretan convent of Neilos Damilas made habits for the monks of the nearby monastery, but in this case the monks were in turn to make habits and shoes for the nuns, a curious arrangement.[140] The nuns at the Sure Hope convent, who made their own habits, were enjoined to take raw materials from the storerooms and to return their finished products at the end of the day; they were to pray and chant psalms as they worked.[141] Some convents sold surplus cloth on the market to generate revenues.[142] Regrettably, there is no firm evidence for the production by Byzantine nuns of lace or embroidery, such as is attested in the post-Byzantine Balkans[143] and as one sees today in Greek convents.[144]

I have found reference to only one other kind of item manufactured in a convent, candles, which were essential for church lighting. Among the sacristan's duties at the Kecharitomene convent was overseeing the manufacture of cotton-wicked wax candles, in a variety of sizes: four ounces, six ounces, one pound, and huge ones weighing six pounds each. The wax came from beehives on monastic property and was produced in such abundance that the convent sold the surplus on the open market.[145]

Although both urban and rural convents often had attached vineyards, wheat fields, vegetable gardens, and orchards, agricultural labor was carried out by hired hands rather than the nuns themselves. Synodal documents from the late Byzantine period suggest that sometimes nunneries found it difficult to manage these properties with their own workers and leased them to outsiders on condition that they cultivate and improve the land. In 1399, for example, there was a dispute between the nunnery of St. Andrew in Krisei and two men who had been paid to cultivate the nunnery vineyard for four years and were to receive one-half the vintage in return.[146] At the rural convent of Damilas on Crete, nuns were permitted to guard and water the vineyard and garden, but this is a rare allusion to female labor outdoors.[147] It may be that when the cultivated properties were outside the convent walls, there were fears for the nuns' safety if they worked in the open air; also, as women they may have been deemed too weak for such labor.

In contrast to these restrictions on manual labor by nuns, male cenobitic monasteries, such as Stoudios and the Great Lavra, greatly encouraged a wide variety of artisanal activities that enabled their institutions to be largely self-sufficient.[148] The relative lack of income sources for convents, on the other hand, may have caused them financial problems, since they were more dependent on hired labor and purchased products. Moreover, although some Constantinopolitan nunneries, such as the Kecharitomene, Lips, and Sure Hope, were populated by nuns from imperial or aristocratic backgrounds and were well endowed with landed properties, others were intended as a residence for women of little means. The Constantinopolitan convent of St. Basil, for example, founded and generously endowed by the father of Gregory Antiochos in the twelfth century, was designated for twelve nuns who were unable to marry for lack of a dowry. All but two of the nuns were required to be literate, and they were exhorted to devote themselves to reading and psalmody, with no mention at all of handwork. Gregory's father was buried in the convent church, and the nuns were also enjoined to assure his annual commemoration on the anniversary of his death.[149]

There is also evidence, especially from late Byzantium, that a number of convents, lacking a sufficient endowment, were relatively poor and partially reliant on charitable donations. Thus, during the famine of 1305–6, the patriarch Athanasios I ordered the distribution of thirty measures of wheat "to all the female convents, and particularly to the poor ones, since they do not have a sufficient livelihood from properties or other revenues, but [are supported] only by the work of their own hands; and there are many of these in the Queen of Cities [i.e., Constantinople]."[150] The fifteenth-century historian George Sphrantzes describes how the convent of Kleraina in the capital had no endowment but relied solely on income from sale of the nuns' handwork and therefore needed support from aristocratic benefactors.[151] At the double monastery of the patriarch Athanasios in Constantinople, the nuns relied totally on the monks for the provision of foodstuffs.

Intellectual Life and Artistic Production

Many nuns were literate and were encouraged to read scripture and ecclesiastical literature in their cells as part of their spiritual devotions. Neilos Damilas, the founder of a Cretan convent, placed unusual emphasis on the benefits of reading for nuns, stating: "I say this, too, that every night you should read aloud at least twice, if not more; for prayer and reading are like two eyes; and Saint Isaac [of Nineveh] sets reading before psalmody."[152] Damilas was also concerned about the monastic library and forbade the nuns to loan out any of the books.[153]

It is important to note that nuns perused the *vitae* of both male and female saints: thus, Irene of Chrysobalanton, who was assiduous in her study of hagiography, was particularly impressed by the *vita* of St. Arsenios the Great, whom she took as a model for her ascetic exercises.[154] When the fourteenth-century patroness Anna Komnene Raoulaina Strategopoulina commissioned a collection of saints' lives for the nunnery of the Mighty Savior (*Soter Krataios*) that she founded in Constantinople, she specified the inclusion in the manuscript of the *vitae* of twelve male saints and only two female saints.[155]

On the other hand, there are some indications that nuns had a predilection for reading the *vitae* of female saints. Thus, the *typikon* of the convent of Sure Hope placed special emphasis on the efficacy of reading the *vitae* of holy women. The abbess is urged to look at the lives of female saints as if they were "living images" that could serve as a model for her nuns; the *typikon* praises the "heroic conduct and wondrous lives" of these holy women.[156] A collection of fifteen lives of holy women, preserved in a fourteenth-century manuscript now in Florence, was clearly intended for an audience of female monastics, since it is prefaced by the heading "Give a blessing, mother," referring to the abbess who was presiding over the reading of these *vitae*. Among the *vitae* were those of Makrina, the sister of Gregory of Nyssa; Theodora of Thessalonike; Empress Theophano; Irene of Chrysobalanton; and Euphrosyne the Younger.[157]

If we turn to literary production in Byzantine convents, it will seem very insignificant in comparison with the works of the nuns of the medieval West, such as Hroswitha of Gandersheim and Hildegarde of Bingen. In contrast with male monasteries, which were important centers for the composition of hagiography, hymnography, theological treatises, and the like, in middle and late Byzantium the authorship of very few surviving texts can be securely attributed to Byzantine women who were either nuns at the time they were writing or were residing in convents without having taken the veil. The most important author in the latter category was Anna Komnene, the imperial princess who composed in the twelfth century a panegyrical history of the reign of her father, Alexios I Komnenos (r. 1081–1118). Anna wrote this work while residing in the Kecharitomene nunnery founded by her mother; she had retired to apartments there after a failed conspiracy to elevate her husband to the throne, as a successor to her father. She did not take monastic vows, however, until her deathbed.[158]

There were a few nun hymnographers, such as Kassia and Theodosia in the ninth century, and Palaiologina in the fourteenth, but only one firmly identified hagiographer, Theodora Raoulaina, a niece of Emperor Michael VIII, and opponent of his religious policy.[159] She wrote a *vita* of two ninth-century monks who were tortured for their support of icon veneration.[160] None of these authors showed a particular predilection for female saints as their subjects; in fact, most of their works were devoted to male saints. Theodora Raoulaina was a *rara avis* indeed, the only Byzantine nun who can be compared with the erudite monks of Byzantium. Before becoming a nun, she copied at least two texts in her own hand, the *Orations of Ailios Aristeides* (Vat. gr. 1899) and Simplikios's *Commentary on the Physics of Aristotle* (Moscow, National Historical Museum, Mus. Sobr. 3649).[161] At the Constantinopolitan convent of St. Andrew in Krisei, where she spent the final years of her life, she devoted herself to intensive reading of classical Greek authors and to building up her library by commissioning the copying of manuscripts. Her wide-ranging interests extended to mathematics and physics. She maintained an active correspondence with the literati of the day; for example, the patriarch Gregory II of Cyprus (1283–89), a classically trained theologian, wrote her around thirty letters. Regrettably, none of her responses to him or to anyone else survive.[162]

In the realm of the visual arts, even less activity is recorded in the nunneries of Byzantium. Women definitely served as significant patrons of religious architecture and commissioned many of the icons, liturgical vessels, and manuscripts necessary for ecclesiastical services in the convent, but there is little evidence that they were producers of art, except possibly in the realm of embroidery and calligraphy.[163]

IDIORRHYTHMIC NUNNERIES

Byzantine nuns were strong supporters of the cenobitic form of monasticism, and therefore it should not be surprising that an idiorrhythmic regime was almost never found in their convents. The only attested example of an idiorrhythmic nunnery is that founded by Neilos Damilas in Crete in 1399, which functioned very briefly under "self-regulating" principles before transitioning to a more traditional cenobitic model. When the convent of the Mother of God Pantanassa at Baionaia was first instituted, there was a paucity of older nuns to train the novices, so Damilas permitted them to be sponsored by the abbess and allowed "each one to be established according to her own wishes, in a private cell and with her own personal handiwork."[164] The nuns were also originally permitted to give to their relatives some of the money earned from their handiwork, most likely spinning, weaving, and sewing. When Damilas wrote his *typikon* around 1400, only a year or so after the convent's foundation, he imposed a more cenobitic lifestyle and closely regulated the nuns' sale of the products of their labor to monks or laymen; they were also enjoined to make the habits for the monks of a nearby monastery.[165] Unfortunately, Damilas does not provide regulations for the refectory, so we cannot be sure whether the nuns took their meals communally. In another holdover from the original idiorrhythmic regimen, they were permitted to have personal possessions.[166]

Elements of an idiorrhythmic regimen can also be found in the special privileges granted by some Constantinopolitan nunneries to women who came from aristocratic and imperial families. At the Lips convent, for example, established by the dowager empress Theodora Palaiologina around 1300, the founder stipulates that her female relatives and other women of "distinguished family" should be exempt from the requirement to take their meals in the refectory and could dine in their private apartments, being waited upon by their personal servants. She acknowledged, however, that if any of them chose to eat "at the common table," this was an admirable course of action.[167] Theodora Synadene may have been implicitly criticizing the permissiveness of Lips when in her *typikon* for Sure Hope she praised her nuns for not having separate apartments and idiorhythmic occupations, but for following a truly cenobitic regimen.[168]

DOUBLE MONASTERIES

The establishment of double monasteries, that is, adjoining male and female monastic institutions, with common property and ruled by a single superior, was a controversial practice in Byzantium. The monks and nuns lived separately, with separate churches and refectories, but their close association made some interaction inevitable.[169] These establishments were prohibited by both civil and ecclesiastical law on several occasions, such as Justinian's novel 123.36 of the year 546 and canon 20 of the Second Council of Nicaea in 787.[170] Canon 20 forbade the foundation of any new double monasteries, but it permitted existing ones to continue to function. Soon after, however, the ban was widened to include all existing double monasteries. A decree of the patriarch Nikephoros I of around 810 dispatched bishops to all corners of the empire to oversee personally the dissolution of double monasteries. It is clear that his primary concern was the sexual temptation posed to male monastics by the proximity of women, since he states that the monks in double monasteries "avoided open cohabitation, but they could not entirely escape indulgence in sexual fantasies."[171] The necessity for repeated prohibitions shows how difficult it was to eradicate this form of monasticism. One reason for the persistence of double monasteries over the centuries may be that this arrangement was advantageous for nunneries, which sometimes benefited from the provision of food by the male monasteries.

An early example is the very large institution (reportedly of 900 male and female monastics) founded around 740 at Mantineon in Paphlagonia by St. Anthousa; it is known from the *synaxarion* notice for Anthousa and from the Georgian *vita* of her disciple, Romanos the neomartyr (d. 780).[172] Unusually in this case, the two monasteries were not adjacent but physically separated; the nuns lived on an island, the monks on the lakeshore.[173] The monks brought food to the nuns, who in turn made habits for the monks.[174] It is noteworthy that Anthousa served as the superior of the monastery as a whole, while her nephew was the administrator of the male complex.

A somewhat different model of double monastery was founded by St. Euthymios the Younger in the ninth century at Peristerai, near Thessalonike. It was a curious endeavor for the middle-aged Euthymios, who had spent much of his previous life as a hermit on Mount Athos and brief periods as a stylite in Thessalonike.[175] He first constructed a cenobitic monastery on the site of a ruined church around 871, and then, fourteen years later, he built a convent for women, entrusting the leadership of the two institutions to his grandchildren, Methodios and Euphemia.[176] In this case, however, the establishments were not technically a double monastery since each had its own superior, and they do not seem to have been adjacent to each other.

During the middle Byzantine centuries, the practice of founding double monasteries seems to have died out. The Palaiologan era, however, witnessed a modest resurgence of the phenomenon, even though patriarch Arsenios Autoreianos (1261–64) had ordered the separation of double monasteries at the very beginning of the period.[177] First of all, Athanasios I (1289–93, 1303–9), the future patriarch of Constantinople, founded a double monastery on Mount Ganos during his residence on that holy mountain, probably in the late 1270s.[178] This monastery, called Nea Mone, is known only from the *vita* of Athanasios by Theoktistos the Stoudite.[179] The text reports that the nuns followed the same rules and regulations as the monks, and that some of the women were superior to the men in their virtue. This foundation of Athanasios is noteworthy, since it was relatively rare for convents to be founded on holy mountains, which often, as at Athos, Latros, and Meteora, forbade the presence of women.

At some point after the accession of Andronikos II in 1282, Athanasios left Mount Ganos for Constantinople. Following a brief stay in the monastery of St. Diomedes, he moved to the monastery of the Great Logariastes; this was the monastery that came to bear his name and was located on the hill of Xerolophos in the southwest corner of the city.[180] In 1289, Athanasios was appointed as patriarch, but he faced much opposition and was forced to resign in 1293. He withdrew to the monastery on Xerolophos for ten years until he ascended the patriarchal throne for a second time in 1303. After his second abdication in 1309, he retired to this same monastery, where he spent his remaining years. The date of his death is unknown, but it was before 1323.

We do not know for sure when a convent was included in the complex on Xerolophos, but it was definitely during Athanasios's lifetime. His *vita* relates that two nuns "from the women's convent, who were consumed by severe and chronic illness," sent word to Athanasios of their desperate plight, asking either to be cured or delivered by death from their suffering. Athanasios advised them to pray to the Virgin, and the next day they were fully recovered. In thanksgiving they came to pay obeisance to the holy man, walking on their own feet; it is not specified, however, whether he came to the convent to see them.[181]

A later allusion to the presence of nuns at Athanasios's Xerolophos monastery is found in a posthumous miracle tale describing the healing in 1326 of a woman from Brousa suffering from demonic possession. She came to Constantinople in search of a cure and was relieved of her symptoms by her visitation to the relics of Athanasios at Xerolophos. She later became a nun at the monastery, taking the name Athanasia in gratitude for her healing; shortly thereafter her husband joined her at the monastery after taking monastic vows.[182] The hagiographical corpus about the patriarch Athanasios provides virtually no information about the structure of the monastery complex, except that the church in the male monastery where Athanasios was laid to rest was dedicated to Christ the Savior.[183]

It is puzzling that this strict patriarch, dedicated to monastic reform,[184] should have founded two double monasteries, when he himself had legislated against the practice.[185] In fact, some decades after Athanasios's death, his foundation fell into decline, allegedly as a result of the laziness of the nuns, who came to depend totally on the monks to provide their food. The situation deteriorated to such an extent that the patriarch Neilos I Kerameus (1380–88), with the consent of the synod, issued an official document (*sigillion*) irrevocably separating the two monasteries and allocating the joint property to the two institutions in proportions reflecting the numbers of monks and nuns: two-thirds of the properties were to go to the male monastery, one-third to the nunnery. Although this is not specified, one assumes that the convent was hereafter to have its own superior.

The patriarchal document preserves important information about the properties of the double monastery and the principles of its original foundation, namely, "the simultaneous unification and separation of the women and men, so that each sex had its own abode and each group led the monastic life separately, but the women were subject to the monks and had the same regimen and lifestyle and were assigned to a single superior. In addition their properties were communal, and their food was also communal, as the men had to provide for their daily meals."[186]

A third double monastery from the Palaiologan period was that dedicated to Christ Philanthropos. It was founded in 1307 by Irene Choumnaina Palaiologina, the sixteen-year-old widow of the despot John Palaiologos, son of Andronikos II, who died four years after their marriage. She promptly decided to take the veil as the nun Eulogia, renovated a derelict monastery located near the sea walls at the eastern tip of Constantinople, and dedicated it to Christ

Philanthropos.[187] Only a short tantalizing excerpt from the *typikon* for her convent survives, a section modeled closely on the rule for the twelfth-century Kecharitomene nunnery that emphasizes the importance of maintaining the cenobitic way of life, with a communal refectory and kitchen, and the same handwork for all the nuns.[188] We know from other sources that there was an adjacent male monastery, also dedicated to Christ Philanthropos, to which Irene's father, Nikephoros Choumnos, retired at the end of his career, while his wife withdrew to the convent.[189]

We learn from the monastic discourses of Theoleptos of Philadelphia that he was the spiritual director for both the monks and the nuns of this institution.[190] He normally addressed the nuns and monks in separate orations, indicating that he met with them separately, either in the church or refectory. He also served as the spiritual director of Irene-Eulogia from the time of her tonsure in 1307 until his death in 1322. Irene-Eulogia was clearly the abbess of the convent, but her position with regard to the male monastery is less certain. Sinkewicz has argued that "the administration of the monastery's endowment and properties probably remained largely in the hands of Eulogia or at least within the Choumnos family. However, beyond that, Eulogia's authority as abbess was restricted to the women's community."[191]

The last double monastery founded in Constantinople was of very modest scale. Towards the end of the fourteenth century an aging couple decided to abandon conjugal life and take monastic vows. The husband took the name Ignatios Theologites, the wife became Makrina. They took up separate residence in two very small monasteries, which seem to have been adjacent to each other as a double monastery complex: Ignatios in the *kathisma* of St. John the Theologian, and Makrina in St. Panteleemon, a dilapidated convent that Ignatios restored. Apparently the *kathisma* of John the Theologian later changed its name to the *monydrion* ("little monastery") of the Theotokos, "Hope of the Hopeless." After some years the couple had a falling out over financial matters, and the patriarch in 1400 decided to divide the two institutions; each party was to receive one half of the common resources and to live quite independently of the other.[192]

Around the same time, a provincial double monastery was functioning in the Macedonian town of Neapolis (Kavalla). We learn of this monastery from the *vita* of Philotheos of Athos (d. ca. 1450), whose family had fled to Macedonia from their homeland in Asia Minor to escape the incursions of the Turks. In the late fourteenth century, Philotheos and his brother were seized by the Ottomans as part of the *devshirme*, "child levy," but they soon escaped to a monastery of the Virgin in Neapolis where they were taken in to be schooled as monks. The monastery is described as having two sections, one for men and one for women, and as being ruled by a male superior. Shortly thereafter, by amazing coincidence the boys' mother, now a destitute widow, sought admission to the same monastery and was soon reunited with her children. The two boys were assigned custodial duties in the nuns' church, and it was here that their mother recognized them. This *vita* also confirms the suspicion that double monasteries were morally perilous, for it tells how one of the nuns tried to seduce the youthful Philotheos, but was rebuffed.[193]

NUNS AND NUNNERIES IN BYZANTINE CULTURE AND SOCIETY

Nuns seem to have made little contribution to artistic and literary production in Byzantium, except perhaps for some hymnography. The foundresses of convents were, however, major patrons of the arts, sponsoring new construction and restoration of churches and monastic buildings, and commissioning their fresco decoration and the production of ecclesiastical furnishings and illuminated liturgical manuscripts.[194]

The literary production of Byzantine nuns is also disappointing in comparison with their Western counterparts: a few letters, hymns, and saints' lives are all that survive.[195] But female monastics, both choir and household sisters, were literate and could read scripture and saints' lives; some young nuns were taught their letters within the convent precincts. Choir sisters learned to chant psalms and sing hymns, and they apparently sometimes gained quite a reputation for their musical skills. A thirteenth-century Greek bishop compared singing nuns with the sirens of old, "who [bewitched] those who sailed by them: [just] so did these [nuns] through the harmony of their melody cast a spell over and charm those who entered [the convent churches] and attended their services. And as it were, they held them fast, bound immovably by the songs of these singers . . . so that they could not leave the churches."[196]

I would argue that one of the most important contributions of convents to Byzantine society (this was also true for male monasteries) was the social services they provided to the poor and infirm who came to their gates for charitable assistance. The poor received alms and handouts of bread, wine, and leftovers from the refectory, and some of the infirm and elderly might be fed and receive long-term nursing care in a nunnery's hospice. Convents also benefited society through their role as a haven for orphans, widows, the elderly, the mentally ill, and for women who could not marry for one reason or another or found themselves in troubled and abusive marriages. They were true shelters for women in distress, who would be assured during their remaining years of food, lodging, medical care, burial, and commemorative prayers within the secure precincts of the cloister walls.[197]

Finally, convents provided a place where women could exercise their talents and perform a variety of functions and administrative duties that would normally be unavailable to them in a private household. Although medical care seems to have been relegated to male doctors, nuns could sing in a choir, organize church services, manage monastic estates, keep accounts, provide counseling, and serve as leaders of sizable institutions. For many women, entrance into a convent provided not only spiritual fulfilment but the opportunity to undertake challenging responsibilities denied to them in lay society.

As in so many aspects of Byzantine civilization, there were ambivalent attitudes towards the ideals that should be pursued by nuns. Some hagiographers celebrated nuns' attempts to disguise their sexual identity through mortification of the flesh and praised them for emulating celebrated male saints of old;[198] *typika* might urge nuns to act "in a manly fashion," "assume a manly and masculine temperament," and "forget feminine weakness."[199] The authors of these regulations adopted masculine metaphors, encouraging the abbess to be like a general, leading her nuns into battle against demons,[200] or like a physician, who healed the spiritual ailments of her nuns.[201] Nuns read the *vitae* of holy men and of female saints, as shown by a manuscript commissioned for a fourteenth-century convent in Constantinople, which included the lives of twelve male and two female saints.[202]

On the other hand, the foundresses of both the Kecharitomene and Sure Hope convents reminded their nuns that because of their "gentle and weak nature" and their "frail nature" they required strong protection by a male guardian.[203] On account of their perceived weakness, nuns were not expected to engage in hard physical labor or in extreme ascetic behavior. In the opinion of a commentator such as Balsamon, nuns epitomized the cenobitic ideal and should not attempt to distinguish themselves from other members of their community. At the same time, there is limited evidence that in some convents the nuns were urged to emulate female saints of the past: they might see their images painted on the walls of the refectory, and the readings in the refectory, and private reading, might focus on holy women as models for imitation. These conflicting views may be one explanation for the relatively small number of nuns, such as Theodora of Thessalonike and Irene of Chrysobalanton, who became known for ascetic feats within the cloister and attained sanctity.

CHAPTER 3

HERMITS AND HOLY MOUNTAINS

Residence in a cenobitic monastery, as described in chapters 1 and 2, was the normative form of monastic life in Byzantium and the mode of separation from the world chosen by the vast majority of men and women who decided to devote their lives to prayer and an ascetic lifestyle. Monks who retreated to monasteries in the countryside or on holy mountains obviously had less contact with laypeople and fewer possibilities for secular temptations than those who lived in urban establishments. But for monks who wished to pursue an even purer and more austere withdrawal from earthly distractions there was yet another option: to live as a solitary in the wilderness, either as a dependent of a *lavra*, an institution that combined elements of communal life and eremitism, or as an independent, unaffiliated hermit.

Curiously, this alternative form of monasticism in Byzantium has attracted relatively little scholarly attention, and there is a paucity of secondary bibliography on the various modes of solitary life.[1] The principal sources for this research are hagiographical, the *vitae* of holy men, whose biases must be recognized, but they nevertheless provide a vivid and consistent picture of the challenges of the eremitic lifestyle. A number of the details can be corroborated by the continuing tradition of hermits living on holy mountains, such as Athos, up to the present day.[2] My almost exclusive reliance in this chapter on hagiography as source material for the eremitic life reflects the fact that a significant number of Byzantine monastic saints lived as hermits for part or much of their career. The freedom of solitaries from the highly regulated regimen of a cenobitic monastery and the oversight of an abbot, who might try to restrain extreme asceticism, meant that hermits could engage in more severe mortification of the flesh and were more likely to be recognized as holy men.

The Greek word for living as a monk, *monazein*, has the root meaning of "being alone"; since the fourth century, the time of Anthony the Great's sojourn in the Egyptian desert, the solitary life has been considered by many to be the highest form of Christian spiritual devotion, but it was possible only for a small number of highly motivated ascetics. During the centuries that followed the formative period of monasticism in Syria and Egypt, a select group of monks pursued an isolated existence in the forests of more northern climes in Anatolia (present-day Turkey) and Balkan lands (modern Greece, Serbia, Republic of Macedonia, and Bulgaria). The Greek word for desert and forest wilderness is the same, *eremos*, the root of the English words "hermit" and "eremitic." The Greek term for "withdrawal," *anachoresis*, gave rise to a synonym for hermit, "anachorete" or "anchorite." Seclusion in the silence and isolation of the wilderness or desert and the lack of distraction by fellow human beings provided optimal circumstances for total focus on prayer and contemplation. The reduction of possessions to an absolute bare minimum, subsistence on a frugal diet, performance of ascetic exercises, such as all-night standing vigils, and endurance of bitter cold and blazing heat were all aspects of self-mortification designed to lead to complete disregard of one's physical body, thus better enabling concentration on spiritual exercises and, for the select few, attainment of a mystical ecstatic union with God. The term used for this spiritual contemplation in tranquility, the primary focus of the solitary monk, was *hesychia*, literally "quietude."

HOLY MOUNTAINS AND SOLITARIES

Between the ninth and fifteenth centuries, hermits could be found in almost any isolated location in the Byzantine countryside, but they were particularly attracted to mountainous territory. In Greece and Anatolia, the dense forests, lofty ridges, deep ravines, natural caves, and vertical cliff faces on mountains such as Athos offered unparalleled possibilities for solitaries to hide away in a secluded spot for years on end. Gradually, such mountains attracted sizable numbers of hermits, and cenobitic monasteries were founded there. As monastic pioneers, both eremitic and cenobitic, began to tame the wilderness by inhabiting caves and building huts, cisterns, and chapels, then full-fledged monasteries, they also hallowed the landscape. They exorcized demons by recitation of prayers and psalms as they walked the mountainous paths, by making the sign of the cross and carving it on rocks, by the celebration of the liturgy, and by attracting pilgrims. Eventually these mountains attained a sacred character and began to be termed "holy," in emulation of earlier holy mountains in the Levant, such as Sinai, Carmel, and Tabor. Among the earliest in the Aegean area were Mount St. Auxentios near Constantinople (founded in the fifth century), Mount Latros near Miletos (founded in the seventh century), Mount Olympos near Prousa (where monasticism began to flourish in the eighth century), and Mount Athos (where the first hermits are attested in the ninth century).[3] The access of women to these holy mountains, as visitors or residents, was sometimes totally prohibited, as on Athos and at Meteora, or restricted, as on Galesion, which had no nunneries at all on the mountain itself but permitted the foundation of a single nunnery at the base of the mountain to accommodate female relatives of monks living in the three monasteries on the slopes above. Female pilgrims were frequent visitors to Lazaros's column, but he strongly discouraged women solitaries, probably out of fear for their personal safety.[4]

The life of the solitary was obviously much more physically and spiritually demanding than that of a cenobitic monk. Common wisdom held that a young monk should first spend a few years in communal life in a monastery, learning to chant the monastic office and accepting the principle of obedience to a superior and a monastic *typikon*, before setting off on his own in the wilderness. The tenth-century *typikon* of Athanasios of Athos gave the following conditions for a monk who wished to withdraw to one of the Great Lavra's five *kellia*: "If he has been previously exercised in obedience, if he has learned to stay in a cell with concentration and strict guard over his mind, if he has learned to pray and keep vigil, to control himself, to exercise abstinence, to meditate, to devote himself to the study of the Scriptures with humility, and attach some importance to working with his hands, then let him be permitted to do this."[5] Athanasios felt that a young monk who had thus gained self-discipline and had been initiated into a rigorous regimen of meditation and prayer would better be able to withstand the physical and psychological perils of a solitary life.

Later, in the fourteenth century, when the youthful Maximos the Hutburner arrived at the Great Lavra on Athos, he asked the resident monks which path he should follow first, that of the hermit or the cenobite? The elders strongly recommended that he remain in the monastery for a while to learn humility and submission to an abbot, before progressing to a contemplative life in the wilderness.[6] It was essential for the would-be solitary ascetic to be trained in abnegation of the will, which was viewed as taking priority over self-mortification. Thus, when Athanasios, the future founder of the Great Lavra on Mount Athos, first took monastic vows on Mount Kyminas in Bithynia, the superior, Michael Maleinos, "sought to restrain his will."[7] When he asked to eat only once a week, the abbot ordered him to take nourishment every three days, and when Athanasios requested permission to sleep in a chair, he was told to sleep on the ground on a straw pallet.[8] After four years of this regimen, the abbot permitted him to move to a hut one mile from the monastery and live as a solitary. But Athanasios remained under the supervision of the abbot, who instructed him to subsist on dry bread and a little water every other day, except during Lent, when he was to eat only every fifth day. He was also expected to attend the liturgy at the monastery on weekends, as was customary for solitaries who belonged to a *lavra*. At this time he would also share a meal in the refectory with the other monks and take back to his hermitage food for the week and supplies for his manual labor.

Some very pious and zealous youths, however, eschewed the trial period in a monastery before embarking on the solitary life and withdrew to the wilderness at the very beginning of their monastic careers.[9] Here they normally became the disciples of an established and experienced hermit, a *geron* (elder), who served as a mentor responsible for their spiritual training. In exchange for providing services, such as foraging for food, hauling water, building fires, and carrying heavy loads, the youths would learn submission and obedience to an elder, and how to pray and chant psalms without the structure of church offices and the liturgy.

THREE LIVES OF HERMITS ON HOLY MOUNTAINS

Let us now look at the specific experiences of three saintly hermits, two from Mount Athos, the third from Mount Latros in Anatolia, who exemplify some of the possible variations in pursuit of the eremitic way of life on a holy mountain.

St. Euthymios the Younger

Euthymios the Younger followed many different paths during his long life (823/24 to 898). After abandoning his young wife and daughter and receiving initial training at a cenobitic monastery on Mount Olympos in Asia Minor, he was invested with the monastic habit. He later moved to Mount Athos, where, in the mid-ninth century, he spent three years in the most rigorous form of the solitary contemplative life. At this time, Athos was in the process of becoming a holy mountain after half a millennium of human abandonment, between the third and eighth centuries. Around 800 its primeval forests and pristine wilderness began to attract solitaries, who remained the sole inhabitants of the craggy peninsula until the tenth century when the first monasteries were established.

So when Euthymios arrived on Athos in 859, attracted by its reputation for tranquility, he found it to be an isolated peninsula, sparsely populated by hermits living either as solitaries or in small groups under the leadership of a *geron*; the monks living in groups were called *kelliotai*, from the Greek word *kellion*, which could refer to a hut in the forest or to a cell in a monastery. As later described by the biographer of Athanasios of Athos, seemingly nostalgic for the simpler, more bucolic form of monasticism, in those early days, the Athonite solitaries

> did not engage in agricultural work, nor were they entangled in business affairs, nor were they distracted by bodily concerns, nor did they own a beast of burden nor an ass nor a dog, but constructed huts of wild grasses and lived in these summer and winter, scorched by the sun and frozen by the cold. If they ever needed to transport something somewhere, they did this themselves. For they would place pads on their shoulders, and, carrying the object, would transport it wherever they wished. Their food was nuts and the fruit of other trees.[10]

Euthymios immediately adopted a rigorously ascetic lifestyle, reportedly subsisting solely on foraged wild plants. For the first forty days of his exercise in self-mortification, he and his companion Joseph became *boskoi*, or "grazers."[11] Although this term, used most often of hermits in the Judean Desert, usually referred to forager monks who lived entirely off the land, the hagiographer Basil specifies that in the case of Euthymios and Joseph it was a more literal description: they actually crawled along the ground on all fours, like wild beasts, munching greens as they went. As Euthymios proposed to Joseph, "Let us think of ourselves as beasts and, crawling on the ground for forty days like grazing animals, *we will feed on grass like cattle* [Daniel 4:29]."[12]

Euthymios's next feat, considered an even higher rung of asceticism, was to seclude himself in a cave without ever going outside. Here he vowed to remain as a recluse (*enkleistos*) for a full three years, without the comfort of fire, after laying in a stock of foraged foods, such as chestnuts, acorns, and the fruit of the arbutus, or wild strawberry, tree.[13] Here he and Joseph refrained from conversation with each other, breaking the silence only with prayers, hymns, and spiritually beneficial tales.[14] Joseph abandoned the cave after the first year, unable to endure the terrible cold, lice, and lack of clothes after their original goat-hair shirts rotted away.[15] But Euthymios persevered on his own, and for two more years endured the assaults of demons who assumed various forms, such as Arab raiders, a hissing serpent, and scorpions. Euthymios eventually prevailed over these demons with the help of prayer and the sign of the cross, and he completed the period of seclusion in accordance with his vow.[16] As is seen so often in the *vitae* of hermits, his protracted residence in a cave and spiritual battles against demons resulted in an exorcism of evil spirits from the site and a purification, even sanctification, of this dark hole in the rocks. In the words of his hagiographer, at the end of his three-year ordeal, "he went out from the cave as if from a holy sanctuary or the vaults of heaven."[17]

Euthymios later spent some time as a stylite on a column in Thessalonike, lived with two other hermits on an island off the coast of Athos, and in a location west of the Holy Mountain became the leader of a group of *kelliotai* who had been driven from Athos by Arab raids. He built cells for his fellow hermits and served as their spiritual mentor, but he himself lived apart in a deep ravine. Toward the end of his life, Euthymios unexpectedly founded twin monasteries on a holy mountain (Peristerai) near Thessalonike, where his grandson and granddaughter became the superiors. As he sensed that death drew near, he left his monastic foundation to return to his beloved Athos and withdrew to an offshore island, where his final abode was, appropriately, a cave.[18]

Thus, the various phases of Euthymios's monastic career included life as a cenobitic monk, as a hermit secluded in a cave, as an urban stylite, as the leader of a group of *kelliotai*, as the founder and superior of a double monastery, and, at the end of his life, return to a cave on an island off the coast of Athos.

St. Paul of Latros

Paul of Latros, an Anatolian hermit who died in 955, likewise experimented in the course of his career with several modes of monastic life. Although he came from the family of a respected naval officer, he fell on hard times after being orphaned and ended up working as a swineherd. He later moved to the holy mountain of Latros (ancient Latmos) on the western coast of Anatolia, near Miletos, and became a servant to the abbot Peter at the cenobitic monastery of Karya.[19] He wanted to become a hermit, but Peter said he was too young and inexperienced.

After Peter's death, the youthful Paul left the monastery with a bosom friend named Demetrios with the intention of living in a cave.[20] The two men ended up arguing, however, over the location of their hermitage. Demetrios was worried about their food supply[21] and preferred to live near a *lavra*, where they could get regular provisions. Paul responded that the Lord would provide and pointed to the nearby oak trees teeming with acorns. Demetrios retorted that the acorns were unripe and deemed inedible even by pigs. Paul insisted that they remain where they were. After going without food for a week, they finally ate some of the unripe and raw acorns, which caused violent abdominal distress and much vomiting of blood and bile. Demetrios said to his companion, "I told you so," and went off to live with an elderly solitary named Matthew, who was provisioned by the *lavra* of Kellibara. When Matthew heard the tale of Paul and the acorns, he suggested that he and Demetrios share with Paul their provisions, consisting of dry rusks or hardtack, a twice-baked bread that would keep indefinitely.[22] Later, Paul ascended to a cave at the top of a rocky natural pillar, where he was provided with food and other necessities by a goatherd named Leo; here he lived as both recluse and stylite. But when Leo went off to Miletos at harvest time, Paul was left without supplies and was saved from starvation only by drinking the oil and water in his lamp.[23]

Paul's fame gradually attracted disciples, as had been the case with Anthony the Great: some settled near his pillar, building huts or residing in caves, and worshipping in a small chapel he had constructed; others preferred the communal life, and built a dormitory and refectory. This was the genesis of the *lavra* of Stylos (Pillar), of which Paul was the founder and spiritual father. He himself, however, remained in his cave on the rocky pillar for a number of years until the influx of disciples proved to be too great a distraction. He retreated once more into the forest, "living among the wild beasts and sharing their food," but later on he accepted regular provisions of food.[24]

Thus Paul began his monastic career in a cenobitic monastery, then spent many years as a solitary, and ended up supervising a group of *kelliotai* at a *lavra*, while living by himself in a cave or cell.

St. Maximos the Hutburner

Like Euthymios, Maximos the Hutburner also lived on Mount Athos, but toward the end of the Byzantine era, in the fourteenth century (fig. 7). He began monastic life dwelling with a group of solitaries on two different holy mountains in Thrace, Ganos and Papikion, but soon moved to Athos. After a few years of training at the Great Lavra, he spent the rest of his life as a hermit, at first adopting extreme measures to avoid contact with his fellow human beings. He lived in temporary structures made of twigs and grasses, and whenever his rude shelter was discovered he would burn it to the ground and move away, building another temporary hut elsewhere. In the words of his hagiographer, "The blessed one never possessed ... any ... material necessity, nor bread, but living like an immaterial being in places untouched by materiality, he thus possessed only the semblance of a small hut, large enough only to contain his

FIGURE 7 Portrait of Maximos the Hutburner from *vita* by Ioannikios Kochylas, Vatopedi 470, fol. 1ʳ (photo: Patriarchal Institute of Patristic Studies, Mone Vlatadon, Thessalonike)

much-suffering body."[25] The same hagiographer recounted that "no one ever visited him to bring provisions," but he would occasionally visit other hermits and get "bread and wine and salt."[26] Another hagiographer reported that for a period of ten years he survived on a foraged diet of plants, acorns, and chestnuts.[27]

Maximos had a change of heart after a life-altering encounter with the famous hesychast monk, Gregory of Sinai, who strongly advised him not to avoid his fellow man, but to associate with them so as to share his spiritual wisdom. So for his remaining years, Maximos stayed in one spot, in a hut or cave relatively close to the Great Lavra, where he had regular visits from fellow hermits, cenobitic monks, and laymen, who would bring him gifts of food, such as bread, fish, octopus, wine, and grapes.[28] These visitors would often sit with him and share the meal, enjoying the opportunity for edifying conversation with such a renowned hermit. On a few occasions solitaries who lived nearby would invite him to their hermitages for a meal, including freshly baked pita bread.[29] His hagiographers emphasize, however, that Maximos always trusted to the Lord to provide; he never kept leftovers or any food supplies in his hut but was totally reliant on gifts from visitors.[30] Once he went eight days without food because no one came to see him; on this occasion he was saved from starvation by visiting a nearby vineyard, where the vinedresser had made himself an onion and bread soup, which he served to Maximos with bread and wine.[31]

Maximos represents one extreme on the spectrum of eremitic life styles: except at the beginning of his monastic career, when he lived with groups of hermits and was briefly a cenobitic monk, he lived alone for most of his ninety-five years; even in his old age, he did not take on a youthful assistant as a servant.

VARIOUS FORMS OF SOLITARY LIFE

Just as there were wide variations in the rules of cenobitic monasteries, so there were many different kinds of hermits. Among these solitaries I would distinguish six types, depending on their degree of isolation and autonomy. I start with the most rigorous form of isolation and asceticism.

1. Totally independent and self-sufficient solitary, living in the wilderness and avoiding all human contact. This was the most extreme form of eremitism, in which the hermit lived in a cave or built himself a hut, and foraged for his food, mostly wild plants. An example is Euthymios the Younger, who lived for forty days by grazing and survived three years on a store of foraged plants and nuts.[32] The hermit Paphnoutios on Mount Galesion reportedly subsisted for three years on water that trickled from the rock outside his cave and the weeds that grew in this moist environment.[33]

2. Other hermits were independent but not self-sufficient. Those who took vows of seclusion were termed *enkleistoi* (literally, "enclosed"), or recluses.[34] Some never left their caves, either chaining themselves to a rock, as Ioannikios,[35] or, as Paul of Latros, living on such an inaccessible cliff face that it was difficult for them to leave their hermitages for any reason. These hermits might pick weeds that grew just outside the cave opening and drink water that oozed from the rocky cliff, but they were often dependent on the good will of fellow hermits, shepherds, or pious visitors who would bring them food and water. Yet other hermits, such as Maximos, lived in huts but were unable to obtain food on their own, perhaps because of old age or out of a principled belief that God would provide. They too were dependent on gifts brought by visitors.

3. A pair of independent hermits, such as Euthymios and Joseph, or Paul of Latros and Demetrios, who were spiritual brothers. They lived in much the same way as types 1 and 2, but they had the advantage of human company and mutual support.

4. An elderly solitary with a young disciple/servant to assist with his physical needs. In this case the disciple was responsible for finding food, by foraging or fishing, or by going to a nearby monastery for provisions. He was also expected to fetch water, build fires, and cook meals.

5. Solitaries associated with a *lavra*, such as the Great Lavra on Athos, the monastery of Christodoulos on Patmos, or Machairas on Cyprus, which provided them with food and weekly liturgical services. These solitaries often went to the monastery on weekends to attend the liturgy and take a meal in the refectory; they would also pick up food supplies, consisting of bread, fruit, and legumes soaked in water, and raw materials for handiwork. They remained under the supervision of the superior of the monastic complex with which they were affiliated.[36]

6. Small groups of solitaries (*kelliotai*), often with a leader (a combination of types 3 and 5). They very often got their supplies from nearby monasteries or *lavrai*.

THE EREMITIC LIFESTYLE

Let me now turn to a more detailed description of certain aspects of the lifestyle of a hermit on a holy mountain, and look first at the types of shelter he inhabited.

Shelter

For the hermit who sought to disassociate himself from the world, residence in a cave was in many ways a logical option, adopted, as we have seen, by Euthymios the Younger, Paul of Latros, and Maximos the Hutburner at one point or another in their monastic careers. Above all, caves were a natural shelter, provided by God for the anchorite who eschewed a built environment.[37] Caves offered protection from the elements, and, if situated high atop a mountain or on a cliff face (fig. 8), they were difficult to access for would-be pilgrims or disciples, prying visitors, brigands, or pirates. These advantages, however, were also disadvantages: the cool air of a cave that was welcome in summer was frigid and damp in winter; the darkness that provided relief from the sun was at the same time gloomy and depressing; the inaccessibility of caves made it difficult

FIGURE 8   The hermitages of Saints Gregory and Anthony, close to *skete* of St. Nicholas of Badov. Meteora, Greece (photo: Hercules Milas / Alamy Stock Photo)

for the hermit to obtain food and water; the same cavernous recesses that discouraged human visitors often attracted wild animals.

Some hermits who chose caves in elevated locations, such as atop a rocky pillar, may have been emulating the pillar saints, who sought to live closer to God. Others may have adopted residence in the tomblike darkness of a cave in order to meditate upon their forthcoming death; such a meditation is one of the rungs on the ladder of monastic virtues described by John of the Ladder, a monastic writer of the seventh century.[38] As was the case with Euthymios the Younger, a number of holy men are described as undergoing spiritual transformation, even transfiguration by heavenly light, in their caves, and as exorcising these caverns from demons with prayers, hymns, and fasting, turning them into holy sanctuaries.[39]

As an alternative to dwelling in caves, whose entrances might be covered by woven branches,[40] some hermits constructed simple huts from wild grasses and twigs. When the eighth-century iconodule St. Stephen the Younger moved out of his cave on Mount St. Auxentios, he built a mostly roofless enclosure that was reportedly twenty-eight by thirty-six inches, barely providing enough room to curl up in a fetal position. His disciples were horrified and thought it resembled a tomb more than a dwelling place. On the eastern side of the structure, Stephen added a prayer niche, with a ceiling so low that he was forced to constantly bow his head when standing there.[41] When Maximos the Hutburner finally settled down in a permanent location on Mount Athos, he made a slightly larger fenced enclosure six feet long and six wide, "not out of rectangular pieces of wood or nails, rivets or stones and boards, but as was his custom, taking brushwood and some grass, he built a cell."[42] These huts no doubt resembled the structures built of twigs, reeds, and brush in modern times by nomadic shepherds, the Sarakatsanoi, which could still be seen in Greece in the first half of the twentieth century.[43] A nineteenth-century traveler, George Bowen, described similar huts constructed by Vlach nomads, consisting "of merely a few poles thatched with straw or green boughs." They might be surrounded by a rock "wall crowned with thorny bushes."[44] As more hermits came to a holy mountain and groups of kelliots were organized, they began to build more permanent structures of stone, including chapels.

Food

My brief summaries of the experiences of the hermits Euthymios, Paul, and Maximos focused in large part on their food provisioning, because, in my view, access to food was the determining feature of the degree of isolation and independence that a hermit could enjoy. The *vita* of Michael Maleinos, a tenth-century abbot of a *lavra*, clearly distinguishes, for example, between his first period of solitary withdrawal, when he lived near the monastery and returned to it on weekends, and the second phase of withdrawal to a more remote spot, when he was dependent on a peasant who brought him dried rusks.[45] A hermit living in a cave on stores of acorns, and other nuts and fruits, could have experienced a total isolation from the world not available to a solitary dependent for food on a visiting goatherd, relative,[46] or fellow monk, or to the hermit who went to a *lavra* every weekend for a refectory meal and participation in the liturgy. Moreover, the hagiographical accounts of these hermits themselves emphasize issues of food security and provide rich details of the foods available to them; although these ascetics were determined to subsist on the most frugal of diets, it is clear that food supply was a genuine concern for even the most committed practitioner of this lifestyle. Sometimes they ran dangerously short of food; at one point Athanasios, abbot of the Great Lavra, sent a hunter with provisions to resupply some hermits who were in dire need.[47] As far as I know, however, no saint's *vita* records the death of a hermit from starvation; they always seemed to be saved at the last minute through the arrival of a visitor bearing food.

The story of Euthymios's foraging on Athos in the ninth century raises the question of how in fact he and his fellow hermits supplied themselves with the necessities of life. Because of the isolation of Athos in the ninth and first half of the tenth centuries, before the foundation of the first cenobitic monasteries, these early hermits could not rely on nearby monastic complexes or villages as a source of provisions, as was customary elsewhere, unless they went outside the bounds of the peninsula. The occasional shepherd or cowherd tending his flocks or herds might have provided them with milk and cheese, as was the case with Blasios of Amorion, who spent a period of time on Athos in the ninth century.[48] Athonite hermits could sometimes obtain supplies of grain from visitors who came to the peninsula to receive blessings from the holy men there; the hermits would give the visitors fruits and nuts they had picked in exchange for wheat and millet.[49] For the most part, however, it seems that these pioneering solitaries on the Holy Mountain had to be self-sufficient in terms of their food supply, foraging on the mountainsides and planting small gardens.[50]

The early tenth-century hagiographer Basil strongly suggests this reality with his story of Euthymios's elderly spiritual father, Theodore, who had asked Euthymios to return briefly to Bithynian Olympos in order to escort him back to Mount Athos, where he wished to spend the remaining years of his life. Basil writes,

> Since ... Theodore's body was suffering as a result of mortification through asceticism and his battles with old age and disease, he needed some small concessions to comfort, but an abode on the Mountain was bereft of these because it lay far from any community of lay people. So the excellent disciple and servant [Euthymios] looked for a place for his superior which could provide both tranquility for the old man and comfort for his body in the same location; he settled him there, after building a hut for him to live in. The name of the place was Makrosina, which was near the villages and permitted easy provision of food for the enfeebled old man. And Euthymios himself ministered to his mentor, providing those things with which Theodore longed to be nourished.[51]

Makrosina is believed to have been near the town of Hierissos, just west of the isthmus of the Athonite peninsula, and thus a place where food could be obtained.[52] The clear implication is that the elderly Theodore would be unable to forage for wild foods and therefore could not reside on Athos itself, but only nearby, close to a population center.

The light human footprint on holy mountains, which forestalled deforestation caused by cutting of firewood, logging, grazing of flocks, and clearing of garden plots, no doubt made them rich islands of biodiversity in the Byzantine period. Certainly, the extreme isolation of the Athonite peninsula, surrounded by the sea on three sides, and its half millennium of abandonment by a human population in late antiquity, must have permitted the growth of virgin forests with massive trees and abundant fauna and flora, conditions that have survived to some extent down to this day, with 1,200 known plant species, including 350 types of mushroom.[53] These environmental conditions make more plausible the claims of hagiographers that some early Athonite hermits survived solely on foraged wild foods. The *vita* of Athanasios of Athos states that the monks lived on nuts and wild fruits, and Euthymios is reported to have collected "acorns and chestnuts and the fruits of the strawberry tree."[54] Oak, beech, and chestnut trees grew (and continue to grow) on Athos in profusion, and their nuts fall to the ground when ripe, making them easily available to foragers. Both chestnuts and acorns can be stored for long periods of time and thus would be a reliable long-term food supply for hermits during the winter months. Chestnuts in particular are an excellent source of starch; it is well known that, once roasted over a fire or boiled in water, they are soft and delicious. Acorns are mentioned in saints' lives as food for hermits and have been eaten by humans throughout history. They can be roasted and eaten like nuts or ground into flour to make bread or pasta. Chestnuts, acorns, and beechnuts do, however, contain tannins, which need to be leached out by boiling in several changes of water so they will not adversely affect the digestive system. We have already seen the dangers of eating untreated or unripe acorns, as mentioned in the *vita* of Paul of Latros, when Paul and his companion ate raw and unripe acorns from holm oaks and as a result suffered severe gastric distress.[55]

Paphnoutios, a hermit on Mount Galesion in the eleventh century, is reported to have survived for three years on the plants that grew in front of his cave.[56] Wild greens (*chorta*) have always been a staple of the Greek diet, usually cooked with oil and vinegar, but also edible in the raw form as a salad vegetable.[57] To this day, dandelion greens, nettles, and mushrooms are collected in large quantities by Athonite monks. Other species of edible plants on Athos are wild asparagus, wild carrots, wild onions, asphodel, and sloe plums.[58] The *vitae* of saints who lived in the Aegean region mention the availability of wild honey[59] and their eating of leeks, lupine beans, fennel, myrtle berries and pears, carob pods, chick peas,[60] and seeds,[61] all found growing in the wild. Hermits who lived near the sea, a lake, or river could also catch fish and octopus with nets or a baited hook,[62] and milk and cheese were another protein source.[63] Visitors might bring rye, millet,[64] and perhaps wheat flour; in any case, some hermits baked their own fresh pita bread.[65] The *vita* of Paul of Latros offers a rare insight into the hankering of hermits for special treats. Thus Paul, who on one occasion developed a craving for lettuce, and at another time for freshly made cheese, was thrilled by the arrival of an unexpected visitor bearing these very foods. These were rare indulgences for Paul, a strict ascetic, who when offered a tasty morsel of food used to mask its flavor by adding milk.[66]

Although subsistence on foraged wild plants was generally praised by hagiographers as a sign of a holy man's capacity for self-abnegation, there are occasional hints of a more critical attitude in the hagiographical literature. For example, in the *vita* of Niphon of Athos, a fourteenth-century hermit who was a contemporary of Maximos the Hutburner, some of his fellow monks and the superior of the Great Lavra criticized him for living in the open air on plants alone. The abbot reminded Niphon that excessive asceticism could lead to conceit, and that moderation was preferable. He told Niphon that there was no need for him to emulate the "grazers" of the Judean Desert from early Christian times. The abbot argued that the desert fathers ate plants because there was no bread in the desert, "but here [on Athos] there is both bread and other food to eat, so to avoid conceit you should be content with these."[67]

Solitaries affiliated with a monastery or *lavra* could either go themselves to fetch their weekly food supply or send a servant. The monasteries provided bread as a staple, and in some cases fresh fruit and dried legumes soaked in water.[68] The late fourteenth-century *vita* of Romylos of Vidin provides a helpful insight into the relationship between solitaries and monasteries. When Romylos first came to Athos, he had no official connection with the Great Lavra, that is, apparently he was not one of the five solitaries designated in the monastic rule who were supported by the Great Lavra. His hagiographer explains that he did not have an annual food allowance (*adelphaton*) from the monastery because he was such a recent arrival. Therefore he was not entitled to receive food supplies there, but instead had to purchase his food from an unspecified source.[69] At one point, his disciple Gregory was able to obtain a bag of dry bread from a leper to sustain his master.[70]

The *vitae* of late Byzantine solitaries offer illuminating insights into the role of youthful disciples in assuring food security for their masters. For example, as a youth, Romylos of Vidin served a feeble old monk who had a delicate stomach and ate primarily fish. So Romylos spent a lot of time using nets to catch fish for his elder's supper. This work was particularly arduous in winter when the pools of water froze over; he had to break up the ice with a shovel and hammer and wade in icy water in order to catch fish in a leather sack. Once, when he spent too much time fishing, the irascible old man heaped ridicule on him and made him spend the night outside in the snow; he was found half dead the next morning, buried in a snow drift.[71]

A major assignment for these young disciples was hiking the steep mountain paths to fetch provisions from a monastery. Thus when Romylos himself became a *geron* with a disciple, he would send the youth to a nearby monastery, probably the Great Lavra, three times a week to help with the baking and bring back fresh bread.⁷² This freshly baked bread was a special treat, still offered to its dependent hermits today by the Great Lavra, for most of the time the hermits subsisted on dry rusks.⁷³ When Athanasios (1305–83), the future founder of the Meteora monasteries, first came to Athos, he served the *geron* Gregory, a strict taskmaster who treated him like a beast of burden. Carrying a pad on his back like a mule's saddle, the young disciple had to walk long distances in all weather to fetch provisions. Once, when caught in a blizzard, he almost froze to death and had to wrap clothes around his feet for snowshoes to complete his journey.⁷⁴

The *vita* of the eighth-century holy man Stephen the Younger reports a variant in the use of young disciples to fetch supplies. When Stephen, the disciple of the *geron* John on Mount St. Auxentios, was away on an errand and John needed provisions, he would tie a message to the collar of his pet dog and send it down the mountain to a convent from which he normally obtained his food supplies.⁷⁵

Water Supply

As with their food supply, hermits' access to drinking water varied widely. One would expect that a nearby water supply would be a primary concern for a solitary deciding on the location of his hermitage. But sometimes hermits seem to have deliberately chosen a waterless spot, perhaps as a deliberate act of self-mortification. This decision in turn might make him dependent on outside assistants, who would necessarily intrude upon his solitary lifestyle. A hermit installed in an inaccessible cave on a cliff had to rely on others to bring him water, unless he could collect rainwater in a pot, dig a small cistern, or find water seeping from a rock. Thus for the hermit Paphnoutios on Mount Galesion, a reportedly waterless mountain near Ephesos, "his drink was the water that trickled down from the rock above it [the cave] and was caught by that below, lying stagnant where it was hollowed out a little."⁷⁶ Sometime later, however, Lazaros arranged for a cistern to be built in or near the cave. In the rainy season it was filled with water, but other times apparently went dry, since Lazaros had to depend on his fellow monks for a weekly delivery of a jug of drinking water and "a few pulses [soaked] in water."[77] The frequently mentioned hermit Paul, who lived in a cave on Mount Latros, felt guilty that visitors had to bring him water from a substantial distance, so he left his cave temporarily and went to a nearby ravine where he prayed for the miraculous appearance of a spring. The next day he asked a local shepherd to dig at the spot, and indeed water gushed forth from the ground.[78] On Mount Athos, Maximos the Hutburner had to walk two miles to a shepherd's trough to fetch water, even though he also reputedly had the ability to transform sea water into potable water.[79] On Mount St. Auxentios, Stephen the Younger, when he was still a youthful disciple in the service of an elderly hermit, carried water up the mountainside for his master.[80] Some hermits, however, did take a local water supply into consideration when deciding upon their abode. Thus, Romylos built a new cell on Athos near a spring with clear water.[81] Luke of Steiris (d. 953) established his final hermitage (on the site of the future monastery of Hosios Loukas) near a spring, which also provided water to irrigate his garden; he increased its flow by clearing away the brush that was blocking it.[82]

Fire

Discussion of the wild foods available to Athonite hermits leads us to the related question of whether these solitary monks used fire. Some of the most ascetic holy men rejected its use, whether for warmth or to cook their food, but others did make use of it, to bake pita bread, for example.[83] Euthymios and his companion Joseph are described as "living without fire" in their cave on Athos, but this was to be expected, since they eschewed all other creature comforts during this period of extreme mortification.[84] In the *vita* of Euthymios, when a group of monks was caught in a snowstorm while ascending Mount Athos, the hagiographer notes that "they did not have fire and none of them was carrying a flint," thus implying that it might be normal for monks to possess flint stones or carry smoldering embers in some sort of protective container or a moss bundle in order to start fires.[85] Other texts make it clear that many hermits did build fires for cooking and warmth; among the duties of their disciples was the cutting and carrying of firewood.[86] The tenth-century Italo-Greek holy man Neilos of Rossano reportedly abstained from all cooked foods while living as a hermit, but elsewhere he is said to have eaten boiled legumes.[87] He also kindled a fire in order to burn an unwanted basket.[88]

Clothing

We know very little about the clothing of solitaries, except for occasional reference to goat-hair tunics,[89] which again suggests contact with goatherds who could have supplied the hermits with goatskins or goat hair for spinning, and with milk and cheese. It is not at all clear, however, who might have tanned the goatskins and sewn them into garments, or how the goat hair was spun and woven into cloth. Kerykos, a hermit on Mount Galesion, is said to have worn "a tunic, a scapular and a holy cowl that he had made with his own hands out of wool," but no more specific information is provided.[90] Stephen the Younger wore a hood and a single leather tunic over heavy iron rings that encircled his body.[91] Hermits also sometimes received clothing and footgear from nearby monasteries.[92]

Material Possessions

One of the hagiographers of Maximos the Hutburner, in emphasizing his immaterial life, provides a list of all the things he did not possess, not "a digging fork or hoe, nor a purse, nor a bench, a table, a pot, flour, oil, or wine, nor any other material necessity, nor bread."[93] The implication is that these were the normal essentials for a hermit: minimal furniture, some food staples, a cooking pot, and gardening tools. Other *vitae* add to this list of objects that might be found in a hermit's cave or hut: a cup,[94] an oil lamp,[95] a reed mat that could be used as a bed covering or as a table cloth,[96] a hand mill for grinding grain,[97] a flint stone for lighting fires,[98] a writing tablet,[99] fishnets and a leather sack for fishing,[100] a hammer,[101] a shovel, mattock, and pickax,[102] wooden barrels or goatskins of wine,[103] and baskets.[104] It is evident that some hermits lived in relative comfort, in comparison with the extreme hardships of Euthymios and Joseph in their cave or Maximos the Hutburner in his grass hut.

Manual Labor

One of the dangers of the eremitic life style was the onset of a type of ennui or depression, called *akedia* in Greek, "acedia" in English. Manual labor was thought to be useful in warding off this type of despondency,[105] so some hermits engaged in the manufacture of objects that could be used by the monastery with which they were affiliated, sold in exchange for food, or given away to pilgrims as *eulogiai*, tokens of spiritual blessing. The *vitae* and *typika* provide very little information on the types of manual labor performed by hermits, but there are a few tantalizing allusions to solitary monks copying manuscripts, carving wooden crosses, and weaving fishnets, baskets, mats, and coverlets from grasses and rushes.[106] The eleventh-century *typikon* for the monastery of Christodoulos on Patmos prescribes that the superior is to provide the raw materials for handwork, and the finished product is to be returned to him by the solitary.[107] Cyril Phileotes (d. 1110) tended a small garden and made woolen head coverings for monks while living as a hermit in a *kellion* near his monastery at Philea in eastern Thrace.[108]

Of course, much physical labor was required in order to sustain a solitary life in the wilderness, but it was rather the hermits' young disciples who did most of the heavy work of cutting firewood, hauling water, carrying supplies, weaving and mending fishnets, and fishing.[109] Luke of Steiris, who was servant to a stylite for ten years, "ceaselessly carried wood and water and tended to the cooking and the table preparations, mending nets and fishing."[110] Some of this labor was very arduous indeed: when describing the five-hour journey of the young disciple Germanos Maroules (d. ca. 1336) to the Athonite monastery of Vatopedi, involving a steep ascent and descent carrying a heavy load, his hagiographer, Philotheos Kokkinos, remarks that he himself had climbed this same mountain ridge only with great difficulty, panting and sweating profusely all the way.[111] In the *vita* of Romylos, he is said to have sent his disciple Gregory to a *geron* to borrow a book, but then punished the disciple because he stopped on the way back to read a chapter![112] Another vivid passage from a *vita* by Philotheos Kokkinos describes how Sabas the Younger ended up carrying his companion's load along with his own.[113]

Spiritual Life

One disadvantage of the anchoritic lifestyle was lack of access to regular church services and reception of the Eucharist, and the scarcity of religious texts. At most a hermit might possess a Psalter, a gospel book, New Testament lectionary, or liturgical book of hymns,[114] but usually he was limited to recitation of the psalms and hymns that he had committed to memory. We can catch only occasional glimpses of the spiritual devotions of hermits through brief allusions in their *vitae*. Thus we know that they routinely chanted morning prayers,[115] engaged in occasional all-night standing vigils,[116] sang hymns to Christ and the Virgin, recounted spiritually beneficial tales to each other,[117] and recited psalms as they walked the steep paths of holy mountains, including the appropriate verses from Psalm 120 (121): "I lifted up mine eyes to the hills."[118] Niphon of Athos used to recite the entire Psalter while standing on one foot.[119] Maximos the Hutburner, who dug his own grave near his cell so that he could meditate on the inevitability of death, "used to repeat by heart the mournful funeral hymns" during his morning prayers while standing next to the grave.[120] Lazaros of Mount Galesion is described as "singing the office" as he made his initial ascent of the holy mountain, and as reciting the entire Psalter as he made a second ascent to take up residence in a cave.[121]

One of the fullest descriptions of the daily spiritual routine of a hermit is found in the *vita* of Neilos of Rossano, who lived periodically in a cave in southern Italy in the tenth century. In addition to performing the manual labor of copying manuscripts, he maintained a busy schedule of prayer, reciting the monastic offices and the Psalter, singing hymns, reading, and making a thousand genuflections daily.[122] He hardly slept but spent most of the night in vigil, reciting psalms, singing the midnight and matins hymns, and making five hundred genuflections.[123] Likewise, in the fourteenth century, Gregory of Sinai gave detailed instructions for the solitary. The twelve hours of the day should alternate between prayer, reading, and psalmody, with two hours off for eating and sleeping. The nocturnal schedule could vary, depending on the experience and discipline of the hermit: beginners should sleep half the night and keep vigil for the remaining six hours; those at an intermediate stage should keep vigil for one or two hours, followed by four hours of sleep, then rise for matins, psalmody, and prayer; the most experienced solitaries were to maintain a standing vigil throughout the night.[124]

The fervor with which hermits observed their nocturnal vigils is vividly described in the *vita* of Luke of Steiris, who as a teenager withdrew to a hut on a mountainside near the Gulf of Corinth. A visitor who secretly observed his nightly regimen reported that he was constantly "genuflecting and pressing his forehead to the earth" until he collapsed in exhaustion. Then "he raised his hands up high along with the eyes of his body and soul and said the familiar *Kyrie Eleison* with total devotion. Then when his body had had time to relax a little, he stood upright again and dedicated himself to prayer until the dawn of the day."[125]

In the fourteenth century, with the rise of the mystical movement known as hesychasm, "prayer of the heart" or "mental prayer," a silent, internal recitation of prayer, became standard practice among solitaries.[126] This type of prayer focused on constant repetition of the short "Jesus prayer": "Lord Jesus Christ, Son of God, have mercy on me." Adepts such as Maximos the Hutburner experienced "rapture of the mind" as a result of this "prayer of the heart," and his mind was "set ablaze with the fire of divinity, and . . . consumed by the divine light."[127]

For some Athonite monks, ascent to the summit of the Holy Mountain offered a profound spiritual experience. After making the arduous climb they would spend the night in vigil atop the 6,600-foot peak and sometimes see visions of the Mother of God, or do battle with demonic forces. On his first such ascent, Maximos the Hutburner remained for three additional days by himself, in fasting, prayer, and singing of hymns, and had a vision of the Virgin instructing him to become a hermit on the slopes of Athos. He was surrounded with divine light and granted celestial bread as sustenance for body and spirit.[128]

In the early days of monasticism on Athos, the Holy Mountain was inhabited only by hermits, with no cenobitic monasteries, and hence no regular church services. Some Athonite hermits, such as Blasios of Amorion, had already been ordained as priests or deacons, and could celebrate the liturgy privately;[129] others, such as Euthymios the Younger, sought ordination specifically so they could celebrate the liturgy;[130] yet others would go on weekends to monasteries outside the peninsula to attend services, but many were forced to forgo participation in any formal liturgical rituals. In the tenth century, when Athanasios of Athos established the Great Lavra, he made provision for five hermits who were formally associated with the monastery; they were to come to the Great Lavra on Sundays to partake of the Eucharist and eat in the refectory.[131] This was standard practice at *lavrai*, such as St. Sabas near Jerusalem and Mount Kyminas in Bithynia, where Athanasios himself had received his initial monastic training.

A passage in the *vita* of David, Symeon, and George of Lesbos describes the yearning for the Eucharist among hermits deprived of access to communion rites; David, while a hermit on Mount Ida near Troy, dreamed of a church where the clergy were celebrating the liturgy. In his dream he longed to enter but was refused entrance. Subsequently, at the prompting of an angelic vision, he was tonsured as a monk and ordained as a priest. He then returned to the wilderness, where he built a chapel and could perform the liturgy.[132]

Over the centuries, hermits devised a number of solutions to the problem of lack of access to the Eucharist. Those who remained continuously in their hermitages took advantage of traveling priests, such as Niphon, who in the fourteenth century made the rounds of outlying monastic cells on Mount Athos for three years, "reciting the regular daily office and celebrating the holy sacrament."[133] Niphon also found a ruined church and got permission from the bishop of Hierissos to restore it and celebrate the liturgy there for anchoritic monks.[134] In tenth-century Anatolia, Paul of Latros, living high up on a rocky pillar, had a ladder constructed so that a priest could climb up and administer the sacrament to him.[135]

In central Greece in the tenth century, Luke of Steiris was so concerned about a hermit's access to the Eucharist that he consulted with the bishop of Corinth, who advised him to obtain a vessel with presanctified bread and place it on an altar in a chapel, or on a clean bench in a monastic cell. Then the hermit should spread out a small veil, place the holy bread on it, and burn incense. Finally, he should sing the psalms of the Typika office or the Trisagion hymn and recite the Creed, kneel three times, and put the bread in his mouth, saying "Amen." He could drink ordinary wine, instead of Eucharistic wine.[136] The problem with this advice was that the bishop assumed that the hermit had access to a source of presanctified bread, a liturgical veil, and incense, which were not among the usual possessions of a solitary.

RELATIONSHIP WITH NATURE

Although hermits consciously sought out the solitude and tranquility of holy mountains, their hagiographers make little reference to their appreciation of the natural beauty surrounding them, no mention of birdsong, of the fragrance of wild flowers, of the sound of a waterfall, or the spectacular views from a mountain peak. An exception is found in the ninth-century *vita* of Ioannikios (d. 846), who had a gift for taming wild animals and seemed to enjoy walking in the woods. He is described on one occasion as leaving his dark cave on a beautiful sunny winter day "to warm up and walk about," and another time as going for a walk in the shady forest with his assistant.[137] He would tame wild animals so that they took food from his hands, and a bear used to come and sprawl on the ground near his guests while they were enjoying an al fresco lunch.[138] Likewise Luke of Steiris, distressed by deer that kept eating the vegetables in his garden, immobilized one of them through the power of his words.[139] He also kept pet snakes and used to throw bread crumbs to sparrows.[140]

A rare reference to a hermit enjoying the view is found in the same *vita* of Luke of Steiris. When he was entertaining two monastic visitors, they sat "by the seashore as the sun was stretching out its pure rays, gazing intently as the gentle breezes ruffled the waves and taking great pleasure at the sight."[141] While Neilos of Rossano was living in a cave, he spent his day in copying manuscripts, reciting the Psalter and the monastic offices, praying, and reading; after vespers, he "would go outside to walk a bit and enjoy the view, and to restore a little his mind which was wearied by the length of the day."[142] The fourteenth-century *vita* of Sabas the Younger by Philotheos Kokkinos describes how Sabas spent some time in a cave in an inaccessible cliff near Thracian Herakleia, which provided a vista over the Sea of Marmara and offered protection from the elements in both summer and winter.[143] I would suggest that for the most part, however, the solitaries in search of spiritual tranquility deliberately disregarded the beauties of nature that surrounded them and turned inward in their search for conversation with God. It is also possible, however, that it was their hagiographers who sought to emphasize holy men's focus on interior contemplation rather than taking pleasure in the natural world.

HERMITESSES

In a society in which women led relatively secluded lives and were viewed as the weaker sex, it was almost inconceivable that a woman should go off by herself to live in an isolated spot as a solitary. Such societal disapproval of hermitesses was also perhaps motivated by the fear that a woman living alone might be exposed to sexual violence, as in the case of three eighth-century female anchorites in the Judean Desert who narrowly escaped being raped by local Arab herders.[144] Nonetheless, a few examples of female hermits are attested in the hagiographic literature.

Two of the earliest hermitesses from the middle Byzantine period may both be legendary, but their stories are still instructive. The tenth-century *vita* of Theoktiste of Lesbos, by Niketas Magistros, is closely modeled on the earlier *vita* of Mary of Egypt, but it may have a kernel of historical fact. Theoktiste, an orphan girl raised and tonsured in a nunnery on Lesbos, was reportedly abducted by Arab pirates in the early ninth century, but she escaped to the deserted island of Paros. Here she lived as a solitary for thirty-five years, subsisting on foraged foods such as lupine seeds and other wild plants, until a visiting hunter discovered her, naked and reduced to skin and bones. After the hunter gave her his cloak, she told him her story and begged him to bring her the Eucharist on his next hunting trip, since she had been deprived of the sacraments throughout her long ordeal. The hunter did bring her the Eucharist on his next visit, and a few days later he found the hermitess lying dead.[145] This tale of Theoktiste, who sorely lamented her inability to partake of communion during her lengthy enforced isolation on the island, suggests yet another possible reason for the small numbers of hermitesses: they were deprived, to an even greater extent than hermits, of access to the liturgical rites that were such a key element of monastic discipline because of their inability to be ordained as priests.

Another hermitess, Euphrosyne the Younger, supposedly lived in the late ninth century. She ran away from her relatives' house in Constantinople and spent three months as a solitary in the outskirts of the capital in an abandoned hut, subsisting on dry bread and water. Here she engaged in nocturnal vigils, prayer in orant position (standing with her arms upraised), and multiple genuflections, and shed tears of contrition. After being discovered, she sailed further up the Bosporos and disguised herself as a man, calling herself the monk John.[146]

The eleventh-century *vita* of Lazaros of Galesion has several references to female solitaries. While Lazaros was on his prolonged journey to the Holy Land and staying at the *lavra* of St. Sabas, he heard about a nun who was living in a cave above a dry river bed.[147] A hermitess nun is also mentioned as living on Mount Galesion at the time of Lazaros's arrival.[148] Another woman, the widow Irene from Ephesus, wanted to live as a solitary in a cell near Lazaros's column of the Savior, but he denied her request and sent her back down the mountain to take vows in a convent.[149] One reason for Lazaros's refusal to grant permission may have been his fear for her personal safety, and he was right to be concerned.[150] For Irene continued to make frequent visits to Lazaros on Galesion, and on one such ascent of the mountain narrowly escaped being raped. We are told that the devil prompted some young men from a nearby village to lie in wait for her and two female companions in order to seize and sexually assault them, but the plot was thwarted when the youths fell asleep, and the women passed by unmolested.[151]

Many of the holy men known to us from hagiography spent at least a portion of their careers as solitaries; the challenges of the anchoritic lifestyle were considered an important part of their spiritual development, and their ascetic feats both facilitated their search for enlightenment and made them worthy candidates for eventual sanctification. There were also disadvantages to the eremitic life, however, such as lack of regular access to the liturgy and the sacraments. Another problem for the independent hermit was the lack of any supervision by a superior; there was no one to whom he might make confession, no one to whom he owed obedience, no one to provide spiritual counsel and support. Since monastics emphasized the abnegation of personal volition, it was considered dangerous to forgo daily adherence to a monastic rule and the orders of an abbot. If hermits lived in small groups, they often did acknowledge the leadership of one of their number; thus, when Euthymios moved his disciples to Brastamon, under the threat of Arab raids, he lived separately in a ravine, but he clearly was supervising the monks living in nearby huts. Also, when a *geron* was paired with a youth new to monastic life as his trainer and spiritual advisor, he demanded total obedience from his young disciple.

Some hermit pairs, such as Euthymios the Younger and Joseph, and Paul of Latros and Demetrios, solved the problem of receiving mutual support by living together and encouraging each other in their asceticism. In both cases, however, the companion eventually proved less steadfast and abandoned his friend. Also striking is the extent to which hermits visited each other in the wilderness; the *vitae* of Maximos the Hutburner and Niphon of Athos, for example, abound with instances of hermits going to each other's huts to share a meal, conversation, and spiritual encouragement. Despondency (*akedia*), however, was a frequent problem for solitaries; one of the most vivid descriptions is the depression suffered by Athanasios of Athos during his year-long residence as a hermit at Melana, as described in chapter 1.[152] The tension between the cenobitic and eremitic forms of monasticism and the debate over which lifestyle was superior continued throughout the Byzantine centuries, and I will discuss this in further detail in the conclusion to this volume.

CHAPTER 4

ALTERNATIVE MODES OF MONASTICISM

Beyond the basic division between cenobitic and eremitic monks, several other varieties of monastic experience were embraced by monks (and more rarely by nuns) of middle and late Byzantium. Some of these modes of life, such as that of a recluse or a stylite, whether pursued within a monastic complex, in an urban environment, or in the wilderness, exemplified a rigorous adherence to the ideal of monastic stability (*stabilitas loci*), that is, residing in a single location throughout one's monastic career. Wandering monks, on the other hand, represented the opposite extreme, as they moved from one monastery or cave to another. Some wandering monks can be considered "holy fools" because they deliberately engaged in shameful or incomprehensible behavior designed to alienate themselves from society. Yet other monks and nuns lived independently in both urban and village environments, shunning obedience to a monastic superior. The common characteristic of all these practitioners of alternative modes of monasticism was individualism, a feature of Byzantine society noted many years ago by Hans-Georg Beck and further developed by Alexander Kazhdan.[1]

RECLUSES (*ENKLEISTOI*)

In chapter 3 we alluded to certain hermits, such as Euthymios and Joseph, and Paul of Latros, who secluded themselves in a cave for a period of time. Such recluses, or *enkleistoi*, literally, "enclosed," solitaries who lived in total seclusion in an enclosed space, deserve special attention since no study has ever been devoted to them.[2] A surprising number of Byzantine holy men spent a portion of their lives in seclusion, but this extreme ascetic endeavor of self-imposed withdrawal to a confined space has been largely overlooked by scholars. This may be in part because of their failure to recognize all the possible distinctions among the forms of cenobitic and eremitic life. Many hermits, for example, lived in caves or wooden huts but left them on occasion to forage for food, draw water from a spring, collect firewood, or even to visit other hermits. Recluses, on the other hand, took private vows to remain enclosed in a cell, cave, hut, chapel, or tower without ever going outside[3] and thus depended on visitors to bring them food and water, unless, like the hermit Paphnoutios on Mount Galesion, they could find edible plants growing right outside the opening of their cave and water dripping down from above.[4] It was also possible to live the life of a recluse in a cenobitic monastery; the monk would either seclude himself in a cell or build a special enclosure in a church from which he never went out. The most extreme form of seclusion was entombment in a gravelike structure, as will be described near the end of this section.

Normally, the ascetic maintained this regimen of seclusion for a fixed period of time, after which he moved on to other forms of monastic experience. Or he might relocate to another place of seclusion, either because of the danger of enemy attack or the oppressive adulation of pilgrims. There are several examples, however, of *enkleistoi* who spent much or most of their lives in seclusion.[5] The indicator words in Greek are the verb ἐγκλείω (I enclose), especially its passive participle, ἐγκεκλεισμένος (enclosed), the adjective ἔγκλειστος (enclosed), the nouns ἔγκλειστρα and ἔγκλειστρον (enclosure), and the noun κάθειρξις (confinement) with its related verb forms. Another telltale word is the adjective ἀπρόϊτος, meaning literally "not going out," and therefore referring to a monk or nun who has taken a vow of seclusion.

This form of monastic asceticism, and the closely related practice of living on top of a column (see section "Pillar Saints," below), is noteworthy in its enforcement for longer or shorter periods of time of the principle of monastic stability. Although this principle was well established in both Byzantine canon and civil law,[6] it was frequently ignored in practice, especially by male monastics. When a cenobitic monk became a recluse, he took to an extreme the monastic principle of enclosure within the walls of a monastery, reducing the area of enclosure to the space of a cell. In essence, he resorted to a hybrid form of monasticism, combining the solitary life with residence in a communal monastery. When a hermit enclosed himself, he reduced his living space from the vast "wilderness" or desert to the narrow confines of a cave or grass hut. Seclusion did not necessarily imply isolation, however. Most recluses (eremitic or cenobitic) depended on the provision of food and water by attendants, received visitors seeking spiritual advice, and some, such as Neophytos, the celebrated twelfth-century recluse on Cyprus, even directed monasteries from their enclosure.

The phenomenon of monastic seclusion or enclosure is much better documented in the medieval West, especially in England, where the practice flourished and was particularly attractive to women, who were called anchoresses.[7] In England the procedure of becoming a recluse was also much more highly regulated than in Byzantium; a would-be anchorite or anchoress had to petition the local bishop for permission to take vows of perpetual enclosure, there was an official ceremony of enclosure performed by a bishop or his deputy, and there were rules of enclosure, such as the well-known thirteenth-century *Ancrene Wisse* (*Guide for Anchoresses*), which prescribed the devotional routine for an anchoress, and periods set aside for rest, meals, and handwork.[8] The enclosure was also much stricter in the West, where the anchorite was literally walled up or bricked up within a cell that was usually attached to a church and had one window facing inside the church and one facing the open air.

The practice of enclosure in Byzantium was more varied, it was more common for monks than nuns, and the recluse does not seem to have been physically prevented from leaving his or her enclosure, but remained within it voluntarily for as long as he or she wished. No special permission seems to have been needed from the ecclesiastical authorities, and usually no ceremony was performed at the moment when the monk entered his enclosure. The Byzantine recluse normally decided to remain in the *enkleistra* for a fixed number of months or years, rather than for life.

Enkleistoi were found in both urban and rural environments, especially on holy mountains. I offer some brief sketches, in roughly chronological order, of those recluses on whom we have more than rudimentary information.

Stephen the Younger

An example of a recluse on a holy mountain was the eighth-century Stephen the Younger, who lived in a cave near the summit of Mount St. Auxentios, located near Constantinople, about seven miles southeast of Chalcedon on the eastern shore of the Bosporos. Originally inhabited by the Syrian hermit Auxentios in the fifth century, the cave served as the residence for a series of recluses over the centuries.[9] At age thirty-one, in the year 745/46, after the death of the recluse John, the iconodule monk Stephen became the sixth recluse to inhabit this cave, "like a bee in a hive." He occupied himself with the manufacture and repair of fishing nets and the copying of manuscripts. Soon disciples flocked to him, and he founded a new monastery, named after St. Auxentios, which he directed from the seclusion of his grotto.[10] We must assume that he received food supplies from his disciples.

Ten years later, at age forty-one, he moved to a much smaller cave at the summit. Here he constructed for himself a very small dwelling (*kellion*), which was twenty-seven inches wide and three feet long. On the west side he built a chapel barely tall enough for a man to stand up in; the rest of the area was open to the sky. Those who saw his new abode were horrified, saying that it resembled the tomb of a dead man more than the dwelling of a monk.[11] And indeed so Stephen intended it to be.

Around 763/64, when Stephen was forty-nine, he was exiled to the island of Prokonnesos in the Sea of Marmara by Emperor Constantine V Kopronymos (r. 741–75) on account of his iconophile views. Here he continued his tradition of living as a recluse and built himself a "small *enkleistron* in the shape of a column."[12] The interpretation of this phrase is uncertain, but it is possible that Stephen adopted for a while the regime of a stylite, or lived on a rocky pillar that resembled a column, or built a structure that looked like a column. In any case, from this temporary abode he continued to direct a group of disciples and his mother, by now a nun. Thus he was secluded as a recluse, but he had the company of his fellow exiles and served as their spiritual leader.

Recluses of the Ninth and Tenth Centuries

Euthymios, a renowned ninth-century hermit (discussed in chapter 3), vowed to spend three years as a recluse in a cave on Mount Athos without ever leaving it. Reportedly, he was able to forage for enough fruits and nuts to lay in a multiyear food supply, and thus he could remain completely incommunicado and not rely on food deliveries by visitors. During the first year of his enclosure he had a companion, Joseph, but for the final two years he lived in total solitude and independence. He exemplifies the purest form of enclosure, without contact with other human beings; as we shall see, however, most recluses were not true solitaries. His term of seclusion was limited to a few years, and it was not lifelong, as in the West.

Another iconodule monk, Ioannikios (762–846), seeking to flee crowds of admirers, sought refuge in a wilderness region of Lydia in western Anatolia, where he enclosed himself in a cave. In order to ensure that he would not break his vow to God of confinement (*katheirxis*) inside the cave for three years, he attached himself to a large rock with a thirty-six-foot chain. The hagiographer provides no information on how he obtained food and water.[13]

Several other ninth-century monks provide examples of recluses at urban or suburban monasteries. Towards the end of his life, Plato of Sakkoudion (d. 814), the uncle of Theodore the Stoudite, spent at least ten years as a recluse in a tiny cell at the Stoudios monastery. It is described as being stifling hot in the summer, like a furnace, because of the sun beating down on its lead roof.[14] Gregory of Akritas, who probably died before 843, lived for many years as an *enkleistos* in a very narrow cell at the monastery of Akritas outside of Constantinople. He did leave his cell in the evening to climb into a large jar full of water in the garden to recite the Psalter![15]

Evaristos (d. 897), a former Stoudite monk, confined himself in a very small enclosure in the left aisle of the church of the Theotokos at the monastery of Kokoroubion in Constantinople. Here he engaged in extreme mortification of the body, wearing heavy irons. He scarcely ate anything and used to suck on a pebble shaped like a chestnut to appease his hunger pangs. He performed standing vigils at night, rarely slept, and did not bathe.[16] Following the death of the abbot Nicholas the Stoudite in 868, he became superior of the Kokoroubion monastery, apparently directing its affairs from his enclosure. He received a substantial number of visitors, many of them seeking relief from incurable diseases, and he was able to heal them with gifts of a link from one of his iron chains or by making the sign of the cross. One miracle tale suggests that Evaristos went to visit the seriously ill wife of a senator (*synkletikos*), the only indication that he ever left his enclosure.[17] Although the text mentions Evaristos leaving his enclosure in the church only this one time, thus implying that he was a recluse for the final thirty years of his life, curiously his hagiographer nowhere refers to Evaristos as a recluse, nor do any of the secondary sources.[18]

Euthymios, the future patriarch of Constantinople (ca. 834–912), used to seclude himself for shorter periods of time in a cell in his monastery at Psamathia: "In his love of spiritual tranquility, the father used frequently to do this [that is, go into seclusion], confining himself for three or four months, sometimes a whole year, to one cell, and though the door stood open he did not go out of it, but waited patiently till the period was accomplished which he had fixed for himself."[19] This passage demonstrates how Euthymios viewed seclusion as a voluntary and short-term ascetic exercise, in contrast to the tradition of permanent enclosure in the West. Euthymios is yet another example of a recluse who also served as superior of his monastery despite periods of confinement.[20]

A less successful ninth-century recluse was the monk Anthony the Younger, who spent nine months in an *enkleistra* in or near Nicaea without ever going outside. The structure is not described, but we know that he maintained absolute seclusion on weekdays, abstaining from food and water, and only on weekends partook of bread and water and received visitors. His hagiographer provides a rare glimpse of the psychological struggles of such isolated recluses, telling us that after a period of nine months a demonic spirit afflicted Anthony with the despondency to which hermits were prone, and he left for a cenobitic monastery on Mount Olympos.[21]

The *vita* of Mary the Younger implies that recluses were a relatively common phenomenon in the ninth century, for we learn that this pious matron "used to give provisions to monks, both those who enclose themselves in caves and those in huts" on the outskirts of Bizye in Thrace.[22] The same *vita* preserves the precious information that the unnamed monk icon-painter who painted the first icon of Mary was a recluse who lived in Rhaidestos.[23]

An early tenth-century recluse is known only from the *vita* of Theodore of Kythera. The elderly Antonios abandoned his colleague Theodore on Kythera after only three months because he could not endure the hardships, but he then lived as a recluse in a hut on the mainland for twenty-three years. When his hut threatened to collapse, he moved to the nearby church of St. John the Baptist, where he died shortly thereafter.[24]

Recluses of the Eleventh and Twelfth Centuries

The *vita* of Symeon the New Theologian has preserved an unusually detailed account of the eleventh-century recluse Philotheos.[25] Together with the eunuch John he founded a monastery in the suburb of Anaplous, located on the European shore of the Bosporos: "After the completion of this monastery, one of the two [Philotheos], who loved God and was fervent for spiritual contests . . . prepared a cell suitable for spiritual tranquillity as an enclosure for himself. He entered into this, closed off all access, and chose to eagerly pursue more advanced contests of spiritual tranquillity."[26] But before he enclosed himself, he made a farewell tour of the most famous churches of Constantinople and also visited several spiritual leaders in order to say good-bye and to seek their advice on his plan of perpetual seclusion. Among the monasteries he visited was Stoudios, where he met with the monk Niketas Stethatos, a devoted disciple of Symeon and his biographer. Niketas gave Philotheos a book containing some of Symeon's works to read and meditate upon during his upcoming years of seclusion.

Before Philotheos took the final step of secluding himself, he underwent a spiritual crisis and had an attack of anxiety. At this point he had a waking vision of the deceased Symeon coming to his cell and insisting upon the necessity of a strict dietary regimen to purify his body and maintain a state of spiritual tranquility. The saint even squeezed Philotheos's stomach in order to reduce its size and appetite.[27] The apparition of the holy man enabled Philotheos to carry out his vow of seclusion with relative ease, as "abstinence came naturally to him and he lived out his enclosed life with minimal needs and a frugal table." He was so grateful to Symeon that the one time he emerged from seclusion was to visit Symeon's tomb in Chrysopolis and take back with him an icon of the saint, more of his writings, and "the encomia written about him," presumably the *vita* penned by Niketas.[28] Philotheos's vow of seclusion until the end of his life resembled Western practice more than Byzantine, where shorter terms of seclusion seem to have been the norm.

Alternative Modes of Monasticism   141

The *vita* of Euthymios, a Georgian monk on Mount Athos, provides rare information on the diet of a recluse and flexibility in his regimen.

The most famous Byzantine recluse of the twelfth century was Neophytos the Enkleistos (1134 to after 1214), whose hermitage can be seen to this day in Cyprus (fig. 9).[29] After introductory training at the cenobitic monastery of Koutsoventis and a pilgrimage to the Holy Land, Neophytos decided to embark on the solitary life at the age of twenty-five and found a suitable cave near Paphos. Here, in his own words, "God gave me this precipice and this smallest of caves, which was deserted and a resting-place of various birds, but to me it appeared desirable because of the solitary nature of the place, and in hope I settled in it alone . . . having discovered that the place was quiet and undisturbed, I started hewing the cave and widening it, and breaking down its unsound parts."[30]

FIGURE 9   Cell of Neophytos the Recluse at his monastery near Paphos (photo: Image Collection and Fieldwork Archives, Dumbarton Oaks, Trustees for Harvard University, Washington, DC)

In the cave, he carved out of the rock a sleeping bench, a desk, an altar on which to celebrate the Eucharist, and a tomb as a *memento mori*, on which he could meditate about his inevitable death. Neophytos used the desk to compose an impressive list of hagiographical and spiritual works. After he had endured about ten years of solitary residence in the cave, the bishop of Paphos ordained him as a priest and persuaded him to take on a disciple, who no doubt was to be responsible for looking after Neophytos's food provisioning and other physical needs; we do not know how Neophytos managed before the advent of this disciple. Soon Neophytos was joined by other monks, who lived in cells hollowed out of the rocky cliff; thus Neophytos became the superior of a small monastery dedicated to the Holy Cross. Toward the end of his life, in order to escape crowds of pilgrims who flocked to his cave, he had a smaller cave prepared, higher up the cliff face, which took the name of the "upper *enkleistra*." He drafted the first rule for his monastery in 1177; this *typikon* was superseded in 1214 by a revised version, shortly before Neophytos died. His final instructions show that he was determined to preserve his solitude and seclusion even in death. Thus he ordered that his body be placed in a wooden coffin and enclosed within the stone tomb carved out in his cell, and that the door in the tomb wall be closed up so that there could be no access to his relics and they would be undisturbed by pilgrims.[31]

From the second *typikon* we learn that it was Neophytos's intention that he be succeeded as superior by his nephew, who should also become an *enkleistos*. It was understood, however, that the superior should primarily serve as a spiritual confessor, while the practical concerns of monastic management were to be handled by the steward (*oikonomos*) and treasurer, "so that the recluse shall always remain quiet and undisturbed."[32] Chapter 15 of the *typikon*, which contains "specific exhortation to the recluse," ordains that he should spend his time in meditation on death, in prayer and reading, simple handwork, and hearing the confessions of the monks.[33] He was also to give spiritual advice to the brethren.

The *typikon* of Neophytos is the only source, to my knowledge, that describes an installation ceremony for a monk who was about to enter his enclosure. Neophytos's successors were to ascend to the cave in the cliff face and enter the *enkleistra* of their renowned predecessor in order to begin life as a recluse while also serving as abbot of the monastery. After the Trisagion hymn, the brethren were to read aloud the prayer Neophytos had written for this occasion. Addressing the Lord, the monks prayed that he would look after "this slave of yours, too, who has forsaken everything by his free will and chosen the life of a recluse and a solitary, so that . . . he may follow in the footsteps of your aforementioned saints [that is, Anthony and Euthymios the Great] and the holy men who shone forth [from the top of] pillars."[34]

As Galatariotou has already observed, it is noteworthy that Neophytos compares himself and other recluses who lived in caves on cliff faces to stylites.[35] His subsequent ascent to a second cave higher in elevation is reminiscent of the stylite practice of moving to a taller column or moving to a column higher up a mountainside.

Late Byzantine Recluses

Sabas the Younger was a fourteenth-century holy man who sequentially embraced many monastic lifestyles, including that of a wandering monk, holy fool, and recluse. He enclosed himself on at least four occasions during the course of his life. While he was engaged on a lengthy journey to the eastern Mediterranean that included a pilgrimage to the Holy Land and Mount Sinai, he confined himself for three years in a cave next to the Jordan River. There are unfortunately no details on how he obtained the necessities of life, only that he was forced by the press of visitors to leave for a remoter region of the desert.[36] Subsequently he enclosed himself in a cave near the *lavra* of St. Sabas, again for a period of three years. Here he engaged in an unusual form of mortification of the body, lying on one side without moving for one year and remaining seated in a chair for a second year. We are told that he survived on bread and water brought to him by a monk helper, only getting up from the chair to relieve himself.[37]

Upon his return to Greece from the Holy Land, he withdrew to a cave near Thracian Herakleia, situated on a cliff face high above the sea. Near the cave was a chapel with a marvelous icon or fresco of Christ. Sabas remained enclosed there, but he did receive visitors from Herakleia, mostly members of the clergy, who brought him food and sought his spiritual advice.[38] But his spiritual tranquility was disturbed by the throng of visitors, so he left for Constantinople, where he became a recluse at the monastery of St. Diomedes. Here he tried to avoid attention by covering most of his face with his cowl, and he refused to receive visitors, even Emperor Andronikos II (r. 1282–1328) and the patriarch Isaias (1323–32).[39] Once again his fame forced him to flee, back to Athos, where surprisingly, after years of solitary wandering or seclusion, he returned to a cenobitic regimen of obedience to a superior at the monastery of Vatopedi.[40] At the very end of his life, he went back to Constantinople, where he spent his remaining days as a recluse at the Chora monastery, dying in 1347 after six years of enclosure in a cell.[41]

With the exception of the twelfth-century *typikon* of Neophytos, texts provide very little information about the physical structures in which recluses sequestered themselves. Several monastic bell towers in Serbia and Greece, however, preserve evidence of spaces set aside as residences for hermits. Typically, a small room served as a private cell (*hesychasterion*) for an eminent elderly monk or retired church hierarch. This room might have an altar niche where the recluse could perform his devotions or have access to a private chapel; at Žiča, for example, a third-floor chapel was accessed by a wooden ladder from a room on the floor below. In some churches an opening in the cell offered a window onto the nave so that the solitary could observe church services. In several cases, surviving fresco decoration depicts stylite saints, thus alluding to the similarity between a recluse secluded in a tower and a pillar saint residing atop a column.[42]

Female Recluses

Female *enkleistoi* are occasionally attested in the middle Byzantine period. Hilaria, the twin sister of George of Lesbos (763/64 to 845/46), "was a holy virgin ... who lived for the sake of the Lord as a recluse in a very small cell" at the church of St. John the Theologian.[43] Her brother George served as her conduit to the outside world and brought her provisions and other essentials. A female recluse named Euphemia received two letters from Theodore the Stoudite shortly after the revival of iconoclasm in 815.[44] She apparently was living in a convent of Stoudite persuasions and considered Theodore as her spiritual father. A repentant prostitute who appears in the *vita* of the ninth-century bishop Theodore of Edessa vowed to spend her remaining years "enclosed in a dark room" weeping for her sins.[45]

The most detailed description of a female recluse is found in the fourteenth-century *vita* of St. Euphrosyne the Younger by Nikephoros Kallistos Xanthopoulos.[46] Euphrosyne, who may be a fictional holy woman, supposedly lived in the late ninth and early tenth centuries, was for a while a transvestite who lived in a male monastery, and ended up living as a recluse in Constantinople during the reign of Leo VI (r. 886–912). She enclosed herself in a tomblike pit, described as a "circular, cave-like dwelling in the ground" and "an underground cave," near the female convent at the Pege monastery.[47] That she thought of this abode as a grave is clearly indicated by a subsequent passage describing Euphrosyne as a woman "who inhabited a subterranean cave in front of the Life-giving Spring, since she deemed it right for herself to live in a grave although she was still alive and her time had not come."[48] Here she weighed down her body with heavy irons, wore a hair shirt, slept on a straw mat, and subsisted on a minimal diet, eating seeds and vegetables once a week. She was attended by a eunuch monk named Nicholas. But she attracted attention and many visitors, including Emperor Leo VI himself, who came to supplicate her for the birth of a male heir. Her prayers apparently bore fruit, and Constantine

(VII) Porphyrogennetos was born to Leo's mistress (and eventual fourth wife), Zoe Karbonopsina, in 905.[49]

Overwhelmed by the popular adulation that followed this miracle, Euphrosyne left her subterranean cave and moved to a nearby abandoned house, next to the Kalagrou Gate, where once more she enclosed herself as a recluse. Here she again dug a tomblike dwelling for herself, two fathoms (approximately twelve feet) wide and deep, and founded a convent for twelve nuns: "Again enclosing herself there, she delivered herself over to an even harsher regimen, devoting herself even more energetically to standing vigils and genuflections and all the other exercises, conversing only with herself and with God."[50]

After many years at the convent near the Kalagrou Gate, Euphrosyne was forced by an attack of "Scythian barbarians," probably Bulgarians, to move again to a safer location. Her final abode was at the monastery of Skepe, where she once more enclosed herself in an "underground dwelling that was very small, so that she could barely stand upright and its breadth extended to about a fathom."[51] Here she increased the intensity of her ascetic regimen, sleeping on a bed of straw infested with vermin and continuing to wear the rusty iron bands that caused festering sores on her flesh. At age sixty-eight she was also afflicted with an illness that resulted in tremors and paralysis of her limbs. Her condition was truly pitiable: "Due to her very narrow and low dwelling both her calves became stuck to the backs of her thighs on both sides so that she could not stand up without pain. Her kneecaps ... were roughened by her continuous genuflections and resembled those of an animal rather than a human being." The hagiographer also describes her bed of straw, her uncombed hair, and her feet that were bare in winter.[52] She could pull herself up to a sitting position only by means of a suspended rope. The text mentions servants who changed her bedding once a year, and a swarm of visitors, but as with many recluses it is not clear who brought her food and water.

The case of Euphrosyne demonstrates once again a frequent theme in the stories about Byzantine recluses—their seclusion in cramped spaces was a *memento mori*. Some *enkleistoi*, such as Neophytos, prepared their tombs in advance within their cells but did not actually live in them, while others, such as Stephen Neolampes (839/40 to 911/12), spent months or years in a gravelike hole, prefiguring their future entombment. At age eighteen, Stephen enclosed himself in the chapel next to the treasury (*skeuophylakion*) of Hagia Sophia, subsisting solely on vegetables; later in his life he spent twelve years in a gravelike trench.[53] Paul of Atroa, the eighth-century predecessor of the superior Peter at the monastery of Atroa, having been forewarned by the Lord of his impending death, had a gravelike structure (termed an *enkleistron*) prepared: "Before his actual burial in a grave, he had constructed for himself a small tomb-like enclosure, whose dimensions were smaller than his body, and enclosed himself in it." Here he spent the last six months of his life. After his death, however, he was buried in the chapel of St. Zacharias, not in his *enkleistron*.[54]

As this brief survey demonstrates, recluses, both male and female, are most frequently attested as a phenomenon of the ninth century, while the existence of male recluses continues to be sporadically documented up to the fourteenth century.

PILLAR SAINTS (STYLITES)

Stylites, or pillar saints, were so named because of their residence atop a column (*stylos* in Greek); they may be considered as an extreme type of recluse, since they lived in a very confined space atop a column and normally remained there for very long periods of time. Stylites were particularly renowned for the arduous form of their mortification of the body.[55] This ascetic practice was virtually unknown in the medieval West; only one instance is recorded, in the *History of the Franks* by Gregory of Tours. He recounts the tale of the sixth-century French deacon Wolflaicus, who ascended a column but was forced by local bishops to give up this exercise in mortification.[56] It is difficult to estimate their numbers in the

Byzantine East; as some indication, the *Prosopographie der mittelbyzantinischen Zeit* lists thirteen stylites for the period 641–867 and twelve for the period 867–1025.[57] But surely numerous anonymous stylites have gone uncounted.

Although individual experiences varied, stylites typically lived on a small enclosed platform at the top of either a reused ancient stone column, one specifically built of masonry for the purpose, or a natural rocky pillar. The height of these columns varied but could reach fifty feet or more.[58] Sometimes stylites resided within a small hut with a window; in the case of Lazaros of Galesion, his hut had no roof, and so he was exposed to the elements all year long. Lazaros's cell was only a few feet in diameter, so that he did not lie down to sleep, but slept sitting in a special chair. A ladder leading up to the platform allowed disciples to bring food and water to the stylite, and it also permitted pilgrims to visit the holy man and receive his spiritual instruction and blessing.[59] Just as recluses, stylites were totally dependent on helpers to bring them food and water and other necessities; Luke of Steiris as a youth became the disciple of a stylite at Zemena in the northern Peloponnesos and spent ten years serving him, carrying wood and water, cooking, catching fish, and mending nets.[60]

Residence atop a pillar symbolized the physical removal of the ascetic's body from earthly distractions and his spiritual ascent toward heaven. But only a select few monks were sufficiently disciplined to embrace the lifestyle of a stylite, and they were thus viewed as among the elite of holy men. In the prologue to his *vita*, the hagiographer of Luke the Stylite presents a hierarchy of saints: on the lowest rung were pious laymen, who resemble roses among thorns; then cenobitic monks; third, hermits; and, at the top, stylites.[61] He writes:

> They have left behind residence below on the surface of the earth, which is trodden in common by all men, viewing it as unspiritual, and have renounced an earthly lifestyle in order to raise themselves aloft upon tower-shaped columns or pillars

that rise to a very great height; and like birds that love the solitude of the air, they build nests and live without shelter or possessions like winged creatures, with regard to their bodies practicing a lifestyle similar to that of the angels and maintaining a superhuman way of life that lasts for very many years.[62]

Stylites are first attested in the fifth century in Syria, where Symeon the Stylite the Elder (ca. 389–459) lived on a succession of ever taller columns at Qalʿat Semʿan, near Aleppo. Other important stylites in late antiquity were Daniel (409–93) in Constantinople and Symeon the Younger (521–92) on the Wondrous Mountain southwest of Antioch. The middle Byzantine era witnessed a modest revival of the phenomenon in both city and countryside: in the ninth century, Euthymios the Younger twice ascended a pillar near Thessalonike for relatively brief periods,[63] while Symeon of Lesbos (ca. 755/56 to 844) lived for decades near the harbor of Mytilene in a hut with window and roof atop a column. The charismatic Symeon attracted the wrath of Lesbos's iconoclast bishop, Leo of Mytilene, because of his popularity with the local people; Leo went so far as to complain to the emperor, "In truth, the stylite is bishop in the diocese assigned to me, not I." Soon thereafter, Leo exiled Symeon briefly to the island of Lagousai, in the southern Cyclades, where he built a pillar, somewhere between fourteen and nineteen feet high.[64]

A lengthy passage in the *vita* of the ninth-century bishop Theodore of Edessa provides important information on the decline of stylites in northern Syria over the centuries.[65] The bishop, a newcomer to the region, had remarked on the large number of built columns in the outskirts of the city, and he was told that they dated to the reign of Emperor Maurikios (r. 582–602). Since all the columns seemed to be abandoned, he asked if any stylite still lived in the vicinity. Theodore was then told that a single unnamed stylite continued the tradition and had supposedly remained on his column for ninety-five years. The two men met, and the stylite told the bishop the story of his life. The chronology of the story may be suspect, but the passage is nonetheless illuminating.

The best-attested stylites of the middle Byzantine period are Paul the Younger and Luke the Stylite in the tenth century, and Lazaros of Mount Galesion in the eleventh. The travails of Paul as a hermit on Mount Latros in the tenth century have already been described in chapter 3. Here I would like to focus on the twelve years he spent on a natural rocky pillar (ἀχειροποίητος στύλος) with a cave at its peak. He could be described as a hybrid recluse/stylite, since he resided in a cave but atop a rocky pillar. After a while, monastic disciples flocked to the pillar and the *lavra* of the Pillar (*tou Stylou*) was founded, which Paul directed from his lofty perch, just as Lazaros was to do on Mount Galesion. But as long as Paul was living in total isolation, he was completely dependent on helpers, such as a local goatherd, to bring him food and water. He also required the services of a priest to administer communion to him; for this reason he had a ladder constructed so a priest could climb up to his cave at the top of the pillar and bring him the Eucharist.[66] This natural pillar had a history of habitation by stylites, since Paul was preceded by a certain Athanasios (who spent twenty-two years there in the first half of the ninth century) and was succeeded by Pachomios.[67]

Luke the Stylite (ca. 900–979), the son of middle-class landowners from the Anatolikon theme (administrative district) in Asia Minor, had a brief career as a soldier and fought in a Bulgarian campaign. During his military service, he came under the influence of two pious fellow soldiers whose spiritual father was a stylite. Luke decided to take monastic vows and was tonsured by the stylite. He embraced his new vocation with extreme asceticism and was ordained a priest at age twenty-four, but somehow he managed to also remain in military service.[68] He then spent three years in the *lavra* of St. Zacharias on Mount Olympos, and two and a half years as a recluse (ἐγκατάκλειστον) in a dark cave he himself excavated on a mountainside, where he remained secluded (ἀπρόϊτος). Next, he constructed a pillar eighteen feet high, atop which he lived for three years, suffering terribly from bitter cold, ice, and snow in winter.[69]

Later he moved to Constantinople and spent the final forty-four years of his life atop a column in the Asian quarter of Eutropios,

FIGURE 10   Luke the Stylite from Menologion of Basil II (Vaticanus gr. 1613), p. 238 (photo: ©Biblioteca Apostolica Vaticana)

south of Chalcedon (fig. 10). Apparently, he sought permission from Michael, bishop of Chalcedon, to reside on the column, and Michael performed appropriate prayers before Luke ascended the ladder to his lofty perch.[70] This is a rare example in the middle Byzantine period in which official Church sanction is attested when a stylite embarked upon his ascetic endeavor. At the beginning, Luke was grievously tormented by the elements and by demonic wasps and stinging insects, but soon he was granted a miraculous dispensation by the Archangel Michael, as the five bronze crosses atop the column began to glow with fiery heat and provide him with warmth and light.[71]

Despite his eighteen-foot elevation above the ground, Luke engaged actively with the local populace, who came to him for assistance, advice, blessings, and confessions. He would give them holy water from his water jug or strips of cloth or blessed bread as *eulogiai*, gifts sanctified by contact with the holy man that could work miracles or bring good fortune. He is described, for example, as bantering with local fishermen who were having a run of bad luck and giving them holy water to sprinkle on their fishing gear, rags from his hand towel to tie to their nets, or pieces of bread to use as bait to ensure a bountiful catch. Luke then would join them in feasting on the freshly caught fish.[72] He also performed healing miracles, curing bodily illness and demonic possession alike. Other objects that had curative powers were the leather belt that girded his loins and a wooden cross he had carved.[73] Luke was occasionally visited by notables; for example, the patriarch Theophylaktos (933–56) used to climb up the ladder to his platform to share a meal with him. He had a monk servant to bring him food and water and run errands for him, and he supposedly lived to be more than one hundred years old.[74]

It is notable that despite his seclusion atop a column, Luke played an active role in the restoration of the Constantinopolitan monastery of Bassianos, which had fallen into serious decline. His hagiographer reports that he did this at the prompting of the patriarch and was called the "new founder" (νέος κτήτωρ) for his contributions, but the *vita* provides no information on the source of funds for the renovation.[75] Luke's *vita* presents the image of a holy man vitally involved with his community, despite his lengthy residence on his lofty perch.[76]

Lazaros of Mount Galesion

Lazaros, who founded a group of monastic communities on Mount Galesion, near Ephesos, in the first half of the eleventh century, and turned it into a holy mountain, was unusual in that he served as superior of several monasteries from atop a series of pillars he erected at increasingly higher altitudes on the mountain. He spent the last forty years of his life as a pillar saint, apparently inspired by a visit in his youth to the shrine of Symeon the Younger, a sixth-century stylite on the Wondrous Mountain near Antioch. Lazaros began his career as a stylite by ascending a built pillar at the small hermitage of St. Marina near Ephesos. At first the hut atop the column was roofed, but then Lazaros had the roof removed in order to "live in the open air on this [pillar] in imitation of the wondrous Symeon."[77]

After seven years at St. Marina, he decided that the pillar was too close to the road and too noisy, so he moved to nearby Mount Galesion, where his monks built for him a pillar dedicated to Christ the Savior, and a monastic complex eventually developed. Before the monastery was constructed, Lazaros was quite isolated and was provisioned only once a week with water and dried legumes that had been soaked in water. Once when he was stung by a scorpion, he jerked his foot and broke the water pot. Unwilling to eat the dried legumes without any water to wash them down, he went hungry and thirsty for days in broiling summer heat. Fortunately, a layman in a nearby village had a vision that Lazaros was dying of thirst and rushed to bring him water, arriving just in time. Thereafter a monk was assigned to reside in a nearby cave so as to be available in case of emergency.[78]

Twelve years later, Lazaros moved further up the mountain to yet another newly constructed pillar; here the monastery of the Theotokos was established. Lazaros evidently lived alone at the pillar of the Theotokos for some time before a monastic community was established, and thus he had the same problems as isolated hermits and recluses with regard to access to the celebration of the liturgy. His hagiographer provides important information on his resolution of this difficulty:

> As our father was alone in that place, he made arrangements for receiving the blessed sacraments, and they built a little drystone apse immediately opposite the pillar; a priest from among the brothers at the [monastery of the] Savior would go and celebrate the holy Eucharist in this [chapel] and so give the blessed sacraments to Lazaros. A [secular] priest called Menas from the village of Samakios also used to go up to the father quite often, as he had great faith in him; on many occasions he too would celebrate the holy Eucharist when so directed by the father, and would give him the undefiled sacraments.[79]

It should be noted, however, that Lazaros had tense relations with the bishop of Ephesos, the see that owned Mount Galesion,[80] and that there was an ongoing power struggle between the charismatic ascetic authority of the stylite on the mountain and the ecclesiastical authority of the metropolitan.

In the early 1040s, Lazaros moved a final time, to the pillar of the Resurrection (where once again a monastery was founded), and here he died in 1053.[81] The text suggests that Lazaros's final pillar was somehow attached to the monastic church so that he could look through a window into the nave during services.

The *vita* of Lazaros also provides evidence for other stylites or would-be stylites on Mount Galesion. The story of the youth Nikon demonstrates the hazards of a life exposed to the elements atop a column. Nikon had taken monastic vows on Galesion as a teenager, and he was soon consumed by the passionate desire to ascend a pillar in imitation of his superior, Lazaros. Lazaros, however, felt that Nikon was too young to embark on this arduous lifestyle and told him he had to spend more time in a cenobitic monastery to learn obedience. Nikon was ordered to refrain from speech for three years and to undertake the exhausting task of descending the mountain on a daily basis to the river at its foot and to carry two heavy pots of water back uphill to the monastery. After Nikon faithfully fulfilled these commands, Lazaros permitted him to ascend the pillar of Petra located near the village at the base of the mountain. But Nikon soon fell ill and died at the age of twenty.[82]

The history of the natural rock pillar of Petra (Greek for "rock") shows that sometimes a tradition was established of several stylites occupying the same pillar in succession, as we have already seen on Mount Latros.[83] At least four of Petra's occupants are known: an anonymous stylite in the early eleventh century, who was succeeded first by the monk Kerykos and then by Merkourios, before the brief residence of Nikon.[84] This column was apparently so close to the village of Galesion that the stylites were bothered by noise and other distractions from the local population, and Lazaros himself decided not to use this column when he left his pillar at St. Marina.

We also know that after Lazaros left the pillar of the Theotokos for that of the Resurrection, Kerykos moved from the pillar at Petra to the column at the monastery of the Theotokos, which Lazaros had previously occupied.[85]

There was even a rare female stylite on Mount Galesion. Lazaros's *vita* reports that shortly after he moved to the pillar of the Theotokos, he heard about "a woman enclosed on a pillar, who had her feet hanging outside through a hole."[86] Not to be outdone by a woman, Lazaros resolved to imitate her despite the pleas of his disciples and his mother, Eupraxia, who was living in a nearby nunnery, so he too "hung his feet out through the wall." But after being rebuked by a monk "from the West" for arrogance and excessive asceticism, he "drew his feet [back] inside the pillar."[87]

Stylites are also attested on the holy mountain of Athos in the late eleventh century but with no details.[88] Also from the end of the eleventh century survives an interesting letter by Symeon, metropolitan of Euchaita in northern Anatolia, addressed to John the monk and *enkleistos*, a youthful stylite.[89] Symeon is surprisingly critical of his addressee's lifestyle, using the standard argument that before embarking upon a solitary lifestyle a young monk should be trained in the discipline of a cenobitic monastery in order to learn obedience and abnegation of the will, and to benefit from the spiritual advice of a superior. Asceticism should be embraced with moderation. Symeon accuses the young stylite of "acting according to his own will" and "fleeing obedience."[90] This type of criticism from an urban prelate is reminiscent of the concerns we saw earlier in chapter 3 about the pitfalls of an eremitic lifestyle and the necessity for a would-be hermit to first be well trained at a cenobitic monastery and to learn submission to authority.

After the eleventh century, stylites are rarely attested by name in Byzantium, but they evidently continued to exist until the period of the Latin conquest of Constantinople in 1204. The twelfth-century archbishop of Thessalonike, Eustathios (ca. 1115–1195/96), in an oration on hypocrisy, criticized the current generation of pillar saints. He praised a few great stylites of the past, "sky-climbers [οὐρανοβάμωνες] who reached heaven by using pillars as ladders," but went on to say: "But this generation sprouts the stylite race like trees in a forest, and these are not trees of life, nor trees of knowledge, but puny little trees indeed."[91] But the same Eustathios addressed to a stylite in Thessalonike a lengthy work praising the ascetic's angelic lifestyle and his column with a view of the sea.[92] He describes the ascent of a column as resembling burial in a grave and enclosure in a cave, but he states that a stylite's life is much more difficult than that of a recluse.[93] Leontios, the future titular patriarch of Jerusalem (1176–85), reportedly planned to ascend the column of Daniel the stylite in Constantinople, but never did so.[94]

In the early thirteenth century, at the time of the Fourth Crusade, the French writer Robert de Clari mentioned that in Constantinople there were stylites living atop two huge columns: "There were two columns; each of which was three times the thickness of a man's arm and fifty *toises* high. And on each of these columns was living a hermit, in tiny huts which were there. And there was a spiral staircase inside the column by which you could climb up the interior of these columns."[95] He also notes that the columns were sculpted on their exterior. Robert must be referring to the two attested historiated columns in Constantinople: the Column of Theodosios I in the Forum of Theodosios (destroyed in the late fifteenth century) and the partially preserved Column of Arcadius in the Forum of Arcadius in the Xerolophos region of the capital.[96]

There do not seem to be any references to stylites after Robert de Clari; apparently this form of extreme asceticism died out by the Palaiologan period (1261–1453).[97]

WANDERING MONKS

Recluses and stylites exemplified extreme fixity of abode, but a third alternative form of monasticism rejected any stability at all. In late antiquity both canon and civil law supported the principle of monastic stability, that is, monks or nuns were admonished to remain for life in the monastery where they had taken vows, unless they received the express permission of their bishop to leave. Basil of Caesarea, for example, forbade monasteries to receive wandering monks without the agreement of the monks' former superiors.[98] A canon of the Council of Chalcedon in 451 sought to place monks under episcopal control,[99] while novel 5 of Justinian explained that the superior of a monastery should not admit a monk who came from another monastery, because such a monastic demonstrated an unbecoming "inconstancy of mind."[100] Late antique patristic writings, such as the works of Neilos of Ankyra, were also critical of wandering monks, calling them *kykleutai* and *gyreutai*, literally, "those who go in circles."[101] Nonetheless wandering and begging monks are well attested in the fourth and fifth centuries, and the profusion of restrictions on such activity suggests that the practice was widespread.[102] Obedient to neither a monastic nor an ecclesiastical superior, these monks were valued by the populace for their spiritual counsel, charismatic behavior, and prophetic utterances, but were criticized by monastic leaders and ecclesiastical authorities for their independence, their failure to perform manual labor, and their material dependency on others.[103]

The tradition of wandering monks continued from the ninth to fifteenth centuries; an important difference from late antiquity, however, was that these vagrant monks often wandered beyond the borders of the shrinking Byzantine Empire, into the Muslim-occupied Holy Land, for example. Our information on these holy men in middle and late Byzantium comes from their *vitae*[104] and from the *typika* of some monasteries that criticized peripatetic monks and rejected the admission of so-called *xenokouritai*, that is, monks of "foreign tonsure," those who had been tonsured in another monastery. The *typikon* for Athos drafted by Emperor John I Tzimiskes in 971/72, for example, condemned monks who "withdraw from their own superiors and do not choose to settle under the obedience of a father . . . , but who prefer to wander in a bold and undisciplined way around the whole Mountain, and to offer their services for hire."[105]

Of particular note is the criticism directed by a "holy woman" at Leo Luke of Corleone, a ninth-century Italo-Greek monk, who early in his career engaged in a wandering mendicant lifestyle. When he asked the woman for provisions, she rebuked him for his lack of stability, saying that true virtue was not to be found by wandering about and that he should enter a cenobitic monastery and imitate the lives of earlier saints. He followed her advice and ended up as the revered abbot of a monastery.[106] If the "holy woman" was a nun, as seems likely, her rejection of a wandering lifestyle would reflect the much stronger tradition of monastic stability in convents in contrast to male monasteries.[107]

Another term for these wandering, mendicant monks seems to have been "brethren in Christ." They appear in several passages of *Vita B of Athanasios of Athos*, who had a more charitable attitude toward them. He recommended that they be offered hospitality in exchange for performing tasks such as cutting up vegetables in the kitchen, slicing bread in the refectory, or holding the bellows in the smithy. These monks were also offered care in the infirmary. In another passage, however, Athanasios criticized his monks for donating their cowls and cloaks to wandering monks, reminding them that these items of clothing were communal property and they had no right to make individual donations, for "charity to strangers is a communal endeavor and all donations are made jointly on everyone's behalf."[108]

A more critical and less charitable attitude is seen in the twelfth-century *vita* of the monk Cyril Phileotes (ca. 1015–1110), where one can find a strong reproach of wandering monks (*kykleutai*) who depended on alms for survival instead of earning their keep through manual labor.[109] Cyril, citing the admonitions of earlier authors, such as the seventh-century Isaiah of Nineveh, urged cenobitic monks not to offer charity to these men, whom he accused of laziness, pride, and gluttony. Moreover, he argued, if they were granted admittance to a monastery, they would set a bad example and upset the normal monastic routine.[110] Cyril did make an exception for those few monks who led this sort of life "for the sake of the Lord" and with spiritual intent, in order to go on pilgrimage, for example, just as Cyril himself had gone to Rome to visit the tombs of the apostles Peter and Paul.[111]

Despite all these criticisms, throughout the middle and late centuries of Byzantium many holy men are depicted positively in their hagiographies as incessant travelers and wanderers, not only moving from one monastic community to another but transitioning back and forth between cenobitic and eremitic life, and undertaking long journeys to the Holy Land for pilgrimage to the holy sites and visits to the celebrated monasteries of the Judean Desert and Mount Sinai.[112]

The motivations for the mobility and long-distance journeys of Byzantine monks vary widely: some moves were necessitated by the danger from Arab or Turkish attacks, but most were voluntary. Monks who were dissatisfied with their monastery wanted to visit others to find an abbot and regimen more suited to their spiritual goals; sometimes they would settle down in a monastery for a year or two or ten, before becoming restless and moving on to another. Or they might wish to go on a lengthy spiritual journey to the Holy Land, not just to see the holy places but also to visit famed monasteries and holy hermits. The *vita* of Sabas the Younger hints at another possible motive for pilgrimages to Muslim lands: the desire to convert Muslims to Christianity. In three separate passages, the *vita* of Sabas describes the veneration in which he was held by the local Muslim people, who sometimes prostrated themselves at his feet. Since Sabas was maintaining a vow of silence, he made no overt efforts at proselytization, but he still managed to impress Muslims by his demeanor and behavior.[113]

As were many hermits, recluses, and stylites, these itinerant monks were dependent for their daily sustenance on the charity of individual pious Christians and ecclesiastical institutions; they relied heavily on the hospitality of monasteries and churches in the lands through which they traveled. The *typikon* of the Constantinopolitan monastery of St. Mamas, for example, made provision for the distribution of food to begging monks at the monastery gate; lay beggars were offered only bread and leftovers, but their monastic brethren received wine, fish, and cheese.[114]

A fourteenth-century hagiographical text, the *vita* of Maximos the Hutburner by Theophanes, sheds light on the lifestyle of a vagrant monk who at an early stage in his life spent a significant amount of time in Constantinople. Maximos, a wandering monk for the first part of his career, went to the capital to pray in its churches and venerate relics of the saints. We do not know how long he stayed in the city, but it must have been several weeks or even months. He is described as spending night after night at the church of the Virgin Hodegetria to venerate its famous icon, "going barefoot and bareheaded, and wearing only one garment made of haircloth which itself was mostly in rags."[115] He visited both Emperor Andronikos II in his palace and the patriarch Athanasios I (1289–93, 1303–9), who urged him to take up residence in his cenobitic monastery on Xerolophos: "But the holy one refused, and stayed in the doorway of the church of the all-pure Lady and Mother of God of Blachernai. He remained there every night like a poor homeless man, in hunger and thirst, in vigil, standing, and prayer, in weeping, shedding a multitude of tears, and endless lamentation."[116]

The story of the youthful Lazaros of Galesion is particularly instructive on the vicissitudes of a wandering monk in the late tenth and early eleventh centuries: while still an adolescent, he became consumed with longing to visit the Holy Land, and he ran away twice from a monastery. Both times he was caught and forced to return, but he finally managed to make his escape. Seeking the company of other pilgrims or of monks, he slowly made his way east, sometimes sleeping in a rural chapel at night and begging bread from local villagers. After making the pilgrimage to the church of the Archangel Michael at Chonai in west-central Anatolia, he stopped for a while at a monastery near Attaleia, where he took monastic vows, and then he went to live as a solitary in a mountain cave. Soon he attracted disciples, and a small community formed around him. Seven years later, he set out again for Jerusalem. After visiting the holy sites and monasteries, Lazaros decided to settle down at the *lavra* of St. Sabas, where he spent at least sixteen years, was ordained priest, and was promoted to a monk of the great habit (*megaloschemos*).[117]

Lazaros decided to leave the Holy Land after the Muslim destruction of the Holy Sepulcher and persecution of Christians in 1009. He made his way through Syria, visiting the site of Symeon the Stylite the Younger's pillar on the Wondrous Mountain, and then continued on to Cappadocia, where he climbed the 12,000-foot Mount Argeas near Caesarea (modern Kayseri). He went on to the shrine of St. Theodore Teron at Euchaita, then made a second visit to Chonai, and finally reached the Aegean coast at Ephesos, the site of the tomb of St. John the Theologian. Here, after a period of about twenty-five years, his travels ended, for he soon ascended his first pillar at the base of nearby Mount Galesion. He had visited many holy sites, lived as a solitary in a cave, taken up residence in several monasteries, and advanced in his monastic career, but he had also spent much time on the road with no possessions or money, never knowing where he would next lay his head or find a crust of bread to eat.[118]

Wandering monks such as Lazaros were sometimes admired as living like true disciples of Christ, without any source of support, but dependent upon God's mercy and the charity of strangers. Sometimes they were offered lodgings, bread and water, an egg, money, a ragged cloak, or a bag.[119] In other places, however, the villagers ignored their pleas for alms, and the monks went hungry and thirsty.[120] Such wandering monks were also subject to sexual temptation, as can be seen from two stories in the *vita* of Lazaros. One traveling monk accepted hospitality from a poor woman and ending up sleeping with her. She turned out to be his long-lost daughter, so that he unwittingly committed the sin of incest along with fornication.[121] On another occasion, a priest's wife tried to seduce a wandering monk, but he was able to resist thanks to the prayers of Lazaros.[122]

After Lazaros settled down and had established a group of three monasteries on Mount Galesion, wandering monks (*kykleutai*) came regularly to visit this holy mountain, seeking food and shelter. His monks scolded him for letting these visitors abuse his hospitality, and they recommended that the vagrant monks be allowed to stay only three days and be made to eat in the guesthouse instead of in the refectory with the resident monks. Lazaros agreed to the three-day limit but, no doubt mindful of his own days as a wandering monk, insisted that the vagrants be allowed to join the monks in the refectory, "for even if they are poor and vagrant, they have been made our brothers through their [monastic] habit and they should not eat with the lay people in the guest house."[123]

A very different kind of wandering monk, who was a contemporary of Lazaros, is described in a group of letters from an eleventh-century writer, Michael Psellos, about an acquaintance of his called Elias.[124] Elias, an amusing but less savory character than Lazaros, was widely traveled in Syria, Anatolia, and Greece, but we learn nothing of his origins. He seems to have taken up his mendicant lifestyle in order to earn money to support himself, his mother, and a "tribe of relatives."[125] He was evidently a man of many talents: a skilled calligrapher, musician, dancer, singer, mimic, and tragic actor, who could play the buffoon and entertain his wealthy patrons.[126] Although he sometimes claimed to fornicate only in his imagination, he apparently had an intimate acquaintance with taverns and brothels. Psellos may exaggerate Elias's peccadillos for comic effect, but the man clearly had a split personality: "During the day he gives himself to God, but he allots the night to Satan."[127]

Paul Magdalino has also brought to our attention instances of fraudulent wandering ascetics who conned the faithful by ostentatious displays of masochism of the flesh or by exhibiting fake wounds caused by the wearing of irons, for example. These fake holy men were ridiculed with vivid satire by twelfth-century observers, such as John Tzetzes and Eustathios of Thessalonike.[128]

In the Palaiologan period, there are many instances of wandering monks and holy men.[129] The future patriarch Athanasios I (1289–93, 1303–9) began his monastic career in his uncle's monastery in Thessalonike and then moved to Mount Athos, where he visited several monasteries before settling down at Esphigmenou.

He then embarked on a pilgrimage to the Holy Land, paid long visits to the holy mountains of Latros and St. Auxentios in Anatolia, and spent eighteen years at yet another Anatolian holy mountain, Galesion. He subsequently moved to Mount Ganos in Thrace, where he established a double monastery, and he finally came to Constantinople, where he resided in a monastery that came to bear his name. He remained in the capital for the rest of his life, serving two terms as patriarch. He was firmly committed to cenobitic monasticism and never lived as a solitary, but he did move restlessly from one holy mountain to another until the final decades of his life.[130]

In the fourteenth century, the peregrinations of another holy man, Sabas the Younger (ca. 1283–1347), were recounted in detail by his hagiographer, Philotheos Kokkinos.[131] Sabas, a native of Thessalonike, became a monk at Vatopedi on Athos, but he was forced to flee around 1308 because of Catalan raids on the Holy Mountain. He then embarked on pilgrimage to the Holy Land but made a very lengthy stopover in Cyprus (at that time under the control of the Lusignan dynasty), where he wandered through cities and countryside for years in the guise of a holy fool. The stories of Sabas's outrageous behavior in Cyprus give us an idea of why the local inhabitants often regarded him with mystification and contempt.[132]

He then moved on to the Muslim-occupied Holy Land, where he lived as a hermit in the desert, and made a side trip to Mount Sinai. He finally decided to return to Athos after a circuitous journey that took him to Crete, Euboea, Athens, and Constantinople; all in all he had been away from Athos for twenty years. Although he returned for a while to the cenobitic monastery of Vatopedi, he still did not settle down, and in 1342 he led a delegation to the capital where he spent his final years as a recluse at the Chora monastery.[133] Thus Sabas not only was absent from Athos for twenty years, but in the course of his career he lived in turn as a cenobitic monk, a hermit, a wandering monk, a holy fool, and a recluse.

As this brief survey has demonstrated, a wandering lifestyle in imitation of the early apostles was adopted by a number of monks throughout the Byzantine centuries; for the most part they were motivated by spiritual purposes to undertake their arduous journeys. After the Arab conquest of the Holy Land and Egypt in the seventh century, and the Turkish occupation of much of Anatolia in the eleventh century, long-distance pilgrimage became more difficult and even dangerous, but many holy men persevered in journeys to visit the Holy Places and famed desert monasteries. They also frequently relocated from one monastery to another, or one hermitage to another, or shifted back and forth between the eremitic and cenobitic lifestyle.

Nuns, on the other hand, tended to stay put in their original cloisters. They not only seldom moved from one nunnery to another except under dire necessity[134] or left their convents to take up eremitic life, but they also very rarely went on long-distance pilgrimage. An exception that proves the rule is the case of the nun in the eleventh-century *vita* of Lazaros of Galesion.[135] We are told that this nun from Constantinople, consumed by an ardent desire to visit the Holy Land, set forth in male disguise on pilgrimage to Jerusalem. En route she made a detour to the holy mountain of Galesion to see Lazaros on his pillar and profit from his spiritual counsel. Lazaros immediately saw through her disguise and scolded her, saying that women should not travel about in this fashion, and that true pilgrimage is possible through prayer alone.[136] She obediently returned to Constantinople. This criticism of pilgrimage sounds strange coming from the lips of a man who spent his early years on an extended journey to the Holy Land; Lazaros was clearly making a gender-based distinction in discouraging the nun from her pious journey.

The greater stability of nuns is yet another indication of their staunch commitment to the cenobitic form of monasticism; many male monastics, on the other hand, seem to have rejected principles of obedience to authority after a few years in a monastery and to have set forth on pilgrimages in search of individual fulfilment and spiritual enlightenment.

HOLY FOOLS

Some monks, especially those with no fixed abode, increased the challenges of their lifestyle and the risk of abuse and humiliation by pretending to be crazy; they are known as "fools for Christ's sake." The phenomenon of "holy fools," that is, monks (and a few nuns in the early Christian centuries) who feigned madness in order to humiliate themselves by attracting mockery and abuse, is well attested in late antiquity, especially in the lands of Syria and Egypt. The best-known practitioner of holy foolery from this period is Symeon, in the sixth century, who, after a lengthy sojourn in the desert, spent the final years of his life in Emesa, where he was targeted with insults and beatings for his antisocial and occasionally sacrilegious behavior.[137] His *vita* by Leontios of Neapolis became a model for all subsequent *vitae* of holy fools.

Canon 60 of the Council in Trullo (691/92) condemned those "who pretend to be possessed" and attests that there must have been a sufficient number of holy fools for them to be a matter of concern to the Church;[138] at the same time, since those condemned are not described as "fools for Christ's sake," a distinction may have been made between genuinely holy men and charlatans. Sergei Ivanov has done masterful research in his *Holy Fools in Byzantium and Beyond* in collecting evidence for the pretense of folly among holy men mentioned in texts of the eighth to fourteenth centuries.[139] For example, he has resurrected from oblivion Paul of Corinth, who lived in the mid-ninth century and is known primarily from a canon in his honor, arguing that he was likely a real person.[140] Yet several of the individuals whom Ivanov discusses are legendary, or semifictional at best, and perhaps tell us more about the hagiography of the late ninth and tenth centuries than about monks who actually feigned holy folly. Thus the mid-tenth-century *vita* of Gregentios deals with an archbishop who lived in southern Arabia in the mid-sixth century, while the contemporary *vita* of the celebrated Andrew the Fool portrays him in a fifth-century setting.[141]

Basil the Younger, who supposedly lived during the first part of the tenth century, is briefly described in his *vita* as a holy fool, but with very little supporting evidence.[142]

When we come to the late tenth and eleventh centuries, we are on firmer ground. The eleventh-century *vita* of Symeon the New Theologian records the remarkable tale of a bishop "from the West," most likely southern Italy, who had accidentally killed his nephew. In atonement for his sin he went on pilgrimage to Rome to confess to the pope, and then on to Constantinople where he was persuaded to enter the monastery of St. Mamas, where Symeon was abbot. Here he took vows as the monk Hierotheos.[143] In addition to imposing on himself severe ascetic feats in order to "crush his spirit," he decided to play the fool for Christ's sake: "In his desire for affliction he would thus pretend to do crazy things, often intentionally damaging or even smashing vessels, so that he might become the target of insults or, if warranted, even be beaten about the head. Then, when he was insulted for this, he would rejoice because he had achieved his goal. He also thirsted to experience whippings, so that as the exterior sack [of his flesh] was beaten, his inner man might be freed from future punishment."[144]

Once when Hierotheos was working in the wine cellar, he accidentally spilled an entire vessel of wine and immediately ran to confess his fault to the abbot Symeon. Symeon realized that Hierotheos was actively seeking humiliation and disgrace, and therefore devised the following punishment for him: he made him sit on top of a load of empty wine jars being carried by a mule and be paraded through the streets of Constantinople.[145] Although Symeon supported Hierotheos's desire for mockery and abuse, he had harsh words for those who feigned folly: "Even those who pretend to be mad [τοὺς τὸν σαλὸν ὑποκρινομένους], who joke and prattle utter nonsense, who adopt indecent poses and thus make people laugh—even those men are revered as if they were impassive and virtuous ... on the assumption that the real purpose of their strutting and gesticulating and chattering is in fact to conceal their virtue and their impassivity."[146]

This criticism of holy fools, especially of fraudulent ones who feigned madness for the sake of personal gain, continued in the twelfth century. The canonist Balsamon, in his commentary on canon 60 of the Council in Trullo, openly condemned "those who pretend to be possessed so that they can derive some profit, and ... those who ... make crazed pronouncements with false, satanic intentions ... it is said that their very pretence is inspired by demons." He complained further that these frauds operate with impunity in the streets of Constantinople, and that gullible people fell victim to their wiles and tried to kiss them as if they were holy men.[147]

One of the most famous holy fools in the Palaiologan period was Sabas the Younger, a wandering monk from Athos who spent many years journeying in Cyprus and the Holy Land. Notably throughout his twenty years of travels in the eastern Mediterranean, he maintained the vow of silence he had made upon arrival in Cyprus. This gave a special character to his pretense of folly, since he could only indicate his feigned mental aberration through his actions rather than through speech, and when questioned he would further infuriate his abusers by his stubborn refusal to answer.[148] The most flagrant incidents of Sabas's behavior as a holy fool occurred on Cyprus. Immediately after arriving, he removed all his clothes and wandered about the island with only a ragged cloth covering his private parts, roaming through cities and wilderness. His vow of silence prevented him from begging, which made it even more difficult for him to obtain food. So he was reduced to eating wild greens in the wilderness or scraps of discarded food in towns and villages.[149]

One day, a woman standing on a balcony admired his body out loud. To teach her a lesson, Sabas immediately climbed into a muddy cistern full of worms and emerged only in the evening, with his body blackened with filth so as to discourage the woman from any further thoughts of carnal temptation.[150] Because of his vow of silence, Sabas was not as provocative as some earlier holy fools and usually maintained a rather meek demeanor, but occasionally he provoked through his effrontery rather than through his diffidence. Once, for example, while on Cyprus, he encountered an arrogant Italian, who suspected him of being a spy and interrogated him about his identity. Sabas enraged the Italian by his failure to respond and by using his walking stick to knock the man's hat off his head. As a result he was severely beaten by the Italian's bodyguards.[151] On another occasion, he wandered uninvited into the refectory of a Latin monastery; the monks did not offer him any food but, suspicious of his intentions as he wandered among the tables, struck him mercilessly and threw him out the door.[152]

Maximos the Hutburner was another Palaiologan holy man who was described as behaving at times as a holy fool. His extreme form of eremitism, in which he moved from one solitary grass hut on Athos to another, burning the huts behind him, was evidently viewed as abnormal behavior by his fellow hermits, who called him deranged. They also viewed him with suspicion because of his claims to have had an ecstatic vision of the Virgin at the summit of Mount Athos, "rejecting him as someone who was deranged and reviling him. But this unerring luminary embraced even this, that is, being called deranged rather than holy.... And so he always pretended to be deranged whenever he talked with people, and he played the fool so as to eradicate from himself the pride and self-conceit which tries to court popularity and so as to bring into flower the humility which preserves the grace of the Spirit."[153]

Most holy fools were not part of a cenobitic community for obvious reasons; their antisocial behavior and resistance to authority made it impossible for them to maintain vows of obedience to a superior. The exception that proves the rule is another Palaiologan monk, Nikodemos of Thessalonike, who spent the last part of his life in the Philokalou monastery in Thessalonike. He was hardly a model monk, however, since, though obedient to the abbot, he spent a lot of time outside the monastery walls, "always engaged in conversations with prostitutes and pretending to participate in boisterous revelry."[154] He used to give food to the prostitutes to persuade them not to defile their beds in intercourse with male customers. His behavior so horrified the abbot that on occasion he would expel him from the monastery. Eventually, when Nikodemos was about forty years old, he was violently attacked by some scandalized inhabitants of Thessalonike. Scarcely breathing, he was carried to the monastery, but the abbot refused to let him inside. He did, however, permit Nikodemos to receive the last rites outside the monastery gates. Here he was buried. Eventually, the fragrance emanating from his tomb led to the excavation of his perfectly preserved remains and the determination of his sanctity.[155]

To the best of my knowledge, holy folly was characteristic only of men in the middle and late Byzantine centuries; I have not encountered any female holy fools in this period.

NUNS DISGUISED AS MONKS

I should include here a brief discussion of a small subset of holy women who donned male monastic garb in order to live either as hermits or in monasteries. They are variously called "cross-dressing nuns," "transvestite nuns," or "nuns disguised as monks."[156] These women are attested most frequently in the late antique period, but a few, such as Mary-Marinos, are difficult to place in a definitive chronological or geographical framework, suggesting a legendary character for at least some of them.[157] Others, such as the fifth-century Matrona of Perge, seem to be historical figures.[158] These women disguised themselves as monks for a variety of reasons: the motherless Mary in order to accompany her father when he entered a monastery; Matrona to escape an abusive husband; Anastasia Patrikia to escape the amorous attentions of Emperor Justinian (r. 527–65). In the last two cases, these women feared discovery if they took vows in a nunnery. Some of these nuns, such as Mary/Marinos, maintained their disguise until death; for others, such as Matrona, it was a temporary measure until they could reassume their own identity and live as nuns in a convent.

Two transvestite nuns, Anna-Euphemianos (eighth to early ninth centuries) and Euphrosyne the Younger (late ninth to early tenth centuries), fall within the chronological limits of this study and deserve special attention since they are less well known than their earlier counterparts.[159] Anna, daughter of a deacon at the church of Blachernai in Constantinople, and a widow, is a puzzling figure, known to us only from a brief biographical notice preserved in a fourteenth-century manuscript, probably the summary of a lost *vita* of the ninth or tenth century.[160] When Anna was widowed and her two children died at a young age, she decided to take monastic vows. After distributing her property to the poor, she was tonsured, apparently while still in Constantinople, by a monk from Bithynian Mount Olympos. At this point she pretended to be following the expected procedures to become a nun, since she is described as wearing a nun's habit. Her real intentions, however, were quite different, as revealed by the monk's habit she wore underneath.[161] She then headed for Mount Olympos, where she removed the nun's habit and entered a male cenobitic monastery, introducing herself as Euphemianos. The abbot, assuming she was a eunuch, had no objection to her admission to his institution. Anna's status as a widow when she fled her home and her concealment of male monastic garb beneath a nun's habit are unique phenomena in tales of transvestite nuns, and the hagiographer makes no attempt to explain her motivation for dressing as a monk instead of entering a convent. One possible explanation may be that she wanted to make a total break from her family and felt that disguise as a monk was the only way to escape detection—she left no word of her whereabouts, and the monk who tonsured her and a faithful family retainer had to track her down on Olympos; the monk persuaded her to move to his *lavra* on Olympos.[162] One could argue that only by cross-dressing as a man could she escape the family ties that continued to bind nuns even in the cloister. Another explanation of her decision to enter a monastery, suggested by Delierneux, might be that no place was available in a nunnery.[163]

Anna/Euphemianos moved three more times, a restlessness more typical of male monks than nuns. As the fame of her miraculous deeds attracted more monks to the *lavra* on Olympos, it became too small to accommodate the burgeoning community. Patriarch Tarasios (784–806) granted to the *lavra* a ruinous property in Constantinople for the foundation of a new monastery, called *ton Abramiton*. Next, after a scandalous incident in which a monk endeavored to see her naked to determine if she was really a eunuch, she moved to a church on the Bosporos. Her final move was to a monastery in the Sigma region in Constantinople. The closing paragraphs of the abridged notice make it clear that she remained in a male monastic environment until her death, but it is unclear to what extent her identity as a woman was revealed; it was certainly suspected and was a topic of discussion. Nor was there any dramatic revelation of her gender after her death, as is found in the *vitae* of some transvestite nuns.

Euphrosyne the Younger, the last transvestite nun attested in Byzantine sources, is a shadowy figure indeed. Although she is described as living during the reign of Leo VI (r. 886–912), the earliest notice of her is the saint's life written in the early fourteenth century by Nikephoros Kallistos Xanthopoulos (d. ca. 1335).[164] This is a time when her healing shrine in Constantinople seems to have been particularly active, since Xanthopoulos's contemporary, Constantine Akropolites (d. 1324), also wrote an *enkomion* in her honor.[165] Although her relics were venerated at a shrine at the monastery of the Skepe, it seems likely that Xanthopoulos has invented the early history of St. Euphrosyne, and that she is a legendary character. His account of the first part of her life, when she lived as a cenobitic monk and hermit somewhere in the Black Sea region, is quite vague, with no reference to a toponym or the name of the monastery where she lived in disguise as a monk.

According to Xanthopoulos, Euphrosyne was an only child, born in the Peloponnesos to her parents after a long period of childlessness. At age six or seven she began her education in a convent where she put on monastic garb, perhaps that of a novice. She then went to Constantinople where she lived with the Agelastos family. As a teenager she ran away from their house and spent three months alone in a nearby millhouse, engaged in prayer and spiritual exercises. She then took a boat to the Black Sea, where she entered a monastery dressed as a man, with the name John. Here she stayed for fifteen years. It is not clear at what point she took monastic vows, but she was so admired in the monastery that the monks wanted to appoint her as their abbot. So she fled into the wilderness and attached herself to a hermit living in a cave, whom she served as a disciple. Among other duties, she used to carry water in a jar for a distance of three miles. After ten years, she decided to return to Constantinople, once more donned a female monastic habit, and entered the convent of the Theotokos of the Pege, just outside the city walls.[166] For the rest of her life, she lived as a recluse in female garb.[167] Euphrosyne seems to have originally disguised herself as a male monk in order to maintain her anonymity and keep her family from finding her, despite the fact that they had sent out a number of servants in search of her. She also transgressed other bounds of normative behavior for a nun by her several changes of abode, her extreme mortification of the body, and her adoption of a reclusive lifestyle.

UNAFFILIATED MONKS AND NUNS IN VILLAGE AND URBAN CONTEXTS

We have seen that many alternative forms of Byzantine monasticism were characterized by individualism, fluidity, and flexibility, in contrast to the more rigid norms of cenobitic life. Especially in the cases of hermits who withdrew to the wilderness and of wandering monks, I have noted that many of them were apparently independent of any authority, whether monastic (an abbot) or ecclesiastical (a bishop). Here I examine a related phenomenon that hitherto has attracted little scholarly attention: the apparent autonomy of certain monks and nuns living in an urban or village environment, either as solitaries or in small groups. The evidence for them is scattered and often difficult to interpret, but I argue that it is sufficient to demonstrate yet another variety of monastic experience.

The information I present is drawn primarily from hagiography and from documents from the archives of Mount Athos and the synod of Constantinople.

House Nunneries

Occasionally, the women in a pious family who decided to take monastic vows did not enter a convent and subject themselves to obedience to an abbess, but they instead remained in their own homes. Two Byzantine sources, one hagiographic, the other documentary, describe what might be called a "house nunnery," reminiscent of early Christian establishments, such as the family monastery founded in provincial Anatolia by Makrina (d. 379), the sister of Gregory of Nyssa, in the fourth century. Gregory's *vita* of Makrina tells how the beautiful, studious girl, the eldest of nine children, was betrothed at age twelve, but when her fiancé died before the wedding, she refused to consider a second engagement and resolved to remain a virgin devoted to God. Maintaining a permanent residence in her house at Annisa with her widowed mother, she embraced a lifestyle resembling that in a nunnery: frequent recitation of the Psalter, constant prayer and singing of hymns, manual labor, rejection of material wealth, and provision of the same food and drink to family members and female slaves: "Macrina, who had already renounced all the conventionalities, brought her mother to her own state of humility. She induced her to place herself on an equal footing with the whole group of virgins, so that she shared with them in equality the same table, the same kind of bed and all the same necessities of life. All differences of rank were removed from their way of life."[168]

She later persuaded her youngest brother, Peter, to renounce the world, and the family home became a kind of "double monastery," with men and women living in separate enclosures, under the leadership of Peter and Makrina, respectively, with Makrina playing the dominant role.[169] This house-monastery also evolved to include individuals who were not part of the original family household.

The early phase of this establishment seems to have been an informal communal association, but it developed into a more organized institution. The members of the community attended church services in the village and were apparently under the spiritual direction of local clergy.[170]

Five centuries later, the *vita* of David, Symeon, and George of Lesbos describes a similar establishment in or near Constantinople. Hypatia (the namesake of a famous fourth-century Neoplatonist scholar in Alexandria) was the daughter of a prosperous Constantinopolitan family. Like Makrina, she was an assiduous student and well-read in scriptures and theological treatises; when she approached marriageable age, she refused to accept a husband and yearned for the monastic life. One night she had a terrifying vision that rendered her mute. Her mother, now widowed, took Hypatia and her sister to visit a holy man named Symeon, a former stylite who was living in the outskirts of the capital. After she spent a week with Symeon, the girl miraculously regained her speech. Thereupon Hypatia's mother decided that the whole family should be tonsured. Symeon came to their house to perform the ceremony: "The blessed one [then] tonsured her [Hypatia] and clothed her mother and the two sisters and the more outstanding of their maidservants with the monastic habit, making their house a holy monastery of virgins; he gave her the name of Febronia, who distinguished herself in the ascetic habit, instead of Hypatia, for she was educated and had great experience in the Scriptures."[171] The resemblance to the story of Makrina and her mother is self-evident; what we do not know is whether this house nunnery was ever officially consecrated by the local bishop. There is also no mention of any hierarchy within this institution, nor do we know if Symeon continued to serve as a spiritual father to the nuns.

A will of the late eleventh century describes, in my view, a similar informal establishment of nuns in an aristocratic household in Constantinople.[172] In 1098, Kale Pakouriane, the young widow of the general Symbatios Pakourianos, had fallen ill and decided to compose a last will and testament. She was a wealthy woman, both on account of her own dowry and family inheritances and the substantial bequests she had received from her husband upon his untimely death sometime in late 1092 or 1093. As was often customary in Byzantium, she had become a nun after being widowed, taking the name of Maria, but she apparently remained at home together with a group of other women, who are all described as nuns: her widowed mother, Xene Diabatene; her sister, Irene; Helena Diaxene (a close friend) and Theodoule; and two freedwomen and former servants, Christina and Maria Oungraina.[173] Again one sees a marked resemblance to the ménages of Makrina and Hypatia-Febronia, a group of female relatives and maidservants who have all taken the veil. There is no reference to any convent in the document, and surely Kale-Maria would have made a bequest to the nunnery in which she resided if she had moved out of her house into a convent. So we can assume that she stayed at home as a nun.

Her house was well equipped to serve as an informal nunnery, since it had a chapel, liturgical books, liturgical vessels, and icons. She and the other nuns also wore monastic habits.[174] Her bequests included four icons, including an icon of Christ, the Virgin Blachernitissa, the Deesis, and the Baptism. At least two of her books were for liturgical use, an Oktaechos and a Panegyrikon, and three others could have been for private devotional use: *The Ladder of John Climax*, almost required reading for monastics; a book of unspecified works of Basil of Caesarea; and a Psalter.[175] Objects of silver listed in the will included a liturgical plate, flagons, an incense burner, a cross, and two lampstands, all of which no doubt adorned her chapel. A silver basin and ewer may have also served liturgical purposes.[176] In addition, Kale-Maria bequeathed a purple liturgical vestment to a monk.[177] One puzzling feature of the legacies is that she gave some luxury objects and garments to the nuns in her household; for example, besides the monastic garments bequeathed to the nun Helena Diaxene, she also specified the donation of her spun-gold bracelet with enamel ornaments, while the nun Christina was to receive a blue cloak.[178] Did she intend for the nuns to wear these items or perhaps to sell them and donate the proceeds to the poor?

At first glance, it seems as if Kale-Maria envisaged the closing down of her monastic household upon her demise (which occurred some time before 1103), since she made bequests of icons, liturgical books, vessels, and vestments to legatees outside the family. If so, perhaps she intended for her mother, sister, and maidservants to enter an established nunnery after her death. On the other hand, it has already been noted that the items listed in her will do not seem to be a complete tally of her possessions, and she may have planned to retain enough liturgical objects in the house and chapel for an informal nunnery to continue for the foreseeable future.

Admittedly, my sample of three house-nunneries is very small, and I have found no comparable male house-monasteries. One possible explanation of this gender discrepancy could be that some Byzantine women, who led circumscribed lives, may have felt more comfortable remaining in their own homes after dedicating themselves to Christ rather than moving to a new environment.

The desire to retain close ties with relatives is seen in the case of the family of Gregory Palamas. After his father died, his mother, Kallone-Kale, entered a convent in Constantinople with her two daughters, while her three sons went off to Mount Athos. Once his mother died, Gregory moved his two sisters to a nunnery in Berrhoia, where he and his brothers also continued to pursue monastic life.[179]

Unaffiliated Nuns

At the beginning of *Vita B of Athanasios of Athos*, we learn that after being orphaned at a young age, he was cared for by an unnamed "virgin and nun," until in his teenage years he left Trebizond and went off to Constantinople for his education. The woman is described as wearing a monastic habit and engaging "in assiduous prayer and fasting," but she has evidently remained in her own household. There is no mention of a convent or other nuns, and it would be highly unusual for a boy to be raised in a nunnery. Athanasios is free to go off and play with other boys and to go to school, so all the evidence points to his living in an ordinary house with his foster mother.[180] This tale of an unaffiliated nun can be paralleled in numerous other sources.

In chapter 2, I made brief mention of a number of rural nuns, who are attested as donors in inscriptions in village churches; these nuns are not identified as belonging to a specific nunnery, and we have no further information about them. We can only speculate that some of them may have taken the monastic habit very late in life or on their deathbed, and continued to live at home, while others may have withdrawn to a solitary hut or cave, or may have lived together in small informal communities.[181]

More information about a village nun can be extracted from the will of Nymphodora, a nun living in 1445 in Siderokausia, a mining village in Chalkidike near the boundary of Mount Athos. She was the eighty-four-year-old widow of Markelos, who abandoned her to become a monk at the Athonite monastery of Xeropotamou, where he made major donations to restore the buildings and was regarded as a "second founder." Nymphodora also took the monastic habit, but it is not specified whether she did this immediately after her husband became a monk or after his death. Evidently she was not living in a convent, since she donated substantial properties to Xeropotamou in exchange for the provision of foodstuffs for the rest of her life, a so-called *adelphaton*. She might, however, have been living in a type of village hermitage, since her will included bequests of two *kellia* with their furnishings, along with the church of St. Nicholas and its contents, such as liturgical vessels and books. Her spiritual gift to the monastery entitled her to the following during her lifetime: on her behalf the monks would sing a hymn to the Virgin at vespers on Monday, celebrate the liturgy every Tuesday, and drink a cup of wine in the refectory. After she died, she would be commemorated annually on the anniversary of her death.[182]

The records of the patriarchal synod of Constantinople provide a considerable amount of evidence for unaffiliated nuns in Constantinople and Thessalonike in the Palaiologan period. A common pattern seems to have been for widows to take monastic vows but remain in their own homes.[183] I have tentatively identified as "unaffiliated" those nuns for whom no monastic institution is named and who retain private property. It is true that Byzantine civil and canon law had conflicting opinions about the possession of property by monks and nuns and their right to bequeath or sell it as they chose, with canon law arguing that after tonsure, all of a monastic's possessions belonged to the monastery and he or she had no right to dispose of them.[184] Monastic *typika* frequently required novices to dispose of all their possessions before they were admitted to monastic life. But the rules varied, and some monasteries were much less strict in their prohibition of personal possessions.[185] Thus retention of property does not necessarily disprove entrance into a monastery. The nuns described below, however, not only still have private property but remain active in family affairs and secular life in a way that would be unusual for cloistered nuns.

I will summarize a few such cases in chronological order.

Euphrosyne Petraleiphina
In 1330, the synod in Constantinople resolved a dispute between the nun Euphrosyne Petraleiphina and her son-in-law about the dowry of her daughter, who had died childless and intestate. At first the son-in-law, Theodore Branas, claimed that his wife wanted him to receive all her property in exchange for arranging commemorative services for her in perpetuity, but Euphrosyne argued that her daughter was too young to make an oral bequest. In the end, because Branas was unable to perform the commemorative services on account of his other duties, the synod awarded the nun the bulk of her daughter's estate.[186] Since the nun Euphrosyne remained active in the management of family affairs and property, it seems unlikely that she was living in a convent.

Elaiodora Sarantene Tzymypinissa

Elaiodora was a nun from a prominent family in Thessalonike who came to plead before the synod of Constantinople in 1348 about the dowry rights of her deceased sister; the latter's second husband was claiming all her property for himself and refusing to give any part of it to the three children from her first marriage.[187] Elaiodora's intense involvement in family affairs and journey to Constantinople suggests that she was not cloistered in a nunnery.

Marina

In 1359, the nun Marina was involved in a dispute over the ownership of her house, which had been unlawfully exchanged by her brother-in-law for a vineyard he had received in his wife's dowry. The synod restored Marina's house to her.[188] She probably would not have retained ownership of the house if she had entered a convent.

Pheronike Aspietissa

In 1392, Aspietissa, called "the most honorable among nuns," appeared before the patriarch to claim ownership of a vineyard.[189]

Hypomone Kalothetina

In 1395, a patriarchal decree to the metropolitan of Thessalonike described the pitiful situation of a nun called Hypomone Kalothetina, who had been divorced by her husband, Kalothetos, on false grounds of alleged adultery.[190] Kalothetos had also murdered the woman's mother before he himself died. The Church had forced Kalothetos to give Hypomone an allowance for one year of wine, wheat, firewood, and thirty *hyperpyra*, but now she found herself destitute. It is clear that she was not living in a nunnery where she would be supported, but was on her own. The synod ruled that because Hypomone had been wronged by her husband's unjust accusations and by his murder of his mother-in-law, she was entitled to receive this allowance for as many years as the duration of their marriage.

Hypomone Kaloeidina

Two years later, another nun named Hypomone, a widow, appeared before the synod with regard to a dispute with her son-in-law, Barzanes, who had failed to respect the terms of his deceased wife's will. One-third of the daughter's property was to go to her mother, Hypomone, to help pay for commemorative services and prayers for the salvation of her soul. We learn that the daughter's property included houses, workshops, a bakery, a vineyard, a garden, and *kellia* associated with a newly built *triklinos*.[191] It seems plausible that Hypomone was residing in one of these *kellia*.

Hypomone Chrysokephalina Kaukanina

A third nun named Hypomone is mentioned in a synodal document as having been the co-owner of a perfume and ointment workshop that was sold in 1400. She was to receive one-third of the sale price.[192]

Theodoule Tzouroulene

Another Palaiologan nun who seems to have been unaffiliated is Theodoule Tzouroulene, who restored a ruined church in Constantinople at her own expense. No connection with a convent is mentioned, and she is reported to have been absent from Constantinople for several years, so she was probably not a cloistered nun. She protested to the synod in 1400 about Kaballarios Kontostephanos, who, during her absence from the capital, planted a vineyard in the churchyard right up to the church building, encroaching on the area of the narthex and cemetery. The patriarch ruled that the vineyard must be removed and confirmed Theodoule's administration of the church during her lifetime.[193] There is no hint as to where Theodoule was domiciled, but since she was responsible for supervising the lighting of lamps and services at the church, it is likely that she lived nearby.

Martha Kanabina (and her husband, Neilos Kanabes)

In a synodal act of 1400, the patriarch confirmed the donation by the nun Martha Kanabina of a garden to an unnamed hospital or hospice (*xenon*) founded by the nun Theodosia Kantakouzene. Theodosia had permitted Martha and her husband, Neilos, who, toward the end of their lives, had agreed to renounce conjugal life and adopt the monastic habit, to purchase from her a garden that she owned, on the condition that upon their deaths it be donated to the *xenon*. We do not know under what circumstances the couple was living, but it was probably in separate locations; Martha is called Neilos's "former wife." They continued to manage the garden during their lifetimes and were probably not cloistered.[194]

Martha

The nun Martha inherited the *kathisma* (monastic cell) of the deceased monk Gennadios, in which she took up residence.[195] She had rights to half of a neighboring garden and was guaranteed access to a well and public road. In 1400, after a dispute with neighbors over an adjacent garden, the synod confirmed Martha's access to the well and highway, and awarded her one-third of the neighboring property with houses and a garden.

Zenobia Phialitissa

In 1401, the nun Zenobia Phialitissa disputed the ownership of her house (in which she was currently residing) with her daughter-in-law, and she brought the case before the synod. The patriarch confirmed her rights to the house and her ability to bequeath it to her grandson Theodore, who was caring for her in her old age.[196]

Kallone Pouzoulou

In the same year, a judgment was made against the nun Kallone Pouzoulou, who had failed to hand over to her adopted daughter the entire dowry that she was due. The nun had moved from Selymbria to Constantinople, was living in a *kellion*, and appears to have no affiliation with a nunnery. Among the objects she had retained were a sheet, a large copper cauldron, and a container for keeping beverages cool; these would be unusual items to find in the cell of a cloistered nun.[197]

Although these unaffiliated nuns are diverse in some ways, they often have certain traits in common: many were widowed, they retained family ties, and maintained control over family properties. These synodal cases may illustrate a tension in Byzantine society between a desire to take monastic vows in old age, especially after the loss of a spouse, and the bonds of family and family property.

A smaller group of unaffiliated nuns presents a very different picture, women who took advantage of their autonomous status to lead immoral lives. It is always possible of course that some of these women were unjustly accused of dissolute behavior; they may have fallen under suspicion because they were living independently.

Thiniatissa

In a patriarchal society such as that of Byzantium it was inevitable that women living on their own, without the oversight of a male guardian, might arouse suspicions; in some cases, those suspicions of immorality on the part of unaffiliated nuns seem to have been justified. A flagrant example is that of the Constantinopolitan nun Thiniatissa, reported in a synodal act of 1353 or 1354.[198] A young hieromonk Ioannikios from the Peribleptos monastery, together with a friend Isaias of similar inclinations, was known to engage in depraved behavior. The two monks went "to the house of the daughter of the late Thiniates, the so-called nun Thiniatissa, who even before she donned monastic garb was reported to be living in a dissolute fashion, not only to the destruction of her own soul, but also to the defilement of many souls who were seduced by her, and after she donned monastic garb in her house and remained in it, her behavior worsened, as she turned her house into a brothel, and made herself a procuress for the younger nuns."[199]

Ioannikios and his friend began to frequent the brothel on a regular basis, bringing along a nun prostitute, until neighbors sounded the alarm and the two monks were caught and prosecuted. For the purposes of our argument, the importance of this synodal act is not so much to reveal the occasionally immoral behavior of nuns living on their own, but to document a clear case of a woman becoming a nun and remaining in her own home after her father's death.

Another dissolute nun appears in the *vita* of Basil the Younger, described as a woman with "lovers beyond number," who invites monastic officials to dinner and is possessed by the demon of fornication. She came to visit Basil with the intention of seducing him, but he saw through her and threw her out of the house. Her elderly companion recounted that "she brought to perdition many souls not only of the laity, but even of monastics." This fornicating nun is not linked with any Constantinopolitan convent, and her behavior was possible because she lived in a private dwelling (οἰκία).[200]

If, as I argue, some or all of these nuns were living on their own, their uncanonical status does not seem to have troubled the ecclesiastical authorities; not a single extant synodal act alludes to their irregular status or suggests that they should retire to a cloistered nunnery. There is limited evidence for a similar phenomenon in southern Italy, where independent nuns are mentioned in documents. These nuns are widows who seem to follow a monastic rule, but continue to administer their property and live at home.[201]

Unaffiliated Monks

I have found many fewer allusions to unaffiliated monks in urban centers or villages. Male monastics were freer to make the choice between entering a local cenobitic monastery, leaving the city for a mountain hermitage, or adopting the lifestyle of a wandering monk; this freedom perhaps diminished the desire for an unaffiliated monastic status.

Basil the Younger
Sometime around the year 900, a solitary wandering monk named Basil was discovered in the wilds of Bithynia and apprehended on suspicion of being a spy. He was brought to Constantinople by imperial officials, and after interrogation and torture, he survived an attempted execution when he was thrown into the sea.

Miraculously saved by two dolphins, he returned to the capital and started a long residence there. During subsequent decades spent in Constantinople, he did not enter a monastery, but instead lived in a series of private homes. He stayed first with a couple of modest means, named John and Helena, and received many visitors who came to hear his teaching, prayers, and prophecies, to receive his blessing, and to be cured of illnesses. The couple provided Basil with a small room and some of his food, but he subsisted for the most part on the wine, bread, and fruit brought by his visitors. In fact, they brought so much food that they would share it with him and with the poor people who flocked to the house.[202]

After the death of John and Helena, Basil moved into the house of a eunuch courtier named Constantine Barbaros, where he had private quarters and the devoted services of an elderly slave woman, Theodora. Here Basil continued his ministry of providing spiritual counsel to visitors, performing miraculous cures, and revealing his powers of clairvoyance and prophecy.[203] He also spent much time at the home of the Gongylios brothers, eunuchs who evidently were also courtiers.[204] A notable feature of Basil's career is the degree to which he avoided involvement with monastic and ecclesiastical institutions. The editors of his *vita* have observed: "By choosing to live in private residences rather than settling down in a monastery, Basil deliberately sets himself apart from the official Church. He is not reported to have attended the liturgy at local churches, and seems to have disassociated himself from the Constantinopolitan clerical hierarchy and monasteries, performing his prayers privately."[205]

Basil thus represents yet another kind of independent monk, a former wanderer who settled down in the capital, enjoying the hospitality of local citizens in exchange for his spiritual counsel and the prestige he offered their households. In this way, he resembles those proponents of an apostolic ascetic lifestyle characteristic of late antiquity, described by Daniel Caner as offering "urban patrons spiritual services in exchange for material support."[206] The story of Basil is found in a hagiographic context, and therefore should be treated with caution as a reflection of reality, but it hardly seems implausible in view of the well-known Byzantine reverence for holy men.

A parallel situation to that of Basil is found in the *vita* of Evaristos, a ninth-century Stoudite monk, who was forced to leave the monastery at the time of the deposition of the patriarch Ignatios in 858 and the accession of Photios. Together with a fellow monk he found refuge in the private home of a pious man named Samuel, who housed and fed the two men "for a very long time."[207]

During the final centuries of Byzantium, in the Palaiologan period, unaffiliated monks are sometimes attested in documentary sources, particularly the acts of the patriarchal synod of Constantinople. The synodal acts occasionally mention, for example, monks who are evidently living on their own in a *kellion* or in a private home.

Kappadokes

This monk, originally from Thessalonike, was accused of practicing magic. He found refuge in the home of an unnamed monk, who sought Kappadokes's assistance in gaining an episcopal appointment. Kappadokes obliged him by writing the Lord's Prayer backwards on a piece of parchment, which the anonymous monk wore sewn to his cloak. The synodal decision about the fate of the two monks is unknown, since the end of the relevant act (1351/52) is missing. For our purposes, however, the most important information in this act is that the anonymous monk was living in a private home where he could offer hospitality to another monk: "He brought him home and offered him hospitality, and wished him to share his roof and his table."[208]

Daniel, the Hieromonk

Another such autonomous monk was a certain Daniel, who in 1389 vowed to the patriarch that, now that he had been ordained a priest, he would no longer make barrels or sell books outside his *kellion*.[209] He was apparently an independent monk who was earning his living as an artisan and merchant.

Methodios

An act of 1400 makes reference to the monk Methodios, who some years previously had made an arrangement with the church of St. Euphemia near the Hippodrome. The church granted him the usufruct for life of a garden plot and a piece of property on which he built himself a *kellion*. He was to pay three *hyperpyra* annually in rent. Methodios cleared the garden plot and planted it; presumably he ate some of the fruits and vegetables produced there and sold the rest for cash to pay for other provisions. But then Methodios realized that his garden did not produce enough income to pay the rent, and he requested a reduction in the annual fee (which was granted).[210]

Anonymous Spiritual Director of Irene-Eulogia Choumnaina

Very little is known about the second spiritual director of Irene-Eulogia Choumnaina, the fourteenth-century princess and abbess.[211] Angela Hero described him as a "hesychast who lived in the outskirts of Constantinople in the company of another monk."[212] A man of considerable education, he used to visit Irene-Eulogia every other month at her convent to offer spiritual counsel. We can surmise that he did not belong to a cenobitic monastery, since he preferred to live in seclusion and was dependent on the princess for food provisions.[213]

THE CURIOUS TALE OF CYRIL PHILEOTES

Cyril, who lived in the Thracian village of Philea in the eleventh century, and was eventually recognized as a saint, demonstrates the extreme fluidity of monastic lifestyles in Byzantium and the difficulty of assigning them to rigid categories. Cyril was a farmer who had been unusually pious since childhood. After he married and had his first child, he resolved to limit conjugal relations with his wife to a few times a year and to lead a semimonastic life at home. He began to fast rigorously, chant psalms seven times a day, make many genuflections, and engage in nocturnal vigils.[214] His ultimate goal was to enter a monastery, but he decided first to learn obedience and humility by going to sea and submitting to the will of the ship's captain. Upon his return home three years later, he announced to his wife that he wanted either to take monastic vows in a monastery or to remain at home, leading a life of spiritual contemplation and abandoning his farmwork. She preferred the second option and told Cyril she would do the necessary labor to support the family. Cyril then built a small cell inside their home, to which he could retire to kneel in prayer and vigil; yet he remained in the company of his wife and children, something very strange and unnatural for a monk, as his hagiographer comments.[215] Here, as a quasi-monk he spent years in fasting, psalmody, and continual prayer, with his body encased in iron rings. Occasionally he would repair neighbors' fishnets in an attempt to avoid the despondency (*akedia*) that was a persistent danger for monks. Sometimes he would withdraw to a deserted lakeshore for greater solitude and ascetic endeavors. He was also granted the "gift of tears," that is, the abundant shedding of tears of compunction.[216]

While maintaining this status of leading a monastic life without taking vows, donning the habit, or swearing obedience to an abbot, Cyril undertook weekly pilgrimages to the shrine of the Virgin of Blachernai in Constantinople, a journey of more than thirty miles each way. He also made longer pilgrimages to the shrine of St. Michael at Chonai in Phrygia and to the churches of Peter and Paul in Rome.[217] Eventually he was tonsured at a monastery founded on family property by his brother Michael, where he spent some time as a recluse and three years as a hermit, taking a vow of silence in a nearby *kellion*.[218] Over the years, Cyril at various times adopted the lifestyle of a hermit, a recluse, a wandering monk, and a cenobite, but he never abandoned his family ties or indeed his bonds with his family property. He epitomizes the many ways one could be a monk; indeed, for many years he followed a monastic regimen of life without donning the habit. He might perhaps be compared with the "holy housewives" who appear in middle Byzantine hagiography, such as Mary the Younger and Thomaïs of Lesbos. Yet these pious matrons led very different lives, suffering brutal and abusive treatment from their husbands; they showed their Christian fervor through church attendance and charitable activities rather than through acts of asceticism and self-mortification, and they never took the monastic veil.[219]

CONCLUSION

In Byzantium there was always a tension between the ideals of cenobitism (life in a communal monastery) and eremitism (life as a solitary); there was also much discussion of the relative values of the two principal modes of monasticism and arguments as to which was superior.[1] The cenobitic monastery was often a self-sufficient, self-contained, and productive economic unit, which provided for the physical needs of its monks. It furnished social and charitable services to the poor and needy, including care for the elderly and widowed, medical treatment, and distribution of food. Cenobitic monks often served as spiritual advisors and confessors for members of the lay community; one of their most important duties was the performance of prayers for the faithful, both while alive and after their deaths, to help ensure the salvation of their souls. The solitary, on the other hand, was often himself dependent on charity and the kindness of others for the essentials of food and even water, and he engaged in little if any social interaction. He was focused on his own communion with the divine, not with prayer for the salvation of others.

But monastic life in Byzantium should not be reduced to a binary opposition between the coenobium and the hermitage. It assumed a variety of forms that can be placed on a broad spectrum of practice, with regimens ranging from strict adherence to a common rule and obedience to a superior in a cenobitic monastery to the total isolation of the hermit in a cave who foraged for his food. Some cenobitic monks practiced extreme abstinence from food, while others were satirized for their obsession with lavish meals.[2] Within a monastery could be found recluses who never left their cells; in the idiorrhythmic monasteries of later Byzantium, monks did not eat in a common refectory, but prepared their own meals in the privacy of their cells; they also might earn a modest income from the sale of handicrafts that they made. As for hermits, some lived in small groups and worshipped at a nearby chapel, others might go to a monastery on weekends to attend the liturgy and enjoy a communal meal. Some monks were stylites who never left their pillars, others spent years traveling on pilgrimage to visit monasteries, holy men, and holy sites. Nuns, on the other hand, were most likely to live in cenobitic nunneries, to remain cloistered, and to observe the ideal of monastic stability.

There was considerable flexibility and fluidity in monastic careers, and the same monk could follow several different regimens over the course of his life. Stability was not highly valued, except in the case of stylites and recluses, and even they sometimes moved around. These different modes of monastic life had only a few features in common: the taking of vows, renunciation of the secular world, celibacy, and a life of prayer and recitation of the Psalter. Asceticism could be practiced in a monastery, but it was more typical of the hermit. Even the monastic habit was worn primarily by residents of monasteries, while hermits were most likely to be garbed in tattered garments made of goat hair or animal skins.

Those Byzantine monks who abandoned cenobitic monasteries for the wilderness were in part expressing their desire for individualism and their rejection of a strictly regimented communal lifestyle. They also believed that a personal search for contact with the divine, facilitated by isolation, asceticism, and constant prayer, was superior to the communal offices and liturgy of the cenobitic monastery. Many of these hermits were noteworthy for their independence and autonomy; in theory, they had to seek permission from their abbot to leave the monastery, but once outside the cloister they were subject to very little authority, answerable to neither abbot nor bishop.[3] This autonomy can also be seen in the little-understood phenomenon of unaffiliated monks and nuns who lived in private homes or individual cells in urban environments or villages.

Alexander Kazhdan has cogently argued that this individualism can also be found inside a cenobitic monastery, where, for example, recluses could follow an eremitic regimen within the cloister, and, according to the twelfth-century canonist Balsamon, many monks failed to follow the rule of communal meals in a refectory and sleeping in a dormitory.[4] Kazhdan also remarks on the "apparent prevalence of eremitic and semifamilial ways of life which allowed the individuals to dispense with the set discipline of a community."[5] He further asserts that "to this degree of individualism in the style of life within the monastic community corresponded the individualism of monastic communities themselves,"[6] as we can see in the great variety of regulations in the *typika* and the absence of monastic orders in Byzantium.

COMMUNAL LIFE OR SOLITARY?

Most monastic rules urged strict adherence to the communal life. Thus the tenth-century rule for the Bulgarian monastery of Rila argued that cenobitism was preferable as a practical matter, as a way of life possible for all: "The communal life is in every way more useful for monks than the solitary one, for solitude is not suitable for the many, but only for a few who are perfect in all monastic virtues. The common life, on the other hand, is useful in general for everybody."[7]

In the thirteenth century, Maximos, the founder of the Boreine monastery in western Anatolia, praised the cenobitic life as definitely superior to the solitary:

The superior ought to direct all the monks practicing asceticism in the monastery to live together in the cenobitic manner.... A common outlook, a common way of thinking, and love of the brothers should be fostered among them. There is no doubt that living by oneself cuts one off from the others. By so being cut off one is preoccupied with oneself and left to one's own devices [*idiorythmei*], and this is totally incompatible with common life. One thinks about and is concerned about one's own good rather than that of another. Peace and union of minds are put aside and destroyed. On the other hand, having things in common binds together and leads to peace and, as mentioned earlier, is the cause of a complete unity of attitudes and of minds.[8]

In 1407, the patriarch Matthew I, in his *typikon* for the monastery of Charsianeites in Constantinople, recognized that there were alternative forms of monasticism, such as the angelic life of the solitary or the lavriotic (lavra-style) combination of solitary and cenobitic life: "For there are many paths of piety for athletes, since our heavenly Father also has 'many mansions' (cf. John 14:2), or rather since there are many paths, therefore there are many mansions."[9]

But Matthew then argued that the *koinobion* was superior because of the establishment of a "community of souls," united by free will, with the abbot as Christ and the monks as disciples. "They own their possessions in common, they have one purpose, their salvation is in common, as is their wealth ... what could be more blessed than this way of life?"[10]

As Paul Magdalino has pointed out, criticism of holy ascetics who lived an unregulated life outside a cenobitic community was particularly prevalent in the twelfth century, especially among members of the Church hierarchy, such as Balsamon and Eustathios of Thessalonike, but also among intellectuals, such as John Tzetzes.[11]

It is a commonplace of many hagiographical texts that life in a *koinobion* is an essential stage of monastic formation, in which the novice learns discipline, obedience to his superior, and abnegation of his will, and is hardened by manual labor. Only after years of training is the young monk deemed ready to attempt the rigors of solitary life, if he so wishes.[12] This was a tradition that goes back to the early centuries of Eastern monasticism, as can be seen, for example, in the *vitae* written in the sixth century by Cyril of Skythopolis, who quotes Sabas the Great as saying that "as the flower precedes the fruit, so the coenobium comes before the anachoretic life."[13]

Many centuries later, the *vitae* of Maximos the Hutburner emphasize this same point. When the young Maximos first arrived at the Great Lavra on Athos in the early fourteenth century, he read the *vitae* of both Peter, the first Athonite hermit, and Athanasios, a solitary converted to cenobitism and the founder of the Great Lavra. In a dilemma as to which model of monasticism he should choose, Maximos consulted the elders of the Great Lavra, who advised him that before becoming a hermit he must first learn in a *koinobion* the qualities of submission (*hypotage*), humility, and obedience as divine tools that would quench the fiery darts of the devil.[14] Similar advice was given to an eleventh-century bishop from southern Italy, who had accidentally killed his nephew and sought to do penance by withdrawing to a solitary life in the wilderness; he was told, however, that it would be more profitable for him "to pursue the monastic life in a cenobitic community and you would derive no little benefit from the negation of your own will."[15]

Although normally the solitary life was considered more challenging than life in the *koinobion*, the *typikon* of Athanasios of Athos painted a different picture, accusing some *kelliotai*, dependent on a *lavra* for their material necessities, of seeking a more liberated and luxurious life than that offered by the *koinobion*: an ill-prepared *kelliotes* should "know precisely that he seeks to live apart and by himself for no other reason but to be able to go here and there whenever he wants and wander about outside his *kellion*, while having unlimited food, drink, and sleep, and no end of relaxation for his flesh."[16] This seemingly unwarranted and exaggerated criticism is surprising, coming from the pen of a former *kelliotes* and hermit, and it demonstrates Athanasios's conversion to a preference for the cenobitic ideal. He concludes that cenobitic monks are in no way inferior to solitaries: "Before God and the angels I bear witness that those who persevere in genuine obedience . . . do not take second place to those carrying on the struggle special to solitude. But they shall be found to be superior and deemed worthy of eternal crowns by the good and impartial Judge."[17]

There was one lurking concern about cenobitic monasteries, and that was homoerotic temptation. Although the matter is very rarely openly discussed, except in the *typikon* of the Phoberos monastery,[18] it is clear that many monastic leaders were concerned that the communal form of monasticism did pose the danger of homosexual relationships, especially between older monks and younger ones. Hence the many prohibitions of the admission of adolescent youths and eunuchs to monasteries.[19] A thirteenth-century act of Demetrios Chomatenos, an archbishop from Epiros, provides unusual insight into the perils presented by monks with insatiable appetites for sex with adolescents.[20] Nephon Gerbenites, a hieromonk from an unnamed monastery, had been a monk for thirty-six years, but he was unable to abide by his vows of chastity. Chomatenos accuses him of fornication, adultery, and even murder; the charges are vague, but the archbishop focuses on Gerbenites's obsession with *paides*, boys or teenagers. He orders him to leave his monastery and adopt the life of a solitary in a place where he will not be tempted by the presence of young men. If one reads between the lines, Chomatenos seems to be arguing that it is easier for a hermit to avoid pederasty because he is not surrounded by temptations, whereas a cenobitic monk must constantly resist the allure of young novices. Thus, the maintenance of sexual purity is not as difficult for a hermit as for a monk in a monastery. Chomatenos does not seem to recognize the reality that many hermits had teenage disciples as servants.

In contrast to the *typika*, which not surprisingly almost uniformly favor cenobitism, hagiography presents a range of attitudes on the question of which mode of monastic life is superior; it gives a positive view of cenobitism in the *vita* of a great monastic founder or superior such as Theodore of Stoudios and praises the solitary life in the *vitae* of holy hermits. After Euthymios, the future patriarch of Constantinople (907–12), became superior of a monastery in Constantinople, he became discontented and considered withdrawing to a holy mountain. He was discouraged from this move, however, by the superior of the Stoudios monastery, who reassured him that if he continued his pattern of extraordinarily compassionate behavior, even though he remained in a *koinobion* in Constantinople, he would be blessed by the holy fathers, for his gift of compassion surpassed "retreat to the mountain or the far desert."[21] Euthymios's anonymous hagiographer clearly believed that charity in an urban environment outweighed asceticism in the wilderness.

Neilos of Rossano (ca. 910–1004), on the other hand, is described by his biographer as preferring the eremitic life for the following reasons:

> He often reflected on the sweetness of spiritual tranquility and the freedom from care that results from poverty, and how the spiritual athlete who lives among brethren does not advance in virtue, but despite himself falls short in his quest. Neilos took all this into account and was much disturbed by his cohabitation with many people. He was annoyed even to meet them, as this distracted him from mental contemplation and the hidden, interior labor, which only the monastic companions of . . . the divinely inspired [desert] fathers had experienced.[22]

Yet surprisingly, Neilos also admitted that he viewed the cenobitic regimen as more demanding than that of the solitary and said that he and his companions were living as hermits because they could not endure the rigors of communal life.[23]

The *vitae* of holy hermits present them as surmounting terrible physical hardships, essentially totally disregarding their bodily needs, and achieving a spiritual focus that sometimes enables them to attain divine enlightenment and ecstatic union with God. They also acquire miraculous powers, such as clairvoyance and prophecy, the ability to heal, to bilocate, to levitate, and even to fly. At the same time, even their hagiographers may reveal a critical attitude toward their heroes and some concerns about their withdrawal from society.

In the ninth century, Ioannikios of Bithynia, for example, came to passionately desire a totally solitary life, for during his thirteen-year residence in a cave he was besieged by pious visitors. So he withdrew to an even more remote region, because he "could not endure being disturbed by interaction with humans, but wished to live immaterially and purely and without distraction and to converse by himself with God alone." After a while, however, he had a vision in which an angel instructed him to return to his original hermitage "so as not to conceal himself, since God had arranged this for the salvation and benefit of many."[24]

Similarly, in the eleventh century, while Cyril Phileotes was living as a hermit, he expressed doubts about his isolation from society because of his inability to provide charity to his fellow humans. He also felt that true humility was impossible if one was living in solitude, as was the spirit of generosity.[25]

These concerns expressed by hagiographers of the middle Byzantine period that hermits' withdrawal from society prevented them from providing charity and spiritual counsel is also found in later centuries. One of the most memorable passages in the late Byzantine *vita* of Maximos the Hutburner by Theophanes is Maximos's encounter with the famous hesychast monk Gregory of Sinai, who rebuked Maximos for his total avoidance of human interaction and urged him to settle down in one place so that he could associate with his fellow humans, share his spiritual wisdom and insights, and teach them by example.[26] Gregory reminded Maximos of Jesus's words, "Let your light shine before men" and not before rocks.[27] In Ioannikios Kochylas's version of the *vita*, Gregory stressed that in the Gospels the disciples are described as ministering to the world and not withdrawing to mountains and wilderness.[28] Likewise, the superior of the Great Lavra criticized Maximos's contemporary, Niphon of Athos, for a lack of humility in undertaking an extreme ascetic regimen in which he survived by foraging for wild plants. He was told this mortification was excessive, and that moderation was preferable.[29]

The debate on the merits of the two main models of monastic life was to continue until the final centuries of Byzantium, as both cenobitism and eremitism continued to thrive. A number of monks tried to combine the two forms of monastic life by becoming *kelliotai* associated with monasteries, where they would go on weekends for liturgical services and a communal meal. One of the clearest descriptions of this hybrid monasticism is found in the *typikon* for the monastery of Christodoulos on Patmos, where the superior maintained close oversight over the twelve solitaries attached to his institution. Here even the solitary should "preserve his subjection and his obedience [to the superior] wholly unshaken." Christodoulos was concerned that the solitaries should observe a regular routine of hymns, prayers, and "inspired spiritual labors," and should also do handwork to ward off despondency. They were to hand their finished handicrafts over to the superior so he could monitor their work. If a solitary failed to observe these rules, he would be brought back to the monastery and demoted to the rank of novice.[30]

On the other hand, as we have seen in the case of Euthymios the Younger, who was successively a solitary, stylite, and cenobite, yet other monks attempted to resolve the dilemma by engaging in several types of monasticism at different stages of their careers. In the memorable words of the biographer of Sabas the Younger, who was at various times a wandering monk, holy fool, hermit, cenobite, and recluse: "Since there are many dwellings in the kingdom of heaven, thus the road of piety which leads thereto must branch into many pathways; it is appropriate for one man to walk one of the paths, for another man—another; for a third man—several of them, and for a fourth man—all of them, if he is able [to do so]."[31]

GLOSSARY

abaton: the principle that a monastery was inaccessible to individuals of the opposite sex

adelphaton: an annual food allowance from a monastery

akedia: a type of despondency or depression, most likely to afflict solitary hermits

enkleistos (*enkleistoi*, pl.): a recluse; a monk or nun who enclosed him- or herself within a confined space, usually for a limited period of time

enkleistra (*enkleistron*): the enclosure in which a recluse lived; it could be a cave, cell, hut, or tower

geron (*gerontes*, pl.): a monastic elder

hieromonk (*hieromonachos*): an ordained monk

hyperpyron: a Byzantine gold coin introduced in the late eleventh century; in late Byzantium it became a money of account

iconoclast: an opponent of icon veneration

iconodule: a supporter of icon veneration

idiorrhythmic: a type of monastery in which monks followed an individualistic rather than a communal regimen, eating in their cells and earning money for their handwork

kathisma: a very small monastery or monastic cell

katholikon (*katholika*, pl.): the main church of a monastery

kellion (*kellia*, pl.): either a cell in a monastery or a hermitage in the wilderness

kelliotes (*kelliotai*, pl.): the inhabitant of a *kellion*, usually a solitary

koinobion: a cenobitic monastery, which emphasized common worship in the church and common meals in the refectory *lavra*: a hybrid form of monastery in which monks lived in dispersed cells at some distance from the monastery, but returned to it on weekends to attend the liturgy and eat in the refectory

metochion: a smaller satellite monastery that is a dependency of a larger monastery

skete: a small monastic settlement, dependent on a mother monastery

stabilitas loci: monastic stability, the obligation of a monk or nun to remain for life in the monastery where he or she had taken monastic vows

stylite: a pillar saint, who lived atop a column

typikon: generic term for a monastic rule

vita: the biography of a holy man or woman

NOTES

PREFACE

1. (60) Charsianeites [B2], *BMFD* 4:1641 (my translation).

INTRODUCTION

1. For a summary of the contents of these rules, see John Thomas in *BMFD*, 1:21–32.

2. Haim Goldfus, "Urban Monasticism and Monasteries of Early Byzantine Palestine: Preliminary Observations," *ARAM Periodical* 15 (2003): 71–79.

3. On the early phases of monasticism in Syria, see Sidney Griffith, "Asceticism in the Church of Syria: The Hermeneutics of Early Syrian Monasticism," in *Asceticism*, ed. Vincent L. Wimbush and Richard Valantasis (New York: Oxford University Press, 1995), 220–45, esp. 220–23 and 235–38.

4. Joseph Patrich, *Sabas, Leader of Palestinian Monasticism: A Comparative Study in Eastern Monasticism, Fourth to Seventh Centuries* (Washington, DC: Dumbarton Oaks, 1995).

5. Peter Hatlie, *The Monks and Monasteries of Constantinople, ca. 350–850* (Cambridge: Cambridge University Press, 2007), 25–132.

6. Gilbert Dagron, "Les moines et la ville: Le monachisme à Constantinple jusqu'au concile de Chalcédoine (451)," *Travaux et Mémoires* 4 (1970): 253n125.

7. Aristeides Papadakis, "Byzantine Monasticism Reconsidered," *Byzantinoslavica* 47 (1986): 40 and n36.

8. See Klaus Belke, "Heilige Berge Bithyniens," in *Heilige Berge und Wüsten: Byzanz und sein Umfeld. Referate auf dem 21. Internationalen*

Kongress für Byzantinistik. London, 21.–26. August 2006, ed. Peter Soustal (Vienna: Österreichische Akademie der Wissenschaften, 2009), 15–24.

9. See Alice-Mary Talbot, "Les saintes montagnes à Byzance," in *Le sacré et son inscription dans l'espace à Byzance et en Occident*, ed. Michel Kaplan (Paris: Publications de la Sorbonne, 2001), 263–75 (with earlier bibliography).

10. Janin, *Grands centres*, 43–50. There has been controversy as to Stephen's death date. In opting for 765, I have followed Marie-France Auzépy's dating in *Vita of Stephen the Younger*, 1.

11. Janin, *Grands centres*, 127–91. The term "Mount Olympos" also includes the plain at the foot of the mountain.

12. See Talbot, "Les saintes montagnes," 265–66.

13. See *Rule of Saint Benedict*.

14. For such an assertion, see Johannes Quasten, *Patrology* (Westminster, MD: Newman Press, 1960), 3:213: "The Basilians are the one great order of the Orient," which is refuted by Cyril Mango, *Byzantium: The Empire of New Rome* (New York: Weidenfeld and Nicolson, 1980), 110, and by John Thomas in *BMFD* 1:22.

15. See *BMFD* 1:21–29.

16. As does John Thomas in *BMFD* 1:10, I am excluding from consideration here the more general monastic rules compiled by Pachomios and Basil of Caesarea in late antiquity.

17. (1) Apa Abraham and (2) Pantelleria Typikon, *BMFD* 1:51–66.

18. For English translation of the so-called Testament of Theodore, see *BMFD* 1:67–83. For the history of its composition, see the definitive article by Olivier Delouis, "Le *Testament* de Théodore Stoudite, est-il de Théodore?" *Revue des études byzantines* 66 (2008): 173–90, and Delouis, "Le Testament de Théodore Stoudite: Édition critique et traduction," *Revue des études byzantines* 67 (2009): 77–109.

19. (4) Stoudios Rule, *BMFD* 1:84–119.

20. *BMFD* 2:608.

21. For discussion of Athanasios of Athos, see chapter 1, section "St. Athanasios of Athos and the Great Lavra."

22. See *ODB* 3:1946–47, s.v. "stauropegion."

23. John Thomas, *Private Religious Foundations in the Byzantine Empire* (Washington, DC: Dumbarton Oaks, 1987).

24. *BMFD* 1:49–50, 3:1093–1106.

25. For further details, see Peter Charanis, "The Monk as an Element of Byzantine Society," *Dumbarton Oaks Papers* 25 (1971): 69–73; and Alice-Mary Talbot, "A Comparison of the Monastic Experience of Byzantine Men and Women," *Greek Orthodox Theological Review* 30 (1985): 19–20, table 2.

26. See Charanis, "The Monk as an Element of Byzantine Society," 63–66.

27. Anthony Bryer, "The Late Byzantine Monastery in Town and Countryside," *Studies in Church History* 16 (1979): 219. See also Talbot, "A Comparison of the Monastic Experience," 18, table 1.

28. Janin, *Eglises CP*.

29. For a useful survey of the written sources for the early period of Byzantine monasticism, up to the tenth century, see Vincent Déroche, "La vie des moines: Les sources pour l'Asie Mineure et les Balkans, ca. 300–1000 apr. J.C.," in *La vie quotidienne des moines en Orient et en Occident, IVe–Xe siècle. I. L'état des sources*, ed. Olivier Delouis and Maria Mossakowska-Gaubert (Athens: École française d'Athènes; Cairo: Institut français d'archéologie orientale, 2015), 275–87.

30. A prime example is the liturgical *typikon* from the Evergetis Monastery in Constantinople; see *The Synaxarion of the Monastery of the Theotokos Evergetis*, ed. and trans. Robert H. Jordan, 3 vols. (Belfast: Belfast Byzantine Enterprises, the Institute of Byzantine Studies, the Queen's University of Belfast, 2000–2007).

31. *BMFD*: http://www.doaks.org/resources/publications/books-in-print/byzantine-monastic-foundation-documents-a-complete.

32. (57) Bebaia Elpis, ch. 4–11, *BMFD* 4:1524–26; (58) Menoikeion, ch. 1, *BMFD* 4:1591–94.

33. See, for example, Robert Jordan's masterful linguistic analysis of this *typikon* or *hypotyposis*, which strongly suggests that the preserved version by Timothy, the second founder of the monastery, was based on an earlier version by Paul, the original founder; see chapter 17 of the introduction, "A Pauline Hypotyposis?" and appendix 1, "The *Typikon* of Paul Evergetinos: A Reconstruction," in *The Hypotyposis of the Monastery of the Theotokos Evergetis, Constantinople (11th–12th Centuries)*, ed. Robert H. Jordan and Rosemary Morris (Farnham: Ashgate, 2012), 127–35, and 217–39.

34. This process is facilitated for users of *BMFD*, which sets passages from earlier *typika* in bold font.

35. For discussion of the use of hagiography as a source for social and economic history, see Michel Kaplan and Eleonora Kountoura-Galake, "Economy and Society in Byzantine Hagiography: Realia and Methodological Questions," in *The Ashgate Research Companion to Byzantine Hagiography* (Farnham: Ashgate, 2014), 2:389–418.

36. See Thomas Pratsch, *Der hagiographische Topos: Griechische Heiligenviten in mittelbyzantinischer Zeit* (Berlin: De Gruyter, 2005).

37. See Denis Sullivan, "The Versions of the Vita Niconis," *Dumbarton Oaks Papers* 32 (1978): 159–73; and *Vita of Nikon*, 7–18.

38. Alice-Mary Talbot, "Fact and Fiction in the *Vita* of the Patriarch Athanasios I of Constantinople by Theoktistos the Stoudite," in *Les Vies des saints à Byzance: Genre littéraire ou biographie historique? Actes du IIe colloque international philologique. Paris, 6-7-8 juin 2002*, ed. Paolo Odorico and Panagiotis Agapitos (Paris: Centre d'études byzantines, néo-helléniques et sud-est européennes, 2004), 87–101; and Talbot, "The Compositional Methods of a Palaiologan Hagiographer: Intertextuality in the Works of Theoktistos the Stoudite," in *Imitatio—Aemulatio—Variatio: Akten des internationalen wissenschaftlichen Symposions zur byzantinischen Sprache und Literatur (Wien, 22.–25. Oktober 2008)*, ed. Andreas Rhoby and Elisabeth Schiffer (Vienna: Österreichische Akademie der Wissenschaften, 2010), 253–59.

39. See *Vita of Theoktiste of Lesbos*, 96; Stavroula Constantinou, "A Byzantine Hagiographical Parody: *Life of Mary the Younger*," *Byzantine and Modern Greek Studies* 34, no. 2 (2010): 160–81.

40. On the *vita* of the patriarch Athanasios, see Talbot, "Fact and Fiction," esp. 87–92. On the *vita* of Palamas, see, for example, Anna Philippidis-Braat, "La captivité de Palamas chez les Turcs: Dossier et commentaire," *Travaux et Mémoires* 7 (1979): 120–22.

41. See https://www.doaks.org/research/byzantine/resources/hagiography-database. The "General Introduction to the Database Project," 2–4, contains information on the project's philosophy of mining "realia" of everyday life from hagiographic sources, which has greatly influenced my own research.

42. The database Άγιολογία Ύστερης Βυζαντινής Περιόδου (1204–1453) may be consulted at http://byzhadb.eie.gr/.

43. The Archives de l'Athos project, carried out primarily by French and Greek scholars, has been ongoing in Paris since the 1930s and has resulted in the publication of twenty-two volumes to date.

44. All the preserved documents of this sort were published in the nineteenth century by Franz Miklosich and Joseph Müller, *Acta et diplomata graeca medii aevi sacra et profana*, 6 vols. (Vienna: C. Gerold, 1860–1890). A new critical edition of the patriarchal acts of the fourteenth century is in preparation in Vienna; to date, three volumes have appeared; see *RPK*. And see *RegPatr* for an essential finding aid for consultation of this material.

45. See, for example, the important article by Ekaterini Mitsiou, "Late Byzantine Female Monasticism from the Point of View of the Register of the Patriarchate of Constantinople," in *The Register of the Patriarchate of Constantinople: An Essential Source for the History and Church of Late Byzantium*, Proceedings of the International Symposium, Vienna, May 5–9, 2009, ed. Christian Gastgeber, Ekaterini Mitsiou, and Johannes Preiser-Kapeller (Vienna, 2013), 161–74.

46. The classic work on this topic is still Anastasios Orlandos, *Μοναστηριακὴ Ἀρχιτεκτονική: κείμενον καὶ σχέδια* (Athens: Hestia, 1958).

47. See Paul Mylonas, *Pictorial Dictionary of the Holy Mountain Athos* (Tübingen: Wasmuth, 2000).

48. See the comments of Olivier Delouis, "Portée et limites de l'archéologie monastique dans les Balkans et en Asie Mineure jusqu'au Xe siècle," in Delouis and Mossakowska-Gaubert, *La vie quotidienne des moines*, 251–74. On page 255, he notes that in general there is very little archaeological evidence for monastic construction in the Balkans before the tenth century. Some of the most important excavations of monasteries in Greece have taken place at the Synaxis Monastery and on Mount Papikion in Thrace, and at Zygos, just west of the boundary of Athos.

49. See Nikos Zekos, *Παπίκιον Ορος: αρχαιολογικός οδηγός* (Makedonia: Synolo/Ekdoses Periphereia An. Makedonias-Thrakes, 2001).

50. Catherine Jolivet-Lévy, "La vie des moines en Cappadoce (VIe–Xe siècle): Contribution à un inventaire des sources archéologiques," in Delouis and Mossakowska-Gaubert, *La vie quotidienne des moines*, 215–49.

CHAPTER 1. Monks and Male Monastic Communities

1. For the reliability of Theodore's letters and catecheses as historical sources, see Vincent Déroche, "La vie des moines," 281.

2. One *vita* is by Michael the Monk, a second perhaps by Theodore Daphnopates, and the third is anonymous (*BHG* 1754, 1755, and 1755d). An English translation of the *vita* by Michael the Monk is being prepared by Robert Jordan and Rosemary Morris for the Dumbarton Oaks Medieval Library.

3. Greek editions of the two *vitae* were prepared by Jacques Noret, *Vitae duae antiquae sancti Athanasii Athonitae* (Turnhout: Brepols, 1982), and an English translation of *vita* B was recently published by Alice-Mary Talbot in Richard Greenfield and Alice-Mary Talbot, *Holy Men of Mount Athos* (Cambridge, MA: Harvard University Press, 2016), 128–367. English translations of the documents about the Great Lavra are to be found in *BMFD* 1:205–31, 245–80.

4. The most complete study of the monastery is the doctoral dissertation by Olivier Delouis, "Saint-Jean-Baptiste de Stoudios à Constantinople: La contribution d'un monastère à l'histoire de l'empire byzantin," 2 vols. (Ph.D. diss., Université Paris I/Panthéon-Sorbonne, 2005).

5. For the most recent biography of Theodore, see Thomas Pratsch, *Theodoros Studites: Zwischen Dogma und Pragma* (Frankfurt: P. Lang, 1998).

6. Delouis, *Stoudios*, 1:232–39.

7. Thomas Mathews, *The Byzantine Churches of Istanbul: A Photographic Survey* (University Park: Pennsylvania State University Press, 1976), 143–58; Mathews, *The Early Churches of Constantinople: Architecture and Liturgy* (University Park: Pennsylvania State University Press, 1971), 19–27.

8. *Vita of Theodore of Stoudios by Michael*, ch. 65, *PG* 99:323C.

9. For detailed discussion of the generation and authorship of this document, and a new critical edition, see Delouis, "Le *Testament* de Théodore Stoudite, est-il de Théodore?" and Delouis, "Le Testament de Théodore Stoudite: Édition critique et traduction." For an English translation of the so-called Testament of Theodore and commentary, see *BMFD* 1:67–83.

10. For an English translation of the *typikon* plus commentary, see (4) Stoudios, *BMFD* 1:84–119.

11. On daily life at Stoudios, see Jules Leroy, "La vie quotidienne du moine stoudite," *Irénikon* 27 (1954): 21–50; Delouis, *Stoudios*, 239–83.

12. (4) Stoudios, ch. 1A, *BMFD* 1:97.

13. John Thomas, "Document Notes [4]," in *BMFD* 1:81.

14. See (3) Theodore Stoudites: Testament, ch. 4, *BMFD* 1:77.

15. *Vita of Theodore of Stoudios by Michael*, ch. 29, *PG* 99:273B–C. The emphasis on artisanal labor seems to have been an innovation of Theodore; certainly no other contemporary monastery supported the same diversity of crafts as Stoudios.

16. (3) Theodore Stoudites: Testament, ch. 5, *BMFD* 1:77. This prohibition was also later observed on Athos.

17. John Thomas, in *BMFD* 1:86.

18. (4) Stoudios, ch. 26, *BMFD* 1:108.

19. Ibid., ch. 37A, 38B, *BMFD* 1:113–15.

20. *Epitimia*, ch. 29, *PG* 99:1736; see also Delouis, *Stoudios*, 1:261–62.

21. See chapter 22 of *Rule of Saint Benedict*, where the monks are enjoined to "all sleep in one place," but in separate beds. A fine example of a very large twelfth-century dormitory is still preserved today at the Cistercian abbey of Fontenay in Burgundy, which was abandoned in 1789 during the French Revolution.

22. See, for example, a passage in Theodore of Stoudios, *Great Catechesis* I.57.24–25, which suggests that there was some sharing of rooms, since Theodore warned that the beds of young monks should not be placed close together, lest their bodies come into contact. For further discussion of this issue and textual references, see Leroy, "La vie quotidienne du moine stoudite," 30–31, who is unsure how to interpret the conflicting and ambiguous evidence. Delouis does not seem to address the matter in his monumental study of the Stoudios monastery. I should like to express my gratitude to Alexis Torrance, who provided me with some of the relevant bibliography on this question, but he himself is uncertain about the sleeping arrangements at Stoudios (personal communication of March 6, 2018).

23. *Vita of Symeon the New Theologian*, ch. 11.

24. (4) Stoudios, ch. 37A, 38B, *BMFD* 1:115.

25. Delouis, *Stoudios*, 1:267–73.

26. Ibid., 1:245–46.

27. Ibid., 1:247.

28. (4) Stoudios, ch. 29, *BMFD* 1:109–10.

29. Ibid., ch. 30, *BMFD* 1:110–11.

30. Ibid., ch. 28, *BMFD* 1:109.

31. The Greek text of the penances (*epitimia*) is in *PG* 99:1733–58; on them, see Delouis, *Stoudios*, 1:275–76.

32. (4) Stoudios, ch. 25, *BMFD* 1:108AB.

33. See the definition by Kallistos Ware, *The Lenten Triodion*, trans. Mother Mary and Archimandrite Kallistos Ware (London: Faber and Faber, 1978), 35–36. I thank Fr. Damaskenos (Jaakko Olkinuora) of the Athonite monastery of Xenophontos for this reference and additional information on *xerophagia*.

34. *Epitimia*, ch. 36, 40; *PG* 99:1737.

35. Ibid., ch. 43–44, 46; *PG* 99:1737–40.

36. Ibid., ch. 86; *PG* 99:1744.

37. Ibid., ch. 71–72; *PG* 99:1741.

38. Ibid., ch. 99–104; *PG* 99:1745–48.

39. Ibid., ch. 105–6; *PG* 99:1748.

40. Ibid., ch. 50 (shoemaker), 61 (tailor), 87 (carpenter), and 109 (weaver); *PG* 99:1740, 1744, 1748.

41. *Vita of Theodore of Stoudios by Michael*, ch. 36, *PG* 99:285B.

42. *Epitimia*, ch. 76–78, 80, 91–92; *PG* 99:1744–45.

43. Ibid., ch. 47–49; *PG* 99:1740.

44. Jeffrey Michael Featherstone and Meridel Holland, "A Note on Penances Prescribed for Negligent Scribes and Librarians in the Monastery of Stoudios," *Scriptorium* 36 (1982): 258–60.

45. The Greek text of ch. 54 in *PG* 99 has ἀντίστιχα (unattested in *Thesaurus Linguae Graecae*), which should be emended to ἀντίστοιχα, meaning "diphthongs"; see Featherstone and Holland, "A Note on Penances," 259 and n3.

46. *Epitimia*, ch. 53–60; *PG* 99:1740.

47. On minuscule script, see *ODB* 2:1377–78. For doubts about its origins in the Stoudios monastery, see Nigel Wilson, *Scholars of Byzantium*, rev. ed. (London: Duckworth, 1996), 66.

48. *ODB* 3:2145.

49. It should thus be contrasted with Mount Latros near Miletos, Mount Galesion near Ephesos, Mount Olympos near Prousa, and Mount St. Auxentios near Constantinople.

50. Note *Vita B of Athanasios of Athos* (ch. 35.2), which states, "Since the seacoast near the monastery [the Great Lavra] lacked any natural harbor whatsoever and was precipitous, it did not permit anchorage ... for the monastery's ships." Also (13) Ath. Typikon, ch. 10, *BMFD* 1:253: "The seashore along the mountain was precipitous and without any

harbors on both sides, to the north, that is, and to the south, for more than eighty miles."

51. *Actes du Prôtaton*, 3.

52. Unfortunately, the hagiographer gives no details of Athanasios's curriculum in "grammar" (*grammatike*), but it must have included the study of classical literature, especially poetry and perhaps rhetoric. My biographical account of Athanasios's formative years is based on his two *vitae*; although the data on his youth cannot be verified, much of the later parts of the *vitae* on his foundation of the Great Lavra can be corroborated by other sources, and on the whole the *vitae* seem reasonably reliable. For the most recent discussion on the two *vitae* and a lost original version, see Dirk Krausmüller, "An Ascetic Founder: The Lost First Life of Athanasius the Athonite," in *Founders and Refounders of Byzantine Monasteries*, ed. Margaret Mullett (Belfast: Belfast Byzantine Enterprises, Institute of Byzantine Studies, Queen's University of Belfast, 2007), 63–86. For an English translation of *vita* B, see Greenfield and Talbot, *Holy Men of Mount Athos*, 128–367.

53. *Vita B of Athanasios of Athos*, ch. 8.1.

54. Michael, who belonged to a prominent family from Asia Minor, became a saint; see *Vita of Michael Maleinos*, 543–68.

55. *Vita B of Athanasios of Athos*, ch. 9.2–10.1.

56. For Athanasios's early days on Athos, see ibid., ch. 13–20.

57. On the early history of monasticism on Athos, see *Actes du Prôtaton*, 17–93, and Denise Papachryssanthou, Ὁ Ἀθωνικὸς μοναχισμός: ἀρχὲς καὶ ὀργάνωση (Athens: Morphotiko Hidryma Ethnikes Trapezes, 1992). These monasteries were likely quite small, however, and were soon abandoned or absorbed by the larger and later foundations; see Delouis, "Portée et limites de l'archéologie monastique," 261–62. For similar doubts about the true state of Patmos at the time of Christodoulos's arrival on the island, see Patricia Karlin-Hayter, "Notes sur les archives de Patmos comme source pour la démographie et l'économie de l'île," *Byzantinische Forschungen* 5 (1977): 189–215.

58. I thank Nathanael Aschenbrenner for this insight.

59. *Vita B of Athanasios of Athos*, ch. 21.1.

60. Ibid., ch. 21.4.

61. Ibid., ch. 22.3.

62. Ibid., ch. 23.1.

63. Ibid., ch. 25.

64. Size, of course, can be variously defined; I have used the criterion of area of buildings within the walled precincts, as calculated by Paul Mylonas, *Pictorial Dictionary of the Holy Mountain Athos*, vol. 1, fasc. 1, what he terms the "covered area." For the Great Lavra this area is 9,750 m². Its closest competitor was Iviron, built in the late tenth century, with a covered area of 9,023 m². Two other tenth-century Athonite monastic foundations were Vatopedi and Xenophontos, with covered areas of 7,715 m² and 5,700 m², respectively.

65. John Thomas in *BMFD* 1:207 and n13.

66. On this, see the analysis of John Thomas in *BMFD* 1:195–96.

67. *BMFD*, 1:207–8.

68. *Actes de Lavra*, Vol. 1, no. 5.13 (τῷ ἁγιωνύμῳ ὄρει).

69. Meyer, *Die Haupturkunden*, 104.8, 29; (13) Ath. Typikon, ch. 6–7, *BMFD* 1:251–52.

70. See (11) Ath. Rule, ch. 22, *BMFD* 1:226. The passages in bold italics are identical with those in the Stoudite rule (both versions A and B); the single word in boldface Roman type is copied only from version B.

71. Delouis, *Stoudios*, 2:481.

72. (11) Ath. Rule, ch. 35, combines the wording of ch. 37 of version A and ch. 38 of version B of the Stoudite rule; see *BMFD* 1:228. The words in bold italics are identical with those in versions A and B, words in plain italics are identical with those in version B.

73. On Athanasios's conversion to the cenobitic ideal, see Delouis, *Stoudios*, 2:480–84, and Jules Leroy, "La conversion de saint Athanase l'Athonite à l'idéal cénobitique et l'influence stoudite," in *Le millénaire du Mont Athos, 963–1963: Études et mélanges* (Chevetogne: Editions de Chevetogne, 1963), 1:101–20. Neither Delouis (who terms it "inexplicable") nor Leroy makes any attempt to explain Athanasios's sudden change of heart.

74. See (13) Ath. Typikon, *BMFD* 1:245–70. Curiously, Athanasios did not acknowledge his debt to Stoudite regulations; see Delouis, *Stoudios*, 2:481–82.

75. *Vita B of Athanasios of Athos*, ch. 25.4.

76. Ibid., ch. 35.4–5.

77. Ibid., ch. 41.1, 42.1, 51.1.

78. (11) Ath. Rule, ch. 30–31, *BMFD* 1:227–28.

79. *Vita B of Athanasios of Athos*, ch. 48.4.

80. Ibid., ch. 29.3.
81. Ibid., ch. 35.2, 40.4, 72.1, 77.1.
82. For Mylopotamos, see *Vita B of Athanasios of Athos*, ch. 49.1, 56.3, 62.1. These satellite or subsidiary monasteries, called *metochia*, followed the same rule as the Great Lavra and acknowledged obedience to its superior, who appointed their priests and stewards; see Nikos Svoronos, "Le domaine de Lavra jusqu'en 1204," in *Actes de Lavra*, 1:56–77.
83. For the island of Neoi, see *Vita B of Athanasios of Athos*, ch. 57.1; for prohibition of flocks, see (13) Ath. Typikon, ch. 53, *BMFD* 1:264.
84. *Vita B of Athanasios of Athos*, ch. 40.2, 54.1, 68.1, 46.1, 60.1. The mention of a hunter (ibid., ch. 52.3–4) is surprising. Could he have been employed to hunt wild game to feed the lay workmen?
85. Ibid., ch. 43.1.
86. Ibid., ch. 43.3–4.
87. Ibid., ch. 36.1.
88. Ibid., ch. 36.3–4.
89. (12) Tzimiskes, preface, *BMFD* 1:235.
90. *Vita B of Athanasios of Athos*, ch. 65–66.
91. See (22) Evergetis in *BMFD* 2:454–506, and Jordan and Morris, *Hypotyposis of the Monastery of the Theotokos Evergetis*.
92. Lyn Rodley has proposed a location in the western suburb of Bahçelievler; see Rodley, "Evergetis, Where It Was and What It Looked Like," in *The Theotokos Evergetis and Eleventh-Century Monasticism*, ed. Margaret Mullett and Anthony Kirby (Belfast: Belfast Byzantine Enterprises, School of Greek, Roman and Semitic Studies, the Queen's University of Belfast, 1994), 17–20. For the most recent discussion of the monastery's location, see Jordan and Morris, *Hypotyposis of the Monastery of the Theotokos Evergetis*, 16–17, and Andreas Külzer, *Ostthrakien (Europe)* (Vienna: Verlag der Österreichischen Akademie der Wissenschaften, 2008), 672–73.
93. See John Thomas, *BMFD* 2:468; and appendix C: "Topical Interrelationships of the Families of the Typika of the Byzantine Monastic Reform Movement," in *BMFD* 5:1717–23.
94. See John Thomas, *BMFD* 2:441–71.
95. Ibid., *BMFD* 2:468.
96. See *ODB* 2:981–82, s.v. "Idiorrhythmic monasticism." There is relatively little information on this form of monasticism in the Byzantine period, and the evidence is scattered; as a result there is virtually

no secondary literature on the subject. On the links between the rise of idiorrhythmic monasteries and the individualism of Byzantine society, see Alexander Kazhdan and Giles Constable, *People and Power in Byzantium: An Introduction to Modern Byzantine Studies* (Washington, DC: Dumbarton Oaks, 1982), 91.

97. An act dated to 1296; see *Actes de Vatopédi*, Vol. 1, act no. 24.2–3.

98. (31) Areia, ch. [T] 10, *BMFD* 3:967.

99. *Vita of Neilos of Rossano*, ch. 71.1: ἰδιορρύθμως προσκαρτερήσαντες τῷ μοναστηρίῳ.

100. *Vita of Lazaros of Galesion*, ch. 17 and n89.

101. Ibid., ch. 147.

102. (21) Roidion, *BMFD* 1:425–39.

103. (21) Roidion, ch. B6, *BMFD* 1:432.

104. *Actes de Vatopédi*, 1, no. 15.99–103, where the name is correctly rendered as "Boreine"; its name was originally misread as "Skoteine," a misspelling still found in *BMFD*; for English translation, see (35) Skoteine, ch. 13, *BMFD* 3:1183.

105. See (60) Charsianeites, ch. B18, *BMFD* 4:1648–50.

106. Ibid., ch. B8, *BMFD* 4:1644.

107. Ibid., ch. [C]3, *BMFD* 4:1653 (my translation).

108. Meyer, *Die Haupturkunden*, 57–64.

109. *Actes de Docheiariou*, 18 and act no. 35, pp. 208–13. In the fourteenth century, the *hyperpyron*, originally a gold coin, had become money of account; see *ODB* 2:964–65.

110. (51) Koutloumousiou, ch. B16, *BMFD* 4:1423.

111. *Actes de Kutlumus*, no. 39.9–14 (p. 146), with revised commentary and notes on p. 393.

112. *Actes du Pantocrator*, 153 and nos. 17.81–82, 22.42 (οὐδὲ ἰδιόριθμον τι κτῆμα τὸν μοναχὸν κτήσασθαι διακελευόμεθα), and 23.28–29 (εἴ τις ... ἰδιόρριθμον κτήσεται κινητὸν ἢ ἀκίνητον ἰδιοποιησάμενος αὐτὸ ὁπωσδήποτε).

113. (59) Manuel II, ch. 1, *BMFD* 4:1618.

114. Graham Speake, *Mount Athos: Renewal in Paradise* (New Haven, CT: Yale University Press, 2002), 109.

115. Ibid., 181–82, 206–7.

116. In the past fifteen years, several important studies on Byzantine eunuchs have appeared; see, for example, Kathryn M. Ringrose, *The*

Perfect Servant: Eunuchs and the Social Construction of Gender in Byzantium (Chicago: University of Chicago Press, 2003); Shaun Tougher, *The Eunuch in Byzantine History and Society* (London: Routledge, 2008); and Charis Messis, *Les eunuques à Byzance, entre réalité et imaginaire* (Paris: Centre d'études byzantines, néo-helléniques et sud-est européennes, 2014).

117. For an example of a father arranging for his son's castration, see the short *vita* of St. Metrios in *SynaxCP*, 721–24, and Ringrose, *The Perfect Servant*, 188–91.

118. On eunuchs and monasteries, see Messis, *Les eunuques à Byzance*, 111–15.

119. (12) Typikon of Tzimiskes, ch. 16, *BMFD* 1:238.

120. (13) Ath. Typikon, ch. 48, *BMFD* 1:263.

121. (15) Typikon of Constantine IX, ch. 1, *BMFD* 1:285.

122. *Théophylacte d'Achrida: Discours, traités, poésies*, ed. and trans. Paul Gautier (Thessalonike: Association de recherches byzantines, 1980), 1:115–17 and 328–29.

123. On the whole episode, see Rosemary Morris, "Symeon the Sanctified and the Re-foundation of Xenophon," *Byzantine and Modern Greek Studies* 33 (2009): 133–47.

124. (59) Manuel II, ch. 13, *BMFD* 4:1621.

125. See Niels Gaul, "Eunuchs in the Late Byzantine Empire, c. 1250–1400," in *Eunuchs in Antiquity and Beyond*, ed. Shaun Tougher (London: Classical Press of Wales and Duckworth, 2002), 199–219. Gaul has calculated that only about 15 of the 30,000 individuals listed in *PLP* were undeniably eunuchs. The decline in the demand for eunuchs in late Byzantium should probably be related to the increasing role of the imperial family at court from the Komnenian period (1081–1185) on.

126. (23) Pakourianos, ch. 17; (24) Christodoulos, ch. A10, *BMFD* 2:541, 583.

127. (29) Kosmosoteira, ch. 3 and 55, *BMFD* 2:800, 824.

128. For Symeon, see Paul Magdalino, "Paphlagonians in Byzantine High Society," in *Η βυζαντινή Μικρά Ασία*, ed. Stelios Lampakes (Athens: Ethniko Hidryma Ereunon, Institouto Vyzantinon Ereunon, 1998), 145; for Arsenios, see *BMFD* 3:974.

129. On Symeon as a eunuch, see Magdalino, "Paphlagonians in Byzantine High Society," and Messis, *Les eunuques à Byzance*, 144–48.

The text of Symeon's *vita* that has come down to us is an abridged version of the original that is reticent about Symeon's castration, but it does provide two important pieces of evidence that he was a eunuch.

130. *Vita of Symeon the New Theologian*, ch. 11.

131. See (3) Theodore Studites, ch. 18, *BMFD* 1:78.

132. *PmbZ* 2, no. 25576.

133. *Vita of Nikephoros of Miletos*, ch. 15.18–20 (my translation).

134. The best discussion of this topic is Shaun Tougher, "The Angelic Life: Monasteries for Eunuchs," in *Byzantine Style, Religion and Civilisation, in Honour of Sir Steven Runciman*, ed. Elizabeth Jeffreys (Cambridge: Cambridge University Press, 2006), 238–52. His research has shown that there were actually fewer monasteries reserved for eunuchs than originally thought.

135. *Vita of Lazaros of Galesion*, 189–90, n435.

136. Janin, *Eglises CP*, 298–300.

137. (19) Attaleiates, ch. 30, *BMFD* 1:348–49.

138. *Vita of Lazaros of Galesion*, ch. 100.

139. Margaret Mullett, "Theophylact of Ohrid's *In Defense of Eunuchs*," in Tougher, *Eunuchs in Antiquity and Beyond*, 177–98.

140. Theophylact of Ohrid, *In Defense of Eunuchs*, 329.9–15. Early and medieval monks (both Greek and Latin) often saw nocturnal emission as a sign of imperfect chastity and sought, by restricting their food and water intake, to "dry up" the excessive liquid that caused emission of semen. See David Brakke, "The Problematization of Nocturnal Emissions in Early Christian Syria, Egypt, and Gaul," *Journal of Early Christian Studies* 3 (1995): 419–60, and *Vita of Neilos of Rossano*, ch. 16.3.

141. Mullett, "Theophylact of Ohrid's *In Defense of Eunuchs*," 186–91.

142. For further discussion, see chapter 2, subsection "Male Staff," 82–83.

143. See Giles Constable in *BMFD* 1:xi–xxxvii.

144. On evolving attitudes to this issue in the West, see *BMFD* 1:xviii.

145. *BMFD* 1:xxiv; *PLP*, statistics compiled by the author from the indices.

146. *BMFD* 1:xx–xxi; Alice-Mary Talbot, "The Adolescent Monastic in Middle and Late Byzantium," in *Coming of Age in Byzantium:*

Adolescence and Society, ed. Despoina Ariantzi (Berlin: De Gruyter, 2018), 83–97.

147. John Thomas, in *BMFD* 1:28.

148. *Vita B of Athanasios of Athos*, ch. 49.1, 57.1. For further examples, see Talbot, "The Adolescent Monastic in Middle and Late Byzantium."

149. "Monastic Schools," *New Catholic Encyclopedia*, accessed June 20, 2017, https://www.encyclopedia.com/religion/encyclopedias-almanacs-transcripts-and-maps/monastic-schools.

150. See Alice-Mary Talbot, "Personal Poverty in Byzantine Monasticism: Ideals and Reality," in *Mélanges Cécile Morrisson* [= *Travaux et Mémoires*, 16] (Paris: Association des Amis du Centre d'Histoire et Civilisation de Byzance, 2010), 829–41.

151. (22) Evergetis, ch. 22, *BMFD* 2:490.

152. *Vita of Lazaros of Galesion*, ch. 138 and n537.

153. See note 21, above, for reference to the *Rule of Saint Benedict*, which stipulates that if possible all monks should sleep in one place.

154. Novel 5.3, lines 29–36 (*CIC* 3:31): "We decree that [the monks] should take their meals together and all sleep together, each of them lying on his own individual pallet, reclining in a single chamber; or if one chamber does not suffice for the multitude of monks, then in two or more chambers, not privately and by themselves, but together, so that they can attest to each other's decorum and chastity" (my translation).

155. *Vita of Paul of Latros*, ch. 17.30.

156. See Maria Dembińska, "Diet: A Comparison of Food Consumption Between Some Eastern and Western Monasteries in the 4th–12th Centuries," *Byzantion* 55 (1985): 453, and tables at end of article; her arguments are based on data from three Western monasteries of the ninth century and three Byzantine monasteries of the eleventh and twelfth centuries.

157. See, for example, the rare specific prohibitions of meat in (20) Black Mountain, ch. 42R, *BMFD* 1:397; (34) Machairas, ch. 115, *BMFD* 3:1155; and the comments of John Thomas in Appendix 2, *BMFD* 5:1696; none of the sixty-one documents in this collection permits the consumption of meat. The *typika* for two Sicilian monasteries of the twelfth century note that during the period of the Arab conquest and occupation of the island, the monks lapsed into meat-eating, but the new founders prohibit the practice. The *Epitimia* of Theodore of Stoudios (II.1, *PG* 99:1748D) do mention a penance for meat-eating, so it was not unknown

even in a Stoudite monastery; this provision also states that exceptions could be made for ailing monks. A meat-eating monk is mentioned in the *Vita of Meletios of Myoupolis by Nicholas of Methone,* 16. And there is the puzzling presence of animal bones in the excavations of some Byzantine monasteries (personal communication of December 28, 2002 from Svetlana Popović).

158. *Rule of Saint Benedict,* chaps. 36, 39.

159. Peter Abelard is a well-known example.

160. For further discussion of this topic, see the section "Eunuchs in Monasteries and Monasteries for Eunuchs," above.

161. Giles Constable, "Preface" to *BMFD* 1:xxvii. For more details on frequency of shaving in Latin monasteries, see Giles Constable, introduction to *Apologiae duae: Gozechini epistola ad Walcherum. Burchardi, ut videtur, abbatis Bellevallis apologia de Barbis,* ed. R. B. C. Huygens [= *Corpus Christianorum, Continuatio Medievalis,* 62] (Turnhout: Brepols, 1985), 114–30.

162. Linda Safran, *The Medieval Salento: Art and Identity in Southern Italy* (Philadelphia: University of Pennsylvania Press, 2014), 78–80.

163. Hans-Georg Beck, *Das byzantinische Jahrtausend* (Munich: Beck, 1978), 213.

164. (28) Pantokrator, ch. 27–28, *BMFD* 2:752–53.

165. The project, under the direction of Vasileios Marinis of Yale University, is provisionally entitled "The Monastery of Hosios Loukas and Its Dependencies: A Network of Foundations in Medieval Byzantium."

166. Morris, "Symeon the Sanctified," 141.

167. See (9) Galesion, ch. 191, *BMFD* 1:161.

CHAPTER 2.   Nuns and Nunneries

1. The very few examples of female hermits are discussed at the end of chapter 3; for the rare instances of female stylites and recluses, see chapter 4.

2. Balsamon, commentary on canon 47 of Council of Carthage, *PG* 138:176CD (my translation): "Only in female cenobitic monasteries are a common dietary regimen and sleeping arrangements observed. Among the Latins, however, such a mode of conduct is maintained. For all the

monks eat and sleep together (Εἰς μόνα δὲ τὰ γυναικεῖα κοινόβια μοναστήρια συντηρεῖται ἡ κοινὴ δίαιτα καὶ κατοικία. Εἰς δὲ τοὺς Λατίνους τέως ἡ τοιουτότροπος διαγωγὴ συντηρεῖται. Πάντες γὰρ οἱ μοναχοὶ ὁμοῦ καὶ ἐσθίουσι καὶ ὑπνώττουσιν)."

3. Eileen Power, *Medieval English Nunneries, c. 1275–1535* (Cambridge: Cambridge University Press, 1922).

4. See Catia Galatariotou, "Byzantine Women's Monastic Communities: The Evidence of the Typika," *Jahrbuch der Österreichischen Byzantinistik* 38 (1988): 263–90, for a convenient survey of the regulations of the *typika*.

5. Also preserved are the *vitae* of two married female saints who never took monastic vows, Mary of Vizye and Thomais of Lesbos. I will discuss in chapter 3 the *vita* of Theoktiste of Lesbos, who was briefly a cloistered nun, but at the age of eighteen she was captured by Arabs and ended up as a hermit on an isolated island. Information on Euphrosyne the Younger will be found in chapter 4, in the section "Recluses (*enkleistoi*)," 145–46. All these holy women are from the middle Byzantine period; the Palaiologan period produced scarcely any female saints, except for Theodora of Arta and Matrona of Chios, whose *vitae* provide little useful information. On female saints, see Alice-Mary Talbot, ed., *Holy Women of Byzantium* (Washington, DC: Dumbarton Oaks, 1996).

6. See Alice-Mary Talbot, "Empress Theodora Palaiologina, Wife of Michael VIII," *Dumbarton Oaks Papers* 46 (1992): 299n40; with further discussion by John Thomas in *BMFD* 3:1256.

7. See discussion in Jordan and Morris, *The Hypotyposis of the Monastery of the Theotokos Evergetis*, 139. The direct source of the Kecharitomene rule may be that of the male monastery of Christ Philanthropos, with which the Kecharitomene was closely affiliated.

8. For more on Theodora, see Alice-Mary Talbot, "Family Cults in Thessalonike: The Case of Theodora of Thessalonike," in *ΛΕΙΜΩΝ: Studies Presented to Lennart Rydén on His Sixty-Fifth Birthday*, ed. Jan Olof Rosenqvist (Uppsala: Uppsala University, 1996), 49–69, with full bibliography; and Michel Kaplan, "La vie de Théodora de Thessalonique: Un écrit familial," in *Approaches to the Byzantine Family*, ed. Leslie Brubaker and Shaun Tougher (Farnham: Ashgate, 2013), 285–301.

9. *Vita of Theodora of Thessalonike*, ch. 22. Athanasia, a ninth-century abbess on the island of Aegina, likewise distinguished herself

from the nuns under her supervision by her strict fasts, normally partaking of bread and water once a day, and during Lent subsisting on a diet of raw greens alone every other day, with no consumption of liquids. She never tasted fruit after taking monastic vows. She also wore a goat-hair tunic, which irritated her skin, and slept on a bed of stones covered with a goat-hair cloth (*Vita of Athanasia of Aegina*, ch. 4–5).

10. *Vita of Theodora of Thessalonike*, ch. 23.

11. Ibid., ch. 28.

12. Ibid., ch. 31.

13. Ibid., ch. 41.

14. Talbot, "Empress Theodora Palaiologina," 295–303. See also *PLP* 21380.

15. See Janin, *Eglises CP*, 307–10; Vasileios Marinis, *Architecture and Ritual in the Churches of Constantinople, Ninth to Fifteenth Centuries* (New York: Cambridge University Press, 2014), 184–90.

16. British Library Additional 22748 (14th c.), in *Deux typica byzantins de l'époque des Paléologues*, ed. Hippolyte Delehaye (Brussels: M. Lamertin, 1921), 106–36; translated into English by Alice-Mary Talbot, "Typikon of Theodora Palaiologina for the Convent of Lips in Constantinople," in *BMFD* 3:1254–86. The document was actually drafted by a ghostwriter, but since the *typikon* is written in the first person, as if the author was the empress herself, we can safely assume that the text reflects her wishes and intentions.

17. (39) Lips Typikon, ch. 40–41, *BMFD* 3:1278.

18. Ibid., ch. 29, *BMFD* 3:1274.

19. Vasileios Marinis, "Tombs and Burials in the Monastery *tou Libos* in Constantinople," *Dumbarton Oaks Papers* 63 (2009): 147–66.

20. Talbot, "Empress Theodora Palaiologina," 297–98, 303.

21. See Dorothy Abrahamse, "Women's Monasticism in the Middle Byzantine Period: Problems and Prospects," *Byzantinische Forschungen* 9 (1985): 38–39.

22. (39) Lips Typikon, ch. 30, *BMFD* 3:1274.

23. Ibid., ch. 39, *BMFD* 3:1277.

24. Ibid., ch. 38, *BMFD* 3:1277.

25. Ibid., ch. 50–51, *BMFD* 3:1281.

26. Delehaye, *Deux typica byzantins de l'époque des Paléologues*, 18–105; English translation by Alice-Mary Talbot, "Typikon of Theodora

Synadene for the Convent of the Mother of God *Bebaia Elpis* in Constantinople," in *BMFD* 4:1512–78. On Theodora Synadene, see *PLP* 21381.

27. The most recent analysis of the Lincoln College Typikon is by Niels Gaul, "Writing 'with Joyful and Leaping Soul': Sacralization, Scribal Hands, and Ceremonial in the Lincoln College Typikon," *Dumbarton Oaks Papers* 69 (2015): 243–71; see also Irmgard Hutter, *Corpus der byzantinischen Miniaturhandschriften: Oxford College Libraries* (Oxford: Oxford University Press, 1997), 5.1–2; Hutter, "Die Geschichte des Lincoln College Typikons," *Jahrbuch der Österreichischen Byzantinistik* 45 (1995): 79–114; Anthony Cutler and Paul Magdalino, "Some Precisions on the Lincoln College Typikon," *Cahiers archéologiques* 27 (1978): 179–98; Carolyn Connor, *Women of Byzantium* (New Haven, CT: Yale University Press, 2004), 277–308.

28. (57) Bebaia Elpis, ch. 124, *BMFD* 4:1556–58. Theodora designated the revenues of certain of her properties for this purpose.

29. Ibid., ch. 93–94, *BMFD* 4:1550.

30. Ibid., ch. 60–64, *BMFD* 4:1540–41.

31. Ibid., ch. 134–43, *BMFD* 4:1561–62. For the icon, see Alice-Mary Talbot, "Female Patronage in the Palaiologan Era: Icons, Minor Arts and Manuscripts," in *Female Founders in Byzantium and Beyond*, ed. Lioba Theis et al. (Vienna: Böhlau Verlag, 2011/12), 260–62 and fig. 1.

32. *Vita of Neilos of Rossano*, ch. 46.3.

33. MM 4:393–96. The convent was Nea Petra in Thessaly.

34. (57) Bebaia Elpis, ch. 9, *BMFD* 4:1526.

35. *Vita of Theodora of Thessalonike*, ch. 8.

36. "Translation of Theodora of Thessalonike," ch. 14–15; translated into English in Talbot, *Holy Women of Byzantium*, 229–30.

37. For more details, see Alice-Mary Talbot, "Late Byzantine Nuns: By Choice or Necessity?" *Byzantinische Forschungen* 9 (1985): 112–13, and Nathalie Delierneux, "Les moniales à Byzance, entre clôture et vie publique (VIIIe–début XIIe siècle)," in *Le saint, le moine et le paysan: Mélanges d'histoire byzantine offerts à Michel Kaplan*, ed. Olivier Delouis, Sophie Métivier, and Paule Pagès (Paris: Publications de la Sorbonne, 2016), 104–5.

38. See, for example, (54) Damilas, ch. 17, *BMFD* 4:1476–77.

39. For further discussion, see Alice-Mary Talbot, "The Byzantine Family and the Monastery," *Dumbarton Oaks Papers* 44 (1990): 119–29.

40. *Vita of Theodora of Thessalonike*, ch. 27–30. On the issue of family ties in this *vita*, see Kaplan, "La vie de Théodora de Thessalonique," 285–301.

41. Her daughter, Anna Komnene, also lived at the convent after being widowed, but she did not take monastic vows until she was on her deathbed; see (27) Kecharitomene, ch. 4, *BMFD* 2:649, 670.

42. For commemorations, see (57) Bebaia Elpis, ch. 113–19, 134–43, *BMFD* 4:1555–56, 1561–62; at (27) Kecharitomene (ch. 76), only tonsured female descendants of Irene could be buried in the exonarthex of the church (*BMFD* 2:704–5).

43. (57) Bebaia Elpis, ch. 135–36, 159, *BMFD* 4:1561, 1568.

44. Ibid., ch. 145, *BMFD* 4:1563.

45. On the sleeping arrangements, see (27) Kecharitomene, ch. 6, 44, *BMFD* 2:671–72, 690.

46. (27) Kecharitomene, ch. 70 and 76, *BMFD* 2:699, 704–5.

47. *BMFD* 4:1515.

48. (57) Bebaia Elpis, ch. 66, *BMFD* 4:1542.

49. Ibid., ch. 149, *BMFD* 4:1565.

50. (47) Philanthropos, ch. 2, *BMFD* 4:1387.

51. For further discussion of this topic, see Alice-Mary Talbot, "Byzantine Women, Saints' Lives, and Social Welfare," in *Through the Eye of a Needle: Judeo-Christian Roots of Social Welfare*, ed. Emily A. Hanawalt and Carter Lindberg (Kirksville, MO: Thomas Jefferson University Press, 1994), 105–22, esp. 117–22.

52. (39) Lips, ch. 50–51, *BMFD* 3:1281. It is curious that most of the staff, except for the laundress, seems to have been male.

53. Ibid., ch. 38, *BMFD* 3:1277.

54. (27) Kecharitomene, ch. 59–64, *BMFD* 2:696–98.

55. Ibid., ch. 71, *BMFD* 2:700–702.

56. (57) Bebaia Elpis, ch. 89, *BMFD* 4:1549.

57. Ibid., ch. 112, 115, 116–17, 119, 142, 149–50, *BMFD* 4:1555–56, 1562, 1565.

58. Ibid., ch. 149, *BMFD* 4:1565.

59. For more detailed discussion, see Talbot, "Late Byzantine Nuns: By Choice or Necessity?"

60. (27) Kecharitomene, ch. 40 (*BMFD* 2:689–90), compared with (22) Evergetis, ch. 9 (*BMFD* 2:478–79). The boldfaced text represents borrowings from the Evergetis document.

61. (27) Kecharitomene, ch. 47 (*BMFD* 2:691), compared with (22) Evergetis, ch. 9–10 (*BMFD* 2:480–81). Again, the boldface represents the Evergetis text.

62. On this, see Alice-Mary Talbot, "The Conversion of Byzantine Monasteries from Male to Female and Vice-Versa," in *ΠΟΛΥΠΛΕΥΡΟΣ ΝΟΥΣ: Miscellanea für Peter Schreiner zu seinem 60. Geburtstag*, ed. Cordula Scholz and Georgios Makris (Munich: Saur, 2000), 360–64.

63. See charts in Talbot, "A Comparison of the Monastic Experience," 19–20, and further discussion of community size in the introduction, 7. One should note, however, that at the double monastery of Athanasios on Xerolophos the number of monks was double that of the nuns; see MM 2:80–83.

64. *Vita of Theodora of Thessalonike*, ch. 31. Theodora is described as sleeping on the floor, on a rush mat and sheepskin.

65. (27) Kecharitomene, ch. 6, *BMFD* 2:671–72.

66. See beginning of this chapter and note 2, above.

67. See *Vita of Paul of Latros*, ch. 17: "one room for sleeping" (τό τε πρὸς ὕπνον οἰκητήριον ἕν).

68. Sharon Gerstel, "Painted Sources for Female Piety in Medieval Byzantium," *Dumbarton Oaks Papers* 52 (1998): 91.

69. See Myrtale Acheimastou-Potamianou, "The Basilissa Anna Palaiologina of Arta and the Monastery of Vlacherna," in *Les femmes et le monachisme byzantin/Women and Byzantine Monasticism: Actes du Symposium d'Athènes, 1988*, ed. Jacques Y. Perreault (Athens: Institut canadien d'archéologie à Athénes, 1991), 43–49.

70. *RPK* 2:278.47–49. For further discussion, see Mitsiou, "Late Byzantine Female Monasticism," 165–66.

71. See Jennifer Ball, "Decoding the Habit of the Byzantine Nun," *Journal of Modern Hellenism* 27 (2009-2010) [=*Byzantium: Essays in Honor of Angela Constantinides Hero* (New York: Hellenic College Press, 2009)], 25–52.

72. *Vita of Matrona of Perge*, ch. 51.

73. For an earlier discussion of this topic, see Talbot, "A Comparison of the Monastic Experience," 1–20.

74. Abrahamse, "Women's Monasticism in the Middle Byzantine Period," 36 and n1. Her tally is based on Janin, *Eglises CP*.

75. My calculations are tabulated from numerous entries in the *PmbZ* indices related to monks and nuns, such as "Mönche" (monks),

"Monachoi" (monks), "Eremit" (hermit), "Gerontes" (elders), "Abbas" (father), "Nonne" (nuns), and "Monache" (nun). These indices, though comprehensive, are difficult to use for comparative statistical calculations. On the one hand, the same individual may be listed several times under different rubrics, such as "monk," "abbot," "hermit." The *PmbZ* volumes (and indices) also include numerous anonymous individuals (who are omitted from *PLP*), thus substantially increasing the numbers.

76. These statistics are based on the indices for professions (*Berufe*) in the list of abbreviations and general index (*Abkürzungsverzeichnis und Gesamtregister*) for the *Prosopographisches Lexikon der Palaiologenzeit* (Vienna, 1996), under the lemmata for "ordained monk," "monk," "nun," "monastic brother," "monastic sister" (*Hieromonachos, Mönch, Nonne,* συνάδελφη, and συνάδελφος).

77. Janin, *Eglises CP*.

78. Janin, *Grands centres*.

79. For example, a sample based on fascicle 3 of the *PLP* indicates that of the total 1,750 listings in this volume, only 144, or 8 percent, were female.

80. The third possibility has been suggested by Maria Sigala, "Η Παναγία η Οδηγήτρια η Εννιαμερίτισσα στη Χάλκη της Δωδεκανήσου," *Αρχαιολογικόν Δελτίον* 55 (2000): 333–34. See also Sharon Gerstel and Alice-Mary Talbot, "Nuns in the Byzantine Countryside," *Δελτίον της Χριστιανικής Αρχαιολογικής Εταιρείας* 27 (2006): 481–90, and Sharon Gerstel, *Rural Lives and Landscapes: Art, Archaeology and Ethnography* (Cambridge: Cambridge University Press, 2015), 148–49, who suggests that some rural women "were able to lead a pious life . . . seemingly, within the confines of a village."

81. Mitsiou has reached the same conclusion on the basis of evidence from the acts of the standing synod (*endemousa synodos*) in Constantinople; see Mitsiou, "Late Byzantine Female Monasticism," 162.

82. *Vita of Lazaros of Galesion*, ch. 74, 164, 201. The nunnery of Eupraxia (named after Lazaros's mother) was actually in the vicinity of Galesion rather than on the mountain itself, while the nunnery of Trichinareai on Mount St. Auxentios was near the base of the mountain, one mile from the male monastery near the summit; see Janin, *Eglises CP*, 45–47, 245. Today two of the surviving six monasteries on Meteora are inhabited by nuns, four by monks.

83. See, for example, *Vita of Theoktiste of Lesbos*, ch. 18. She was a nun at a convent on Lesbos when she was captured by Cretan Arabs while visiting her sister's village for Easter. Athos, as a peninsula, was particularly vulnerable to Arab attack; see, for example, *Vita of Euthymios the Younger*, ch. 24.3 and 25.1–5, and *Vita B of Athanasios of Athos* (ch. 13.2), which mentions "the attacks of the most godless Cretans which used to occur in the old days, for they would lurk in rocky inlets and rob passersby and murder many monks on the Mountain." Christodoulos of Patmos had to flee Mount Latros in the late eleventh century because of attacks by Seljuk Turks; see (24) Christodoulos, ch. A5, *BMFD* 2:580.

84. (31) Areia, ch. M3, *BMFD* 3:961.

85. Act of John Apokaukos, ed. Athanasios Papadopoulos-Kerameus, in "Συνοδικὰ γράμματα Ἰωάννου τοῦ Ἀποκαύκου, μητροπολίτου Ναυπάκτου," *Byzantis* 1 (1909): 14–20; translated by Alice-Mary Talbot in "Affirmative Action in the 13th Century: An Act of John Apokaukos concerning the Blachernitissa Monastery in Arta," in *ΦΙΛΕΛΛΗΝ: In Honour of Robert Browning*, ed. Costas Constantinidis et al. (Venice: Istituto ellenico di studi bizantini e postbizantini di Venezia, 1996), 405.

86. Gerstel, *Rural Lives and Landscapes*, 149.

87. MM 1, no. 200, p. 454 (my translation), where her name is rendered as "Pyriana." The change to "Syriana" is made by *PLP* 27170.

88. See *ODB* 3:1941, s.v. "Stability, monastic," with the relevant bibliography, and chapter 1 herein in section "Comparison of Cenobitic Monasticism in Byzantium and the Medieval West," 48.

89. For example, (27) Kecharitomene, ch. 54; (39) Lips, ch. 20 (*BMFD* 2:695, 3:1271), which permitted the admission of virtuous nuns who had been tonsured at other convents (*exokouritides*). At Lips, no probationary period was required, but the new arrivals were required to familiarize themselves with the *typikon* of the convent they had just joined.

90. *Vita of Theodora of Thessalonike*, ch. 36.

91. Georgios Sphrantzes, *Memorii 1401–1477*, ed. Vasile Grecu (Bucharest: Editura Academiei Republicii Socialiste România, 1966), XVIII.2–4; translated into English by Marios Philippides, *The Fall of the Byzantine Empire: A Chronicle by George Sphrantzes, 1401–1477* (Amherst: University of Massachusetts Press, 1980), 37–38. By coincidence, the Thessalonican convent was the same institution that St. Theodora had refused to leave in the late ninth century.

92. For further discussion of issues of enclosure and *abaton* with extensive bibliography, see Delierneux, "Les moniales à Byzance," 106–12.

93. (27) Kecharitomene, ch. 17, *BMFD* 2:679.

94. (57) Bebaia Elpis, ch. 76–77, *BMFD* 4:1545–46.

95. (39) Lips, ch. 15, *BMFD* 3:1270.

96. Theoleptos, *Monastic Discourses*, Homily 18, ch. 3–4, pp. 310–11.

97. Irene-Eulogia Choumnaina's spiritual director gave her permission to attend the funeral of an aunt; see Vitalien Laurent, "La direction spirituelle à Byzance: La correspondance d'Irène-Eulogie Choumnaina Paléologine avec son second directeur," *Revue des études byzantines* 14 (1956): 79.

98. Vitalien Laurent, "La direction spirituelle des grandes dames à Byzance: La correspondance inédite d'un métropolite de Chalcédoine," *Revue des études byzantines* 8 (1950): 63–84. Laurent remarks that Eulogia (to be distinguished from Irene-Eulogia Choumnaina), who was apparently able to visit at will her spiritual confessor in Chalcedon, enjoyed unusual freedom from rules of enclosure because of her high rank in the nobility.

99. MM 1:223. See also the two nuns cured at the shrine of the patriarch Athanasios: Eugenia from Kroulla in Bithynia, and Magdalene, daughter of Theodore Gabalas; see Alice-Mary Talbot, *Faith Healing in Late Byzantium: The Posthumous Miracles of the Patriarch Athanasios I of Constantinople by Theoktistos the Stoudite* (Brookline, MA: Hellenic College Press, 1983), chaps. 37–39. It should be noted that, in contrast to monks, nuns did not embark on long-distance pilgrimages; see further discussion in chapter 4, section "Wandering Monks," 164.

100. MM 2:409 (no. 585), 506 (no. 654), 509 (no. 655).

101. (57) Bebaia Elpis, ch. 54, *BMFD* 4:1538.

102. Emperor: (39) Lips, ch. 7, *BMFD* 3:1267; patriarch: (57) Bebaia Elpis, ch. 26, *BMFD* 4:1530.

103. (27) Kecharitomene, ch. 70, *BMFD* 2:699–700. The precinct of the Kecharitomene convent did not have sufficient room for a cemetery, so the nuns were buried on the grounds of the nearby convent of the Theotokos tes Kellaraias.

104. *Vita of Irene of Chrysobalanton*, ch. 13, 21.

105. Angela Hero, "Irene-Eulogia Choumnaina Palaiologina, Abbess of the Convent of Philanthropos Soter in Constantinople," *Byzantinische Forschungen* 9 (1985): 146; Hero, *A Woman's Quest for Spiritual*

Guidance: The Correspondence of Princess Irene Eulogia Choumnaina Palaiologina (Brookline, MA: Hellenic College Press, 1986), epistles 15–16. See note 97, above, for a rare exception to her seclusion.

106. (39) Lips, ch. 16, *BMFD* 3:1270.
107. (27) Kecharitomene, ch. 17, *BMFD* 2:679–80.
108. Mature and married priests: (57) Bebaia Elpis, ch. 79, *BMFD* 4:1547; preference for elderly eunuchs: proclamation of patriarch Arsenios, ch. 16, *PG* 119:1144D–1145A.
109. (27) Kecharitomene, ch. 15, *BMFD* 2:678.
110. (39) Lips, ch. 11, *BMFD* 3:1268–69.
111. (27) Kecharitomene, ch. 16, *BMFD* 2:679.
112. (54) Damilas, ch. 9, *BMFD* 4:1473.
113. (39) Lips, ch. 11, *BMFD* 3:1269; (57) Bebaia Elpis, ch. 105–11, *BMFD* 4:553–54.
114. (27) Kecharitomene, ch. 57, *BMFD* 2:696.
115. (39) Lips, ch. 35, *BMFD* 3:1276.
116. Ibid., ch. 51, *BMFD* 3:1281. The staff included doctors, a nurse, druggists, various attendants, a cook, and a blood-letter.
117. (27) Kecharitomene, ch. 14, *BMFD* 2:677–78. At the convent of Anargyroi, the steward could be either a eunuch or a man of respectable character; see (40) Anargyroi, ch. 5, *BMFD* 3:1292.
118. (39) Lips, ch. 25–26, *BMFD* 3:1272–73.
119. *Vita of Irene of Chrysobalanton*, ch. 15, pp. 66–75.
120. (39) Lips, ch. 4, *BMFD* 3:1267.
121. Ibid., ch. 4–5, *BMFD* 3:1267.
122. (57) Bebaia Elpis, ch. 27–36, *BMFD* 4:1531–33.
123. See, for example, the response of the canonist Balsamon that abbesses, just like unordained monks, were prohibited from hearing confessions; Rhalles-Potles, Σύνταγμα 4:477.
124. (57) Bebaia Elpis, ch. 129–30, *BMFD* 4:1559–60.
125. Ibid., ch. 54–55, *BMFD* 4:1538–39.
126. These were documents from the *endemousa synodos*, the permanent standing synod of bishops in Constantinople that conducted the business of the patriarchate. Among other issues, it dealt with canonical discipline, marriage, and inheritance, and disputes over monastic and ecclesiastical property.
127. See MM 2, no. 650, pp. 499–501; *RegPatr* 6, no. 3211.

128. There does not seem to be an English term to describe this monastic official, who was responsible for the physical aspects of church services, such as the lighting of lamps and candles, but also might be involved with the training of the choir sisters. See below in this section for a more detailed description, 86.

129. For the female staff, see (27) Kecharitomene, ch. 11, 19–29, *BMFD* 2:674–75, 680–85.

130. I stress this point because some scholars have suggested that most of the household nuns were illiterate; see, for example, Claudia Rapp, "Figures of Female Sanctity: Byzantine Edifying Manuscripts and Their Audience," *Dumbarton Oaks Papers* 50 (1996): 316. Those who carried out menial tasks, such as cleaning or working in the kitchen, may indeed not have been educated, but their supervisors surely had to have some knowledge of reading and writing.

131. (57) Bebaia Elpis, ch. 72, *BMFD* 4:1544.

132. Ibid., ch. 68, *BMFD* 4:1543.

133. Ibid., ch. 49–53, *BMFD* 4:1537–38; (27) Kecharitomene, ch. 32, *BMFD* 2:686.

134. (57) Bebaia Elpis, ch. 95, *BMFD* 4:1550.

135. See *Ormylia: The Coenobium of the Annunciation*, ed. S. A. Papadopoulos (Athens: Interamerican, 1992), 19–20, figs. 98–101. The nunnery is currently committed to organic farming.

136. *Vita of Theodora of Thessalonike*, ch. 23. The *typikon* for Sure Hope describes bread made from scratch, beginning with grinding wheat into flour; see (57) Bebaia Elpis, ch. 70, *BMFD* 4:1543.

137. *Vita of Theodora of Thessalonike*, ch. 37.

138. (57) Bebaia Elpis, ch. 66, *BMFD* 4:1542, where nuns are enjoined to do no handwork for themselves, not even a "cord of wool."

139. *Vita of Theodora of Thessalonike*, ch. 28, 41, and *Vita of Romanos the Neomartyr*, ch. 1 and 4.

140. (54) Damilas, ch. 8, *BMFD* 4:1472.

141. (57) Bebaia Elpis, ch. 95–96, *BMFD* 4:1550–51. At Kecharitomene habits were purchased on the open market (Kecharitomene, ch. 52, *BMFD* 2:694).

142. See *Vita of Athanasios, patriarch of Constantinople*, ch. 34, p. 43.13–17, which states that some poor convents derived their sources of income not from property or crops but from "the work of their hands."

A passage in the *Chronicle of Sphrantzes* (XVIII, ch. 5) notes that the nuns of the Kleraina convent supported themselves by their "handwork" (ἐργόχειρον), misleadingly translated by Philippides (*The Fall of the Byzantine Empire*, 38) as "needlework."

143. See the cautionary remarks of Pauline Johnstone, *The Byzantine Tradition in Church Embroidery* (London: Alec Tiranti, 1967), 57–64.

144. See, for example, Papadopoulos, *Ormylia: The Coenobium of the Annunciation*, 129–58 and figs. 94–96.

145. See (27) Kecharitomene, ch. 19, 59, *BMFD* 2:680, 696–97.

146. *RegPatr* 6, nos. 3073, 3215; MM 2:506–9; see Alice-Mary Talbot, "Agricultural Properties in Palaiologan Constantinople," in *Koinotaton Doron: Das späte Byzanz zwischen Machtlösigkeit und kultureller Blüte (1204–1461)*, ed. Albrecht Berger et al. (Berlin: De Gruyter, 2016), 188–89, 192–94, on this case and the acts regarding properties of the nunneries of Pausolype and Magistros.

147. (54) Damilas, ch. 16, *BMFD* 4:1476.

148. See chapter 1, sections on "Theodore and the Monastery of Stoudios," 19–20, and "St. Athanasios of Athos and the Great Lavra," 30–38, for detailed discussion of this point.

149. Jean Darrouzès, "Notice sur Grégoire Antiochos (1160 à 1196)," *Revue des études byzantines* 20 (1962): 83–92. See also Janin, *Eglises CP*, 59–60.

150. *Vita of Athanasios, patriarch of Constantinople*, ch. 34, p. 43 (my translation).

151. *Chronicle of Sphrantzes*, XVIII, ch. 4–5, trans. Philippides, 38. An example of such a donation is the will of Theodore Sarantenos (ca. 1326), which provided for charitable gifts to poor convents and nuns; see Georgios Theocharides, *Μία διαθήκη καὶ μία δίκη βυζαντινή: ἀνέκδοτα βυζαντινὰ ἔγγραφα τοῦ ΙΔ΄ αἰῶνος περὶ τῆς Μονῆς Προδρόμου Βεροίας* (Thessalonike: Hetaireia Makedonikon Spoudon, 1962), 24.138.

152. (54) Damilas, ch. 13, *BMFD* 4:1475.

153. Ibid., ch. 20, *BMFD* 4:1477. To the best of my knowledge, this is the only reference to a library in a convent.

154. *Vita of Irene of Chrysobalanton*, ch. 5, pp. 16–17. Irene is said to have been "so devoted to the Divine Scriptures and so engrossed by the Lives of the Fathers . . . that she seemed a mouthpiece of the God-inspired words."

155. Athos, ms. Pantokrator 6. See Spyridon Lampros, *Catalogue of the Greek Manuscripts on Mount Athos* (Cambridge: Cambridge University Press, 1895), 1:92–94, no. 1040; Talbot, "Female Patronage in the Palaiologan Era," 260, 271–72.

156. (57) Bebaia Elpis, ch. 30, 132, *BMFD* 4:1531, 1560.

157. See Rapp, "Figures of Female Sanctity," 319–20, 335–42.

158. See Lynda Garland, *Byzantine Empresses: Women and Power in Byzantium, AD 527–1204* (London: Routledge, 1999), 198, and Angeliki Laiou, "Observations on the Life and Ideology of Byzantine Women," *Byzantinische Forschungen* 9 (1985): 76.

159. On Palaiologina, see *PLP* 21339. On Theodora Raoulaina, see *PLP* 10943; Alexander Riehle, "Theodora Raulaina als Stifterin und Patronin," in Theis et al., *Female Founders in Byzantium and Beyond*, 299–315; Alice-Mary Talbot, "Bluestocking Nuns: Intellectual Life in the Convents of Late Byzantium," in *Okeanos: Essays Presented to Ihor Ševčenko on His Sixtieth Birthday by His Colleagues and Students*, ed. Cyril Mango and Omeljan Pritsak (Cambridge, MA: Harvard Ukrainian Institute, 1983) [= *Harvard Ukrainian Studies* 7 (1983)], 605–6 and 615–16; Donald Nicol, *The Byzantine Lady: Ten Portraits, 1250–1500* (Cambridge: Cambridge University Press, 1994), 33–47. According to Nicol (36–37), Theodora became a nun sometime after her husband's death around 1274.

160. *Vitae of Theophanes the Confessor and Theodore*, 4:185–223, and 5:397–99; see also Nicol, *The Byzantine Lady*, 44–45.

161. Both these manuscripts were copied before 1274, while she was still a married laywoman.

162. Nicol, *The Byzantine Lady*, 43–44.

163. See the remarks of Annemarie W. Carr, "Women as Artists in the Middle Ages: 'The Dark Is Light Enough,'" *Dictionary of Women Artists* (London: Fitzroy Dearborn, 1997), 1:14–17, and Talbot, "Bluestocking Nuns," 618.

164. (54) Damilas, ch. 6, *BMFD* 4:1470–71.

165. Ibid., ch. 7–8, *BMFD* 4:1471–72.

166. Ibid., ch. 2, *BMFD* 4:1468–69.

167. (39) Lips, ch. 40–41, *BMFD* 3:1278.

168. (57) Bebaia Elpis, ch. 149, *BMFD* 4:1565.

169. On double monasteries in Byzantium, see *ODB* 2:1392, s.v. "Monastery, double," with earlier bibliography. See also Ekaterini Mitsiou,

"Frauen als Gründerinnen von Doppelklöstern im byzantinischen Reich," in Theis et al., *Female Founders in Byzantium and Beyond*, 333–43.

170. See *CIC* 3:619–20, and *Decrees of the Ecumenical Councils*, ed. Norman P. Tanner (London: Sheed and Ward, 1990), 1:153–54.

171. *Vita of Nikephoros, patriarch*, 66.

172. *Vita of Anthousa of Mantineon*, 13–19; *Vita of Romanos the Neomartyr*, 393–427.

173. *Vita of Romanos the Neomartyr*, 409.23–410.3.

174. Ibid., 410.8–10. A similar example is found in the fourteenth century at the double monastery of Athanasios on Xerolophos, where the monks furnished food to the nuns (see further below in this section at 95–96).

175. See *Vita of Euthymios the Younger*, ch. 16–26.

176. Ibid., ch. 27–37.

177. *RegPatr* 4, no. 1374, §16.

178. He went to Mount Ganos during the patriarchate of John XI Bekkos (1275–82).

179. *Vita of Athanasios, patriarch of Constantinople*, ch. 11 (p. 17.1–16), ch. 16 (p. 21.22–23).

180. Janin, *Eglises CP*, 10–11 and 331, lists the two monasteries separately, but Albert Failler asserts that they are one and the same; see *Georges Pachymérès, Relations historiques*, ed. Albert Failler (Paris: Les Belles Lettres, 1999), 3:122–23 and n89.

181. *Vita of Athanasios, patriarch of Constantinople*, ch. 33, pp. 42–43.

182. Talbot, *Faith Healing in Late Byzantium*, ch. 64–69, pp. 114–21. The hagiographer provides such a detailed description of her symptoms that we can identify her affliction as what is today called Tourette's syndrome.

183. *Vita of Athanasios, patriarch of Constantinople*, ch. 39, p. 48. It should be noted that the "Rule of Athanasios I," whose translation by Timothy Miller appears in *BMFD* 4:1495–1504, is not a *typikon* for Athanasios's own monastery on Xerolophos, but rather a bold attempt to produce a universal rule for Byzantine monasteries. For an annotated edition of the Greek text, see Timothy S. Miller and John Thomas, "The Monastic Rule of Patriarch Athanasios I," *Orientalia Christiana Periodica* 62 (1996): 353–71.

184. See John L. Boojamra, *Church Reform in the Late Byzantine Empire: A Study for the Patriarchate of Athanasios of Constantinople* (Thessalonike: Patriarchikon Hidryma Paterikon Meleton, 1982).

185. See item no. 1 in his unedited and undated patriarchal letter (ἔνταλμα) to all the metropolitans, forbidding double monasteries, in Vat. Gr. 2219, fol. 137v, and *RegPatr* 4, no. 1747.

186. MM 2:80–83 (my translation); see Ekaterini Mitsiou, "Das Doppelkloster des Patriarchen Athanasios I. in Konstantinopel: Historisch-prosopographische und wirtschaftliche Beobachtungen," *Jahrbuch der Österreichischen Byzantinistik* 58 (2008): 87–106.

187. Janin, *Eglises CP*, 527–29.

188. Philipp Meyer, "Bruchstücke zweier *typika ktetorika*," *Byzantinische Zeitschrift* 4 (1895): 45–58, with Greek text at 48–49. My English translation is to be found in *BMFD* 4:1383–88.

189. See Nikephoros Choumnos's testament in *PG* 140:1481.

190. Theoleptos, *Monastic Discourses*, 19, 24.

191. Ibid., 20. The editor, Sinkewicz, entertains (19) the possibility that the Philanthropos was a mixed monastery, in which the monks and nuns attended services and meals together, rather than a double one. This suggestion is based on his apparent misunderstanding of a passage in discourse 9, which he thinks might be addressed to a mixed audience of monks and nuns, but it was clearly addressed to monks, as can be seen by the use of masculine participles and pronouns.

192. MM 2, nos. 585, 611, and 628, pp. 407–10, 445–46, and 468–69; *RegPatr* 6, nos. 3144, 3190, 3239; Janin, *Eglises CP*, 156, 386, 177.

193. *Vita of Philotheos*, ch. 2–3, pp. 616–27.

194. See Alice-Mary Talbot, "Building Activity in Constantinople under Andronikos II: The Role of Women Patrons in the Construction and Restoration of Monasteries," in *Byzantine Constantinople: Monuments, Topography and Everyday Life*, ed. Nevra Necipoğlu (Leiden: Brill, 2001), 329–43; Talbot, "Female Patronage in the Palaiologan Era."

195. For more on this subject, see Talbot, "Bluestocking Nuns," 604–18.

196. See my translation of John Apokaukos's text in Talbot, "Affirmative Action," 404–5.

197. See some concrete examples in Talbot, "Late Byzantine Nuns," 103–17, and Talbot, "Byzantine Women, Saints' Lives, and Social Welfare," 105–22, esp. 117–22.

198. For example, St. Irene of Chrysobalanton imitated the ascetic exercises of Arsenios the Great, in her standing vigils with upraised arms;

see *Vita of Irene of Chrysobalanton*, ch. 5, pp. 16–19. St. Paraskeve the Younger was praised for having a "masculine spirit" despite her "weaker nature"; her *vita* is unpublished, but see the translated extract by Claudia Rapp, "Figures of Female Sanctity," 324.

199. (57) Bebaia Elpis, ch. 27, *BMFD* 4:1531.
200. Ibid., ch. 28, *BMFD* 4:1531.
201. Ibid., ch. 33, *BMFD* 4:1532.
202. Athos, ms. Pantokrator 6, commissioned by Anna Komnene Raoulaina for the nunnery of Christ Krataios; see Lampros, *Catalogue of the Greek Manuscripts on Mount Athos*, 1:92–94, no. 1040.
203. See (39) Lips, ch. 3, *BMFD* 3:1266, and (57) Bebaia Elpis, ch. 18, *BMFD* 4:1528.

CHAPTER 3. Hermits and Holy Mountains

1. Among the few exceptions are Denise Papachryssanthou, "La vie monastique dans les campagnes byzantines du VIIIe au XIe siècles: Ermitages, groupes, communautés," *Byzantion* 43 (1973): 158–80, and Alexander Kazhdan, "Hermitic, Cenobitic and Secular Ideals in Byzantine Hagiography of the Ninth through the Twelfth Centuries," *Greek Orthodox Theological Review* 30 (1985): 473–87.
2. Speake, *Mount Athos: Renewal in Paradise*, 225–30.
3. For more on holy mountains, see Soustal, *Heilige Berge und Wüsten*; Talbot, "Les saintes montagnes à Byzance"; and the chapter on mountains in Veronica della Dora, *Landscape, Nature, and the Sacred in Byzantium* (Cambridge: Cambridge University Press, 2016), 147–75.
4. For Irene, a would-be hermitess on Galesion, see "Hermitesses" section at the end of this chapter. It should also be noted that a female stylite lived on this holy mountain at the time of Lazaros; see section "Pillar Saints (stylites)" in chapter 4, 155.
5. (13) Ath. Typikon, ch. 40, *BMFD* 1:261.
6. *Vita of Maximos by Theophanes*, ch. 6.1–2. Likewise in the ninth century, when the youthful Ioannikios first arrived at the Agauroi monastery on Bithynian Mount Olympos and asked the abbot to recommend a good place to live as a hermit, "the father . . . knew that it would be unreasonable [to expect] someone not previously trained in ascetic struggles . . .

to attain, at the very beginning, the loftiest [goal of] solitary contemplation." So he was told to first spend two years in a cenobitic monastery before moving into a cave; see *Vita of Ioannikios by Peter*, ch. 8–10.

7. *Vita B of Athanasios of Athos*, ch. 9.2.

8. Ibid.

9. Examples are Maximos the Hutburner, who went first to live with hermits on the holy mountains of Ganos and Papikion before moving to Athos (*Vita of Maximos by Theophanes*, ch. 3–4), Sabas the Younger (*vita*, ch. 6–8), and Germanos Maroules (*vita*, ch. 9), who upon arrival on Athos were directed by a *geron*.

10. *Vita B of Athanasios of Athos*, ch. 13.1–2.

11. On the *boskoi*, see John Wortley, "Grazers (βοσκοί) in the Judaean Desert," in *The Sabaite Heritage in the Orthodox Church from the Fifth Century to the Present*, ed. Joseph Patrich (Leuven: Uitgeveij Peeters en Departement Oosterse Studies, 2000), 37–48, and Rehav Rubin, "The *Melagria*: On Anchorites and Edible Roots in Judaean Desert," *Liber Annuus* 52 (2002): 347–52, who translates the previously unidentified Greek term *melagrion* as "asphodel." Euthymios's forty-day period of "grazing" no doubt was based on the practice of Judean Desert monks who spent the forty days before Easter wandering in the desert and surviving on wild plants, at a time of year when desert vegetation is most abundant; see Rubin, "The *Melagria*," 349–50, and Price, *Lives of the Monks of Palestine*, 53.

12. *Vita of Euthymios the Younger*, ch. 17.2.

13. For a more detailed discussion of *enkleistoi*, see chapter 4, section "Recluses (*enkleistoi*)." For a contemporary website on "grazing hermits" who found their food by foraging, see https://citydesert.wordpress.com/2014/01/04/boskoi-the-grazing-hermits/, accessed July 26, 2016.

14. *Vita of Euthymios the Younger*, ch. 19.1. It is probably not a coincidence that in this ascetic feat Euthymios was emulating his namesake, Euthymios the Great, who also retired to a cave in the desert and survived on plants growing nearby; see Price, *Lives of the Monks of Palestine*, 11.

15. Papachryssanthou (*Actes du Prôtaton*, 33) suggests that Euthymios's rigorous self-mortification was more extreme than that usually practiced on Athos, since Joseph was unaccustomed to such a regimen, but this story provides no information about the practices of other hermits on the Holy Mountain.

16. For a roughly contemporary parallel, see the *vita* of George, bishop of Mytilene (d. ca. 820–21), who spent six years in a cave on Lesbos without any human interaction. He differed from Euthymios, however, in that he left his cave every two to three days to gather wild plants for nourishment; see *Vita of George of Mytilene*, ch. 3, pp. 34–35, a passage copied from the *vita* of John the Hesychast, ch. 11.

17. *Vita of Euthymios the Younger*, ch. 22.1.

18. Ibid., ch. 23–37.

19. On Latros, see Ephe Ragia, *Λάτρος: Ένα άγνωστο μοναστικό κέντρο στη δυτική Μικρά Ασία, με λεπτομερή σχολιασμό των εγγράφων του αρχείου της μονής Θεοτόκου του Στύλου* (Thessalonike: Ekdotikos Oikos Antone Stamoule, 2008).

20. *Vita of Paul of Latros*, ch. 8. Demetrios is described as σύμψυχος, lit. "united in soul."

21. For a parallel from the hagiography of earlier Judean Desert monks, see the *Vita of Symeon the Fool*, where Symeon wants to live in total isolation, and his companion John is worried about what they will eat. Symeon explains, "[We shall eat] what those called the Grazers eat"; see *Vita of Symeon the Fool*, 67.1–3 (Greek text); and English translation by Derek Krueger, *Symeon the Holy Fool: Leontius' Life and the Late Antique City* (Berkeley: University of California Press, 1996), 141.

22. *Vita of Paul of Latros*, ch. 9–10.

23. Ibid., ch. 13. For a parallel to the provisioning of Paul, when Sabas the Younger was living in a cave near Thracian Herakleia, he received food from lay and clerical visitors from the city (*Vita of Sabas the Younger*, ch. 54.1–4).

24. *Vita of Paul of Latros*, ch. 20.

25. *Vita of Maximos by Theophanes*, ch. 10.2.

26. Ibid., ch. 11.1.

27. *Vita of Maximos by Niphon*, ch. 2.1.

28. For gifts of bread, see *Vita of Maximos by Theophanes*, ch. 24.1; *Vita of Maximos by Niphon*, ch. 18.2; for fish, *Vita of Maximos by Niphon*, ch. 11.3, 19.1; *Vita of Maximos by Theophanes*, ch. 26.7; for octopus, *Vita of Maximos by Niphon*, ch. 18.2; for wine, *Vita of Maximos by Niphon*, ch. 11.2, 18.2; *Vita of Maximos by Theophanes*, ch. 24.1; for grapes, *Vita of Maximos by Niphon*, ch. 15.3; *Vita of Maximos by Theophanes*, ch. 26.6.

29. See *Vita of Maximos by Niphon*, ch. 11.4, and *Vita of Maximos by Theophanes*, ch. 26.3.

30. *Vita of Maximos by Niphon*, ch. 30.2. The *Vita of Maximos by Theophanes* (ch. 20.3, 26.4) contradicts this, stating that Maximos had dry rusks in his cell.

31. *Vita of Maximos by Niphon*, ch. 30.1.

32. Another example is David of Lesbos, who reportedly survived for thirty years in the wilderness of Mount Ida by eating "wild greens that grew naturally from the earth and acorns he found lying about, with [only] pure spring-fed streams to drink from"; see *Vita of David, Symeon and George*, ch. 5. See also *Vita of Niphon of Athos*, ch. 4.1.

33. *Vita of Lazaros of Galesion*, ch. 39–40.

34. For a fuller discussion of *enkleistoi*, see chapter 4, section "Recluses (*enkleistoi*)"; and *ODB* 1:699–700.

35. Ioannikios chained himself to a rock in a cave for three years; see *Vita of Ioannikios by Peter*, ch. 39.

36. For specific references in *typika*, see (13) Ath. Typikon, ch. 40–46, *BMFD* 1:261–62; (24) Rule of Christodoulos for Patmos, ch. A23–24, which specifies that the solitaries' food is to be uncooked (with the exception of bread, we assume), *BMFD* 2:590–92; (34) Machairas, ch. 152, *BMFD* 3:1162.

37. For a more detailed analysis of caves as sacred spaces and the relationship of hermits to their cave dwellings, see della Dora, *Landscape, Nature and the Sacred in Byzantium*, 176–202, and Alice-Mary Talbot, "Caves, Demons and Holy Men," in *Le saint, le moine et le paysan: Mélanges d'histoire byzantine offerts à Michel Kaplan*, ed. Olivier Delouis, Sophie Métivier, and Paule Pagès (Paris: Publications de la Sorbonne, 2016), 707–18.

38. Rung 6, "On remembrance of death"; see *PG* 88:793–802; translated into English by Colm Luibheid and Norman Russell, *John Climacus: The Ladder of Divine Ascent* (New York: Paulist Press, 1982), 132–35.

39. For more on this, see Talbot, "Caves, Demons and Holy Men," 713–14.

40. *Vita B of Athanasios of Athos*, ch. 13.1.

41. *Vita of Stephen the Younger*, ch. 20.

42. *Vita of Maximos by Theophanes*, ch. 16.3.

43. Georgios Kavvadias, *Pasteurs-nomades méditerranéens: Les Saracatsans de Grèce* (Paris: Gauthier-Villars, 1965).

44. *Handbook for Travellers in Greece* (London: John Murray, 1884), 2:143.

45. *Vita of Michael Maleinos*, ch. 12–13.

46. Luke of Steiris, for example, was assisted by his sister Kale, who lived near his hermitage in order to serve him. For example, she weeded his garden and, when he moved to a dry and waterless island, brought bread to him; see *Vita of Luke of Steiris*, ch. 30, 52.

47. *Vita B of Athanasios of Athos*, ch. 52.2–4.

48. The *Vita of Blasios of Amorion*, for example, mentions Blasios's interaction with cowherds (βουκόλοι) tending their herds on Athos (ch. 24, 667F).

49. *Vita B of Athanasios of Athos*, ch. 13.2.

50. There is no specific evidence in Byzantine texts for a hermit planting a vegetable garden on Mount Athos, but a parallel can be found in the *Vita of Luke of Steiris* in the tenth century (ch. 28, 30, 41, 54–55). This tradition goes back to Anthony of Egypt; see ch. 50 of the *Vita of Anthony*. A curious detail is that Luke grew in his garden cumin (ch. 30), a spice used in monasteries to make a nonalcoholic hot drink in lieu of wine.

51. *Vita of Euthymios the Younger*, ch. 22.2.

52. On the location of Makrosina, see note on ch. 22.2 of *Vita of Euthymios the Younger*, in Greenfield and Talbot, *Holy Men of Athos*, 667.

53. On the flora and fauna of Mount Athos, see Spyros Dafis, *Treasures of Mount Athos: Nature and Natural Environment in Mount Athos* (Athos: Holy Community of Agion Oros, 1997), http://pemptousia.com/2012/09/nature-and-the-natural-environment-of-mount-athos/.

54. *Vita of Euthymios the Younger*, ch. 18.2.

55. *Vita of Paul of Latros*, ch. 9.

56. *Vita of Lazaros of Galesion*, ch. 39.

57. For the *chorta* eaten by Sabas the Younger when he was a solitary on Cyprus, see ch. 17.65–67 of his *vita*. David of Lesbos reportedly survived for years on Mount Ida by foraging for wild greens and acorns and drinking spring water; see *Vita of David, Symeon and George*, ch. 5.

58. See Dafis, *Treasures of Mount Athos: Nature and Natural Environment in Mount Athos*, passim. Wild asparagus is also mentioned in the *Vita of Neilos of Rossano*, ch. 28.3.

59. The collection of wild honey from cliffs on Mount Galesion is mentioned in the *Vita of Lazaros of Galesion*, ch. 13. It was in fact local villagers who came to harvest the honey, but it would certainly have been

accessible to hermits. Lazaros mentions a stock of honey in the monastery, but it is unclear if it was from the cliffs or from domestic beehives. The *Vita of George of Mytilene* (p. 35.3–5) states that George would emerge from his cave every two or three days to forage for *melagria*, but this passage is cited verbatim from the earlier *vita* of John the Hesychast by Cyril of Skythopolis, so it should probably be discounted. *Melagrion* was a wild plant foraged by monks in the Judean Desert; for its identification as asphodel, see Rubin, "The *Melagria*."

60. Wild leeks and chick peas: *Vita of Lazaros of Galesion*, ch. 131 and 40; lupine beans and fennel: *Vita of Theoktiste of Lesbos*, ch. 11 in Greek text, *AASS* Nov. 4:228; ch. 15 in English translation; myrtle berries and wild pears: *Vita of Neilos of Rossano*, ch. 16.1, 30.1; carobs: *Vita of Theodore of Kythera*, 288.220.

61. In the *Vita of Euphrosyne the Younger*, ch. 11, the hermit who takes her on as a disciple explains that it is very difficult for him to procure food, for there is no nearby water supply, nor are there edible plants such as hermits usually eat. He says his food comes from "wild seeds" (*spermata*), but it is possible that here *spermata* has a more generic meaning, such as fruits or nuts.

62. See *Vita of Niphon of Athos*, ch. 6, and *Vita of Maximos by Niphon*, ch. 11.3, for the fish, and *Vita of Maximos by Niphon*, ch. 18.2, for the octopus brought to Maximos as a present. In the *Vita of Luke of Steiris* (ch. 22–23), on two occasions fish leap out of the Gulf of Corinth onto the shore to offer themselves as a tasty meal.

63. *Vita of Maximos by Niphon*, ch. 5.2, and *Vita of Paul of Latros*, ch. 21.

64. For millet, viewed as humble food, see *Vita of Niphon*, ch. 17.1; Romylos of Vidin's *geron* had a few rye grains in his cell, which he ate boiled in water as a cereal (*Vita of Romylos*, ch. 8).

65. *Vita of Maximos by Theophanes*, ch. 26.3.

66. *Vita of Paul of Latros*, ch. 21.

67. *Vita of Niphon*, ch. 4.1.

68. See (24) Christodoulos, ch. A24, *BMFD* 2:591; (34) Machairas, ch. 152, *BMFD* 3:1162.

69. This policy may have been enacted to exert pressure on new arrivals on Athos to spend time in a cenobitic monastery before adopting the solitary life. I thank Nathanael Aschenbrenner for this suggestion.

70. *Vita of Romylos*, ch. 13.
71. Ibid., ch. 6–7, 10.
72. Ibid., ch. 20.
73. There are many references to rusks (*paximades* or *paxamatia*) in the *vitae*; see, for example, *Vita of Ioannikios by Peter*, ch. 68 (*AASS* Nov. 2.1:429A), *Vita of Maximos by Niphon*, ch. 18.1, *Vita of Maximos by Theophanes*, ch. 20.3 and 26.4, and *Vita of Niphon*, ch. 2. Ioannikios evidently had an abundant supply, since he was able to bless sixty pieces and give them away as tokens of blessing (*eulogiai*).
74. *Vita of Athanasios of Meteora*, 243.
75. *Vita of Stephen the Younger*, ch. 14.
76. *Vita of Lazaros of Galesion*, ch. 39.
77. Ibid., ch. 53 and notes 252 and 258.
78. *Vita of Paul of Latros*, ch. 16.
79. *Vita of Maximos by Theophanes*, ch. 28.2 and 24.1. Peter of Atroa had to carry water a half mile uphill to his cave, a tiring exercise; see *Vita of Peter of Atroa*, ch. 18.
80. *Vita of Stephen the Younger*, ch. 13.
81. *Vita of Romylos*, ch. 21.
82. *Vita of Luke of Steiris*, ch. 54–55.
83. *Vita of Maximos by Theophanes*, ch. 26.3.
84. *Vita of Euthymios the Younger*, ch. 19.1.
85. Ibid., ch. 36.3.
86. Ibid., ch. 11.
87. *Vita of Neilos of Rossano*, ch. 15.1, 16.1.
88. Ibid., ch. 31.1.
89. See, for example, *Vita of Euthymios the Younger*, ch. 25.1, and *Vita of Ioannikios by Peter*, ch. 29. Maximos the Hutburner is said to have possessed only one garment and no shoes (*Vita by Theophanes*, ch. 11.1). Neilos of Rossano wore the same belted goat-hair garment for a full year (*Vita of Neilos*, ch. 17.3).
90. *Vita of Lazaros of Galesion*, ch. 160.
91. *Vita of Stephen the Younger*, ch. 20.
92. See, for example, (37) Typikon for Mount St. Auxentios, ch. 11, *BMFD* 3:1227.
93. *Vita of Maximos by Theophanes*, ch. 10.2. A similar phrase in ch. 16.3 adds a needle to the list of objects he did not have.

94. *Vita of Ioannikios by Peter*, ch. 13.
95. *Vita of Niphon*, ch. 5.2; *Vita of Paul of Latros*, ch.13.
96. *Vita of Maximos by Niphon*, ch. 29.1; *Vita of Maximos by Kochylas*, ch. 67.26–29; *Vita of Paul of Latros*, ch. 14; *Vita of Stephen the Younger*, ch. 20.
97. *Vita of Luke of Steiris*, ch. 49.
98. *Vita of Paul of Latros*, ch. 13.
99. *Vita B of Athanasios of Athos*, ch. 15.1.
100. *Vita of Romylos*, ch. 6.
101. Ibid.
102. Pickax and mattock: *Vita of Ioannikios by Peter*, ch. 40, 49; shovel: *Vita of Romylos*, ch. 6.
103. *Vita of Maximos by Niphon*, ch. 11.4; goatskins for wine: *Vita of Ioannikios by Peter*, ch. 13.
104. *Vita of Neilos of Rossano*, ch. 31.
105. See (13) Ath. Typikon, ch. 40, *BMFD* 1:261; (24) Rule of Christodoulos for Patmos, ch. A23, *BMFD* 2:591.
106. Copying of manuscripts: *Vita of Stephen the Younger*, ch. 17; *Vita B of Athanasios of Athos*, ch. 19.2, which tells how Athanasios would copy Psalters and sell them to earn money to buy bread; Germanos Maroules copied manuscripts when he was a *geron's* disciple (*Vita of Germanos Maroules*, ch. 10.38–40); Neilos of Rossano was an indefatigable copyist of manuscripts; see his *vita*, ch. 9.2, 17.3, 20.1, 32.1. Carving: *Vita of Ioannikios by Peter*, ch. 68; weaving and mending of fishnets: *Vita of Stephen the Younger*, ch. 17; weaving of rushes: (34) Rule for Machairas, ch. 152, *BMFD* 3:1162; *Vita of Maximos by Niphon*, ch. 29.1. *Vita of Maximos by Kochylas* (ch. 67.26–29) adds the detail that the bedcovering woven by Maximos was also used as a tablecloth.
107. (24) Rule of Christodoulos, ch. A23, *BMFD* 2:591; (34) Rule for Machairas makes a similar provision that the finished handwork is to be handed in to the steward (ch. 152; *BMFD* 3:1162). See also ch. 12 of the *Vita of Michael Maleinos*, who hands over his handwork on weekends when he returns to the monastery from his hermitage. The same generic term, *ergocheiron*, is used as for nuns' textile production and could refer to artisanal crafts, such as weaving of baskets and mats from reeds, or to calligraphy.
108. *Vita of Cyril Phileotes*, ch. 23.4.

109. For the fishnets and fishing, see *Vita of Romylos*, ch. 6, and *Vita of Luke of Steiris*, ch. 35; for carrying wood, see ibid., ch. 35.

110. Slightly modified translation of *Vita of Luke of Steiris*, ch. 35. See also *Vita of Euphrosyne the Younger*, ch. 11, where Euphrosyne, disguised as a male monk, carries water and firewood for her *geron*.

111. *Vita of Germanos Maroules*, ch. 10.43–62.

112. *Vita of Romylos*, ch. 18.

113. *Vita of Sabas the Younger*, ch. 12.

114. When Athanasios left Mount Kyminas for Athos, among the few possessions he took with him (*Vita B of Athanasios of Athos*, ch. 12.3) were a gospel book and a Praxapostolos (a New Testament lectionary containing the Acts and Epistles). When Theodore went to Kythera to live as a hermit with his companion Anthony, he had four books that he considered essential: a Psalter, a gospel book, a New Testament lectionary (Apostolos), and an Oktoechos; see *Vita of Theodore of Kythera*, 287.193–94. Paul of Latros also had a gospel book in his cave (*Vita of Paul of Latros*, ch. 43). In the *Vita of Neilos of Rossano* (ch. 31.2), the hermit Stephen is required to hand over his Psalter to an elder from a nearby monastery, who has lost his copy.

115. *Vita of Maximos by Theophanes*, ch. 16.3. When Athanasios of Athos was a solitary for a year at Melana, he made his morning prayer at the third hour; see *Vita B of Athanasios of Athos*, ch. 21.4.

116. *Vita of Maximos by Theophanes*, ch. 8.2. When Athanasios of Athos was a solitary on Mount Kyminas in Bithynia at the beginning of his monastic career, he kept "vigil with prayer and words of praise on all the dominical feast days and every Sunday from sunset until the third hour"; see *Vita B of Athanasios of Athos*, ch. 10.1.

117. *Vita of Euthymios the Younger*, ch. 19.1.

118. Singing of hymns, *Vita of Maximos by Theophanes*, ch. 9.4; recitation of psalms while walking, ibid., ch. 14.3; singing of hymns and chanting of psalms, *Vita of Paul of Latros*, ch. 13–14.

119. *Vita of Niphon*, ch. 1.2.

120. *Vita of Maximos by Theophanes*, ch. 16.3.

121. *Vita of Lazaros of Galesion*, ch. 41 and 53.

122. *Vita of Neilos of Rossano*, ch. 15.3.

123. Ibid., ch. 17.2.

124. See *Philokalia*, 4:233–34.

125. *Vita of Luke of Steiris*, ch. 17.
126. See *Vita of Maximos by Theophanes*, ch. 7.2, 8.2, 9.2, 15.2–3.
127. *Vita of Maximos by Theophanes*, ch. 15.3, 5.
128. Ibid., ch. 9.
129. *Vita of Blasios of Amorion*, ch. 23, 667F; Blasios went to the Holy Mountain equipped with liturgical vestments and sacred vessels for the sacrament. See also Alexander Kazhdan, "Hagiographical Notes," *Byzantinische Zeitschrift* 78 (1985): 53–55.
130. His hagiographer emphasizes that Euthymios was ordained as a deacon, not out of "vainglory" but on account of his blameless desire to "partake of a canonically sanctified holy communion in the wilderness;" see *Vita of Euthymios the Younger*, ch. 24.1.
131. *Vita B of Athanasios of Athos*, ch. 22.3; see also (13) Ath. Typikon, ch. 37, 42, *BMFD* 1:260–62. These *kelliotai* were to receive an annual allowance of up to five measures of grain, plus three gold coins. They were to obey the superior of the Great Lavra, and each was permitted to have one disciple/servant in his charge.
132. *Vita of David, Symeon and George*, ch. 6–7.
133. *Vita of Niphon*, ch. 3. Niphon was appointed by the superior of the Great Lavra to perform this service.
134. *Vita of Niphon*, ch. 4.
135. *Vita of Paul of Latros*, ch. 15.
136. *Vita of Luke of Steiris*, ch. 42. In this context, the term *Typika* does not refer to monastic rules but to select psalms (102 and 145) recited as a liturgical service when the liturgy is not celebrated. The service could be performed without a deacon or priest. The Trisagion (literally, "thrice-holy") hymn was sung at the beginning of the Eucharistic celebration. On this passage from the *vita* of Luke, see also Kazhdan, "Hagiographical Notes," 54, and Robert F. Taft, *A History of the Liturgy of St. John Chrysostom*, Vol. 6, *The Communion, Thanksgiving, and Concluding Rites* [= *Orientalia Christiana Analecta*, 281] (Rome: Pontificium Institutum Studiorum Orientalium, 2008), 398–403. I thank Elena Velkovska for this reference.
137. *Vita of Ioannikios by Peter*, ch. 48–49.
138. Ibid., ch. 51.
139. *Vita of Luke of Steiris*, ch. 19.
140. Ibid., ch. 26.
141. Ibid., ch. 22.
142. *Vita of Neilos of Rossano*, ch. 15.3.

143. *Vita of Sabas the Younger*, ch. 53.

144. See *Vita of Stephen the Sabaite*, ch. 94–95, *AASS* Jul. 3:541–42; the story of Irene recounted just below; and Angeliki Laiou, "Sex, Consent, and Coercion in Byzantium," in *Consent and Coercion to Sex and Marriage in Ancient and Medieval Societies*, ed. Angeliki Laiou (Washington, DC: Dumbarton Oaks, 1993), 109–221, esp. 143, 164–67.

145. *Vita of Theoktiste of Lesbos*.

146. For more on Euphrosyne, see chapter 4, sections "Recluses (*enkleistoi*)," 145–46, and "Nuns Disguised as Monks," 171–72. She is known only from two *vitae* written by Nikephoros Kallistos Xanthopoulos and Constantine Akropolites many centuries after her lifetime; for her life as a hermitess, see Xanthopoulos's *Vita of Euphrosyne the Younger*, ch. 5–8.

147. *Vita of Lazaros of Galesion*, ch. 18.

148. Ibid., ch. 62.

149. Ibid., ch. 56–57.

150. Such a concern was expressed by the devil when he visited Matrona of Perge, who was living as an ascetic in an isolated region near Beirut. He urged Matrona to seek refuge in Beirut, warning her of the danger of rape; see *Vita of Matrona of Perge*, ch. 17.

151. *Vita of Lazaros of Galesion*, ch. 56.

152. See chapter 1, section "St. Athanasios of Athos and the Great Lavra," 29, and *Vita B of Athanasios of Athos*, ch. 21. See also *Vita of Ioannikios by Peter*, ch. 11.

CHAPTER 4 Alternative Modes of Monasticism

1. Beck, *Das byzantinische Jahrtausend*, 213; Kazhdan and Constable, *People and Power in Byzantium*, esp. 25, 28–29, 33–34. See my concluding chapter for further discussion of this concept.

2. See my short entry in the *ODB*, 1:699–700, with no bibliography attached.

3. For the *enkleistos* Isaiah in a tower at Nikomedeia, see *Vita of Theodora the Empress*, ch. 3, p. 365 and n33.

4. *Vita of Lazaros of Galesion*, ch. 39.

5. See, for example, Eustathios, a recluse in the village of Tzoullos in Bithynia (*Vita of Ioannikios by Sabas*, 360A.8–12), and Philotheos,

discussed below in the section "Recluses of the Eleventh and Twelfth Centuries," 140.

6. See, for example, canon 4 of the Fourth and canon 21 of Seventh Ecumenical Council (Tanner, *Decrees of the Ecumenical Councils*, 1:89, 154); and novels 5.4, 5.7, and 123.42 of Justinian (*CIC* 3:32, 33, 623).

7. See, for example, Tom Licence, *Hermits and Recluses in English Society, 950–1200* (Oxford: Oxford University Press, 2011), and Ann K. Warren, *Anchorites and Their Patrons in Medieval England* (Berkeley: University of California Press, 1985).

8. See Robert Hasenfratz, *Ancrene Wisse: Introduction*, accessed May 12, 2016, http://d.lib.rochester.edu/teams/text/hasenfratz-ancrene-wisse-introduction.

9. See *Vita of Stephen the Younger*, ch. 11, p. 102.15–24, for a list of the succession of monks who lived in this grotto.

10. Ibid., ch. 17–18. See also Marie-France Auzépy, introduction to *Vita of Stephen the Younger*, pp. 16–17, who suggests that this new monastery was associated with the convent of Trichinareai on the lower slopes of the mountain as a double monastery, of which the abbess served as superior.

11. *Vita of Stephen the Younger*, ch. 20, p. 112.26–113.8.

12. Ibid., ch. 47 (my translation of the Greek phrase στυλοειδὲς μικρὸν ἐγκλειστρον). Auzépy (p. 247) translates as "une cellule de reclus étroite comme une colonne." In ch. 54 (p. 153.27) he is called a μοναχὸς ἐγκεκλεισμένος (enclosed monk).

13. *Vita of Ioannikios by Peter*, ch. 39, Greek text, p. 407.

14. *Laudatio of Plato of Sakkoudion*, ch. 32–33.

15. *SynaxCP* 374.3–14.

16. *Vita of Evaristos*, ch. 19–21.

17. Ibid., ch. 32.

18. See, for example, *PmbZ* 1, no. 1618, and the van de Vorst introduction to the Greek text (*Vita of Evaristos*, 288–95).

19. My slightly modified version of the translation by Patricia Karlin-Hayter in *Vita of Euthymios the Patriarch*, 42–43.

20. Yet another example of an *enkleistos* in a Constantinopolitan church is the ninth-century Joseph the Hymnographer, who early in his monastic career spent some time as a recluse in the church of Antipas. See *Vita of Joseph the Hymnographer*, ch. 5.18–20.

21. *Vita of Anthony the Younger*, ch. 27, pp. 205–6. Athanasios of Traianos, who also probably lived in the ninth century, followed a similar regimen, remaining incommunicado except for Saturdays and Sundays; see *SynaxCP*, 727–728.41.

22. *Vita of Mary the Younger*, ch. 5, Greek text, p. 694A (my translation). It should be noted that Angeliki Laiou's translation in Talbot, *Holy Women of Byzantium* (p. 260) as "immured" instead of "enclosed" is misleading, since it implies that these monks were permanently walled up. As stated above, there is no evidence in Byzantium for such a practice of permanent and irrevocable enclosure. We should also remember that, according to Angeliki Laiou, this *vita* was probably not written until the eleventh century (see pp. 242–45), and its information may reflect conditions of this later period.

23. *Vita of Mary the Younger*, ch. 18, Greek text, p. 699B.

24. *Vita of Theodore of Kythera*, 288.

25. *PmbZ* 2, no. 26642.

26. My very slightly modified version of the translation of Greenfield in the *Vita of Symeon the New Theologian*, ch. 145.

27. *Vita of Symeon the New Theologian*, ch. 146.3–148.1.

28. Ibid., ch. 148.2.

29. Catia Galatariotou, *The Making of a Saint: The Life, Times and Sanctification of Neophytos the Recluse* (Cambridge: Cambridge University Press, 1991).

30. My slightly modified version of (45) Neophytos, ch. 4–5, *BMFD* 4:1351. No *vita* of Neophytos survives, but fortunately his *typikon* contains some autobiographical passages.

31. (45) Neophytos, ch. 24, *BMFD* 4:1369.

32. Ibid., ch. 9, *BMFD* 4:1353.

33. Ibid., ch. 15, *BMFD* 4:1357.

34. My very slightly modified version of (45) Neophytos, ch. 14, *BMFD* 4:1356–57.

35. Galatariotou, *The Making of a Saint*, 104–5.

36. *Vita of Sabas the Younger*, ch. 32–37.

37. Ibid., ch. 47–48.

38. Ibid., ch. 53–54.

39. Ibid., ch. 54–55.

40. Ibid., ch. 57–58.

41. Ibid., ch. 69–70.

42. On the residence of recluses in bell towers, see Slobodan Ćurčić, "Monastic Cells in Medieval Serbian Church Towers: Survival of an Early Byzantine Monastic Concept and Its Meaning," in *ΣΟΦΙΑ: Sbornik statei po iskusstvu Vizantii i Drevnei Rusi v chest' A.I. Komecha*, ed. A. L. Batalov et al. (Moscow: Severnyi palomnik, 2006), 491–514.

43. *Vita of David, Symeon and George*, ch. 12, Greek text, p. 223.16–18; *PmbZ* 1, no. 2580. The church was apparently on Lesbos, but it is not otherwise attested.

44. Theodore of Stoudios, *Letters*, vol. 2, epistles 387, 413; *PmbZ* 1, no. 1688.

45. *Vita of Theodore of Edessa*, ch. 60, p. 61.1–5.

46. See *Vita of Euphrosyne the Younger*, and *PmbZ* 1, no. 1712, *PmbZ* 2, no. 21800. Xanthopoulos may have based his account on a *vita* that is now lost. But it is curious that his narrative of miracles at her shrine contains only healings from the Palaiologan period and not from the era of Leo VI. His revised version (*metaphrasis*) of the anonymous tenth-century *Miracles of the Pege*, on the other hand, includes miracles from the sixth to tenth centuries and then additional ones from his own time; see Alice-Mary Talbot, "Two Accounts of Miracles at the Pege Shrine in Constantinople," in *Mélanges Gilbert Dagron* [= *Travaux et Mémoires* 14] (Paris, 2002), 605–15.

47. See *Vita of Euphrosyne the Younger*, ch. 16–17. The male monastery of the Source (Pege), which was in fact outside the walls of Constantinople, housed a miraculous spring, and Xanthopoulos wrote a lengthy account of the healings that occurred there during the reign of Andronikos II. Nowhere in his *Logos* on the Pege does he mention a female convent in the vicinity, so the *vita* of Euphrosyne is the only evidence for such an institution. On the monasteries of Euphrosyne and Pege, see Janin, *Eglises CP*, 130–31, 223–28.

48. *Vita of Euphrosyne the Younger*, ch. 25, trans. Rosenqvist and Talbot (forthcoming).

49. Ibid., ch. 16–17, 24–26. For the straw mat and hair shirt, see ch. 32 and 33.

50. Ibid., ch. 28, trans. Rosenqvist and Talbot (forthcoming).

51. Ibid., ch. 34.

52. Ibid., ch. 34.

53. See *SynaxCP* 292.11–14, 29–37.

54. *Vita of Peter of Atroa*, ch. 11.3–6 (my translation).

55. They were also sometimes termed *kionitai*, from *kion*, another Greek word for column.

56. Gregory of Tours, *History of the Franks*, trans. Ernest Brehaut (New York: Norton, 1969), 194–96.

57. See *PmbZ* indices, s.v. "Styliten."

58. In an attempt to avoid contact with the hordes of pilgrims who visited him at Qalʿat Semʿān, the stylite saint Symeon the Elder kept raising the height of his column. The figures given in his three *vitae* for the height of his final column range from 36 to 40 cubits, that is, from 54 to 60 feet; see Robert Doran, *The Lives of Symeon Stylites* (Kalamazoo, MI: Cistercian Publications, 1992), 17.

59. For an introduction to stylites, see the article in *ODB*, 3:1971, s.v. "Stylite." Hippolyte Delehaye, *Les saints stylites* (Brussels: Société des Bollandistes, 1923), remains the fullest treatment of the subject and contains many of the key texts but is obviously outdated. I am not aware of any subsequent survey of the topic.

60. *Vita of Luke of Steiris*, ch. 35.

61. Ibid., ch. 2, p. 196.27–197.16.

62. Ibid., ch. 2, p. 197.8–16 (my translation).

63. See the *Vita of Euthymios the Younger*, esp. ch. 23–24, 36.2 and 37.2–3. He did this in conscious imitation of Symeon the Stylite, probably Symeon the Younger, who lived in the sixth century.

64. For Symeon of Lesbos, brother of David and George, as a stylite, see *PmbZ* 1, no. 7178, and the *Vita of David, Symeon and George*, ch. 10 and 17.

65. *Vita of Theodore of Edessa*, ch. 54–68.

66. *Vita of Paul of Latros*, ch. 15, p. 114.9–13. Much more information is available on the liturgical life of earlier stylites; see the important article of Susan A. Harvey, "The Stylite's Liturgy: Ritual and Religious Identity in Late Antiquity," *Journal of Early Christian Studies* 6, no. 3 (1998): 523–39.

67. For Athanasios, see *Vita of Paul of Latros*, ch. 13, and *PmbZ* 1, no. 681; for Pachomios, see *Vita of Paul of Latros*, ch. 23, and *PmbZ* 2, no. 26217.

68. *Vita of Luke the Stylite*, ch. 5–6.

69. Ibid., ch. 9–10.
70. Ibid., ch. 10–11.
71. Ibid., ch. 13.
72. Ibid., ch. 16. As compensation for his assistance, Luke asked the fishermen to give him one-tenth of their catch.
73. Ibid., ch. 18–19.
74. Ibid., ch. 22–23, 38.
75. Ibid., ch. 39.
76. Luke's column was subsequently inhabited by another, anonymous stylite, who perished by drowning when the column was knocked down by the tidal wave that occurred following the earthquake of October 26, 989. See Leo the Deacon, *History*, bk. 10, chap. 10, p. 218; see also *PmbZ* 2, no. 30743.
77. *Vita of Lazaros of Galesion*, ch. 31. The hagiographer is most likely referring to Symeon the Stylite the Younger, who lived on the Wondrous Mountain, rather than Symeon the Elder; see *Vita of Lazaros of Galesion*, n170.
78. *Vita of Lazaros of Galesion*, ch. 53–55.
79. Ibid., ch. 64.
80. See, for example, Greenfield's introduction to *Vita of Lazaros of Galesion*, pp. 36–38.
81. For Lazaros's successive foundation of pillars and monastic communities on the holy mountain, see Greenfield's introduction to the *Vita of Lazaros of Galesion*, pp. 29–31.
82. *Vita of Lazaros of Galesion*, ch. 174–75.
83. See in this section on pillar saints, at 150.
84. See *Vita of Lazaros of Galesion*, pp. 29–30, ch. 159, 175 and n681.
85. Ibid., ch. 159.
86. Ibid., ch. 59. The same participle (ἐγκεκλεισμένη) is used of her as we find used with regard to *enkleistoi*. For possible references to female stylites in the early Byzantine period, see Hippolyte Delehaye, "Les femmes stylites," *Analecta Bollandiana* 27 (1908): 391–92, and Anna Lampropoulou, "Εἰδήσεις γύρω ἀπὸ τὸ γυναικεῖο στυλιτισμὸ στὸ Βυζάντιο," *Theologia* 61 (1990): 187–99.
87. *Vita of Lazaros of Galesion*, ch. 59–60.
88. *Diegesis* of Alexios I Komnenos, ed. Meyer, *Die Haupturkunden*, 163.31.

89. Kariophilis Mitsakis, "Symeon Metropolitan of Euchaita and the Ascetic Ideal in the Eleventh Century," *Byzantina* 2 (1970): 301–34. The monk is specifically identified as a stylite at 322.16–17.

90. Ibid., 309, 311, 322, 324–25.

91. Eustathios, *Opuscula*, XIII, ch. 38, p. 97 (also in *PG* 136: 405C–408A). My translation is a modified version of that found in Paul Magdalino, "The Byzantine Holy Man in the Twelfth Century," in *The Byzantine Saint*, ed. Sergei Hackel (London: Fellowship of St. Alban and St. Sergius, 1981), 60.

92. Eustathios of Thessalonike, "Ad stylitam quendam Thessalonicensem," *PG* 136:217–64 (also in Eustathios, *Opuscula*, 182–96). This work has not received the attention it deserves and merits further study.

93. Eustathios, "Ad stylitam," ch. 27, 52 and 56.

94. *Vita of Leontios of Jerusalem*, ch. 37–38, pp. 74–75.

95. This is my English version of the modern French translation of Jean DuFournet, *Robert de Clari: La conquête de Constantinople* (Paris: Honoré Champion, 2004), 183, who emends the *huis* (door) of the manuscript to *vis* (spiral staircase). Both Peter Noble, ed. and trans., *Robert de Clari: La conquête de Constantinople* (Edinburgh: Société Rencesvals British Branch, 2005), 109, and Edgar H. McNeal, *The Conquest of Constantinople* (New York: Columbia University Press, 1936), 110, also suggest substituting "spiral staircase" for "door." Note the ambiguity of the imperfect verb *manoit*, rendered "demeurait" (was living) by DuFournet, "lived" by Noble, and "used to live" by McNeal.

96. See Janin, *Constantinople byzantine*, 81–84. I am indebted to Ruth Macrides for discussion of the passage from Robert de Clari and her assistance with the identification of the two columns. Robert has most probably exaggerated the height of the columns, since 50 *toises* would be equivalent to about 300 feet, whereas surviving similar columns generally range from 100 to 150 feet high.

97. Delehaye (*Les saints stylites*, cxxxiv) implies the existence of stylites in late Byzantium by citing an unpublished letter (in a fourteenth-century manuscript) addressed to a stylite by Symeon, metropolitan of Euchaita, but Symeon in fact dates to the eleventh century; see note 86, above. It seems significant that there is no listing for "stylite" in the indices for "Berufe" in the *Prosopographisches Lexikon der Palaiologenzeit*.

98. Basil of Caesarea, *Long Rule* 36, *PG* 31:1008–9.

99. Canon 4 of the Council of Chalcedon; Tanner, *The Decrees of the Ecumenical Councils*, 1:89.

100. Justinian, novel 5, ch. 7, *CIC* 3:33; see Donald Nicol, "*Instabilitas loci*: The Wanderlust of Late Byzantine Monks," *Studies in Church History* 22 (1985): 195.

101. *Gyreutes* is translated by *PGL* as "vagabond, restless person," *kykleutes* as "vagrant monk." For Neilos, see, for example, his *De octo spiritibus malitiae*, ch. 13, *PG* 79:1160A.

102. See Daniel Caner, *Wandering, Begging Monks: Spiritual Authority and the Promotion of Monasticism in Late Antiquity* (Berkeley: University of California Press, 2002). Maribel Dietz, *Wandering Monks, Virgins and Pilgrims: Ascetic Travel in the Mediterranean World, A.D. 300–800* (University Park: Pennsylvania State University Press, 2005), deals primarily with monastics from the Iberian peninsula.

103. See Caner, *Wandering, Begging Monks*, introduction.

104. See especially Elisabeth Malamut, *Sur la route des saints byzantins* (Paris: CNRS, 1993), and Nicol, "*Instabilitas loci*."

105. (12) Tzimiskes, ch. 8, *BMFD* 1:237. See also (19) Attaleiates, ch. 30 (*BMFD* 1:348), (30) Phoberos, ch. 52 (*BMFD* 3:929), and (31) Areia, ch. [T]10 (*BMFD* 3:967).

106. See *Vita of Leo Luke of Corleone* (in Latin), *AASS* Mar. 1, 99–102, ch. 5, p. 99EF.

107. See further discussion at end of this section, at 164.

108. *Vita B of Athanasios of Athos*, ch. 40.3, 41.1, 49.1–4.

109. Cyril was from a monastery in the village of Philea in eastern Thrace, about thirty miles northwest of Constantinople.

110. *Vita of Cyril Phileotes*, ch. 24.

111. Ibid., ch. 20.5, 24.8.

112. See Malamut, *Sur la route des saints byzantins*; Nicol, "*Instabilitas loci*," 193–202.

113. See *Vita of Sabas the Younger*, ch. 31.20–70, 41.31–35, and 50.33–48. In the first passage describing the "barbarian" who guided Sabas to Sinai, the hagiographer comments that the Arab had a "soul capable of receiving the good seed." I thank Mihail Mitrea for these references. For further discussion of these passages, see also Marie-Hélène Congourdeau, "La terre sainte au XIVe siècle: La *Vie de Sabas de Vatopédi* par Philothée Kokkinos," in *Pèlerinages et lieux saints dans l'antiquité*

et le Moyen Âge, ed. Béatrice Caseau, Jean-Claude Cheynet, et al. (Paris: Association des Amis du Centre d'Histoire et Civilisation de Byzance, 2006)," 129–31. As an anonymous reviewer of this book has suggested, it is also possible that Sabas kept silent because he knew it might be dangerous to attempt to convert Muslims to the Christian faith.

114. (32) Mamas, ch. 13, *BMFD* 3:1004.

115. *Vita of Maximos by Theophanes*, ch. 4.2.

116. Ibid., ch. 5.

117. *Vita of Lazaros of Galesion*, ch. 4–18. Investiture with the "great habit," including a cowl and scapular, symbolized attainment of the highest rank of monastic profession.

118. Ibid., ch. 19–31.

119. Ibid., ch. 23–24, 26, 28, 199, 233.

120. Ibid., ch. 27–28.

121. Ibid., ch. 63.

122. Ibid., ch. 156.

123. Ibid., ch. 150.

124. George Dennis, "Elias the Monk, a Friend of Psellos," in *Byzantine Authors: Literary Activities and Preoccupations: Texts and Translations Dedicated to the Memory of Nicolas Oikonomides*, ed. John W. Nesbitt (Leiden: Brill, 2003), 43–62.

125. Elias, epistle 2, translated in Dennis, "Elias the Monk,"49.

126. Elias, epistle 9, translated in Dennis, "Elias the Monk," 57: "he displays sublime musical talent, singing a great deal and delighting in rhythms and melodies."

127. Elias, epistle 8, translated in Dennis, "Elias the Monk," 56.

128. Magdalino, "The Byzantine Holy Man in the Twelfth Century," 54–55.

129. Nicol, "*Instabilitas loci*," 193–202.

130. See Athanasios I, *Correspondence*, xvii–xviii, for a summary of his travels.

131. See Congourdeau, "La terre sainte au XIVe siècle," 121–33.

132. See further discussion in section "Holy Fools," below, at 167–68.

133. See *PLP*, no. 27991 (s.v. "Τζίσκος, Σάβας") and Alice-Mary Talbot, "Children, Healing Miracles, Holy Fools: Highlights from the Hagiographical Works of Philotheos Kokkinos (1300–ca. 1379)," *Bulletin of the Bysantinska Sällskapet* 24 (2006): 59–61.

134. See the references to nuns tonsured in other convents (*exokouritides*) in the index to the *BMFD* 5:1969, under "nuns (types of)." See also the earlier discussion in chapter 2, subsection "Monastic Stability," 78–79.

135. Alice-Mary Talbot, "Female Pilgrimage in Late Antiquity and the Byzantine Era," in *Acta Byzantina Fennica*, n.s., 1 (2002): 81.

136. *Vita of Lazaros of Galesion*, ch. 95.

137. See Krueger, *Symeon the Holy Fool*; Sergei Ivanov, *Holy Fools in Byzantium and Beyond* (Oxford: Oxford University Press, 2006), 104–22.

138. *Discipline générale antique, I.1, Les conciles oecuméniques (IIe–IXe siècles)*, ed. Périclès-Pierre Joannou (Grottaferrata: Tipographia Italo-Orientale "S. Nilo," 1962), 196.

139. Ivanov, *Holy Fools*, 139–219.

140. Ibid., 142–47.

141. See *Vita of Gregentios*, and, on the supposed date of Andrew and the date of composition, *Vita of Andrew the Fool*, 1:38–56.

142. See *Vita of Basil the Younger*, pt. 1, ch. 39, pp. 148–51.

143. *Vita of Symeon the New Theologian*, ch. 52–57; Ivanov, *Holy Fools*, 175–78.

144. *Vita of Symeon the New Theologian*, ch. 55.

145. Ibid., ch. 56.

146. Symeon the New Theologian, Catechesis XXVIII, in Symeon the New Theologian, *Catecheses* 3:156–59; English translation in Ivanov, *Holy Fools*, 183.

147. Rhalles-Potles, *Syntagma*, 2:441; English translation in Ivanov, *Holy Fools*, 212–13.

148. For a summary of Sabas's acts of holy folly, see Ivanov, *Holy Fools*, 225–32, and André-Jean Festugière, "Etude sur la vie de s. Sabas le Jeune qui simulait la folie," in *Vie de Syméon le Fou et Vie de Jean de Chypre*, ed. André-Jean Festugière (Paris: P. Geuthner, 1974), 223–52; see also *Vita of Sabas the Younger*, and its modern Greek translation, Ἁγίου Φιλοθέου Κοκκίνου Βίος Ἁγίου Σάββα τοῦ Βατοπεδινοῦ (Hagion Oros: Hiera Megiste Mone Vatopaidiou, 2000).

149. *Vita of Sabas the Younger*, ch. 17, 19.

150. Ibid., ch. 20.

151. Ibid., ch. 21.

152. Ibid., ch. 24.

153. *Vita of Maximos the Hutburner by Theophanes*, ch. 10.
154. *Vita of Nikodemos of Thessalonike*, ch. 4.
155. Ibid., ch. 5–7.
156. Evelyne Patlagean, "L'histoire de la femme déguisée en moine et l'évolution de la sainteté féminine à Byzance," *Studi Medievali*, ser. 3, 17 (1976): 597–623.
157. See *Vita of Mary/Marinos*, 1–12.
158. See *Vita of Matrona of Perge*, 13–64.
159. Nathalie Delierneux, "Anna-Euphémianos, l'épouse devenue eunuque—continuité et évolution d'un modèle hagiographique," *Byzantion* 72 (2002):105–40, notes the neglect of Anna in twentieth-century studies of transvestite nuns (107). I thank an anonymous reviewer for bringing this article to my attention.
160. Ibid., 107–9; the article also includes a French translation of the *synaxarion* notice, 109–12. An English translation by Vasilis Marinis can be found in *Vita of Anna/Euphemianos*, 53–69.
161. I am following the interpretation of Marinis, in *Vita of Anna/Euphemianos*, 58–61, rather than that of Delierneux, "Anna-Euphémianos," 110.
162. See *Vita of Anna/Euphemianos*, 53–69.
163. Delierneux, "Anna-Euphémianos," 121.
164. A new edition of the Greek text of the *Vita of Euphrosyne the Younger* and an annotated English translation of the *vita* of Euphrosyne are currently in preparation by Jan Olof Rosenqvist and Alice-Mary Talbot.
165. For the *enkomion* by Akropolites, see François Halkin, "Éloge de Ste Euphrosyne la Jeune par Constantin Akropolite," *Byzantion* 57 (1987): 56–65. See also Ilse Rochow, "Die Vita der Euphrosyne der Jüngeren, das späteste Beispiel des Motivs der weiblichen Transvestitentums (*monachoparthenia*) in der byzantinischen Hagiographie," in *Mir Aleksandra Kazhdana: K 80-lettiiu so dnia rozhdenniia*, ed. Aleksandra A. Chekalova (St. Petersburg: Aleteiia, 2003), 259–71.
166. *Vita of Euphrosyne the Younger*, ch. 16. Her reported admission to the Pege monastery as a nun is improbable, since it seems to have been a male institution throughout its history; see Janin, *Eglises CP*, 223–28.
167. For further details on her life as a recluse, see section "Recluses (*enkleistoi*)" at the beginning of this chapter, at 145–46.

168. *Vita of Makrina*, 59.

169. See Kevin Corrigan, *The Life of Saint Macrina by Gregory, Bishop of Nyssa* (Toronto: Peregrina, 1989); Susanna Elm, *"Virgins of God": The Making of Asceticism in Late Antiquity* (Oxford: Clarendon, 1994), 78–105; and Daniel F. Stramara, "Double Monasticism in the Greek East, Fourth through Eighth Centuries," *Journal of Early Christian Studies* 6, no. 2 (1998): 269–312, which deals in large part with the monastery at Annisa.

170. Elm, *"Virgins of God,"* 100.

171. *Vita of David, Symeon, and George*, ch. 19, p. 196. The *vita* describes events of the ninth century, but its date of composition is uncertain. For further discussion of this episode, see Alexander Alexakis, "A Meeting of Hypatia of Alexandria with St. Febronia of Nisibis in the Life of St. David, Symeon and George of Lesbos," in *Byzantine Religious Culture: Studies in Honor of Alice-Mary Talbot*, ed. Denis Sullivan, Elizabeth Fisher, and Stratis Papaioannou (Leiden: Brill, 2012), 19–30.

172. The will is preserved at the Athonite monastery of Iviron, and published in *Actes d'Iviron*, vol. 2, no. 47.

173. See Alice-Mary Talbot, "Une riche veuve de la fin du XIe siècle: Le testament de Kalè Pakourianè," in *Impératrices, princesses, aristocrates et saintes souveraines*, ed. Elisabeth Malamut and Andreas Nicolaïdès (Aix-en-Provence: Presses universitaires de Provence, 2014), 206–7.

174. The fact that Kale-Maria made bequests of her monastic garments seems to indicate that she was not in an established nunnery, where such habits would belong to the community as a whole.

175. *Actes d'Iviron*, vol. 2, no. 47.20–21, 25–26, 30. The Oktaechos (also spelled Oktoechos or Octoechos) was a book containing hymns for the Sunday office; the Panegyrikon contained appropriate sermons for Church feast days.

176. Ibid., no. 47.21, 24–28; Talbot, "Une riche veuve de la fin du XIe siècle," 208–9.

177. *Actes d'Iviron*, vol. 2, no. 47.34.

178. Ibid., no. 47.40–42.

179. See *PLP* references, nos. 6107 (Epicharis), 7195 (Theodote), 10503 (Kallone), 21546 (Gregory Palamas), 21547 (Theodosios Palamas), 21550 (Makarios Palamas).

180. *Vita B of Athanasios of Athos*, ch. 2–3.

181. See Gerstel and Talbot, "Nuns in the Byzantine Countryside," and Gerstel, *Rural Lives and Landscapes*, 148–49.

182. *Actes de Xéropotamou*, no. 30.

183. Mitsiou, "Late Byzantine Female Monasticism," 167–70, discusses some of the evidence but reaches a somewhat different conclusion. Although she admits that some of the nuns attested in the synodal documents lived in their own houses (e.g., 169n73 and 170), she assumes that most of the nuns mentioned in these documents without affiliation with a specific convent did in fact reside in nunneries.

184. Rosemary Morris, "Reciprocal Gifts on Mount Athos in the Tenth and Eleventh Centuries," in *The Languages of Gift in the Early Middle Ages*, ed. Wendy Davies and Paul Fouracre (Cambridge: Cambridge University Press, 2010), 176–77.

185. See Talbot, "Personal Poverty in Byzantine Monasticism."

186. MM 1, no. 69, pp. 149–51, no. 70, pp. 155–56; *RegPatr* 5, nos. 2153, 2156.

187. MM 1, no. 126, pp. 283–84; *RegPatr* 5, no. 2304.

188. MM 1, no. 170, pp. 382–83; *RegPatr* 5, no. 2409.

189. MM 2, no. 557, p. 363.6–34; *RegPatr* 6, no. 2910.

190. MM 2, no. 485, pp. 238–39; *RegPatr* 6, no. 2988.

191. MM 2, nos. 549 and 550, pp. 347–52; *RegPatr* 6, nos. 3061, 3063. The term *triklinos* may refer to a barn or granary; see *LSJ*, s.v. "τρίκλινος." The *kellia* are mentioned on p. 349.9.

192. MM 2, no. 555, pp. 358–59; *RegPatr* 6, no. 3111.

193. MM 2, no. 579, pp. 395–99; *RegPatr* 6, no. 3138.

194. MM 2, no. 578, pp. 394–95; *RegPatr* 6, no. 3137.

195. MM 2, no. 599, pp. 427–29; *RegPatr* 6, no. 3159.

196. MM 2, no. 684, pp. 564–65; *RegPatr* 6, no. 3247. The term *kathisma*, which has several meanings in Greek, normally refers to a very small monastic establishment, and here seems to be identical with a *kellion*.

197. MM 2, no. 652, pp. 502–5; *RegPatr* 6, no. 3213.

198. *RegPatr* 5, no. 2339; *RPK* 3, no. 205, pp. 176–83.

199. *RPK* 3, no. 205, p. 178; for Ioannikios, see *PLP*, no. 8811, for Isaias, *PLP*, no. 6738, for Thiniatissa, *PLP*, no. 7738.

200. *Vita of Basil the Younger*, pt. 1, ch. 36–38.

201. See Annick Peters-Custot, *Les grecs de l'Italie méridionale post-byzantine (IXe–XIVe siècle): Une acculturation en douceur* (Rome: École française de Rome, 2009), 198–99.

202. *Vita of Basil the Younger*, pt. 1, ch. 10–13, 23, 25.

203. Ibid., pt. 1, ch. 26, 33.

204. Ibid., pt. 3, ch. 11.

205. Ibid., p. 15.

206. Caner, *Wandering, Begging Monks*, 15.

207. *Vita of Evaristos*, 307.12–22.

208. MM 1, no. 153, pp. 342–44; *RegPatr* 5, no. 2334 (my translation).

209. MM 2, no. 408, p. 134; *RegPatr* 6, no. 2857. The editor, Jean Darrouzès, notes that he was not forbidden to make barrels, but only from making them in a public space.

210. MM 2, no. 560, p. 370; *RegPatr* 6, no. 3116.

211. See the discussion of her in chapter 2, section "Double Monasteries," 96–97.

212. Hero, "Irene-Eulogia Choumnaina," 131.

213. Ibid., 131n36, 133, and 138.

214. *Vita of Cyril Phileotes*, ch. 2–4.

215. Ibid., ch. 5–6, 21.3

216. Ibid., ch. 6–8.

217. Ibid., ch. 14, 18, 20.

218. Ibid., ch. 21–23.

219. See the *Vita of Mary the Younger* and *Vita of Thomaïs of Lesbos*.

CONCLUSION

1. For good discussion of this tension, see Kazhdan, "Hermitic, Cenobitic and Secular Ideals," 473–87.

2. E.g., *Ptochoprodromos*, poem IV, Greek text, 139–75, German translation, 199–217.

3. Here I disagree with Kazhdan, who calls eremitism "individualism without independence"; see Kazhdan, "Hermitic, Cenobitic and Secular Ideals," 477. His formulation might apply to lavriot hermits or to those who lived in a small group with a leader, but not to completely isolated hermits, such as Maximos the Hutburner.

4. See Kazhdan and Constable, *People and Power*, 25.
5. Ibid., 33.
6. Ibid.
7. (6) Rila, ch. 10, *BMFD* 1:131.
8. (35) Skoteine [= Boreine], ch. 13, *BMFD* 3:1183.
9. (60) Charsianeites, ch. B2, *BMFD* 4:1641.
10. Ibid., ch. B3, *BMFD* 4:1642.
11. Magdalino, "The Byzantine Holy Man in the Twelfth Century." See also the remarks of Rosemary Morris, *Monks and Laymen in Byzantium, 843–1118* (Cambridge: Cambridge University Press, 1995), 293–94, that in the twelfth century there was a view that "eccentricity and even individuality in the monastic life was doctrinally suspect."
12. See, for example, the story of Athanasios of Athos in his formative years at the *lavra* of Mount Kyminas, in chapter 1, section "St. Athanasios of Athos and the Great Lavra," 28.
13. See Wortley, "Grazers," 45 and n39.
14. See *Vita of Maximos by Theophanes*, ch. 6; *Vita of Maximos by Kochylas*, ch. 16, pp. 532–33. See also chapter 3, section "Holy Mountains and Solitaries," 104–5.
15. *Vita of Symeon the New Theologian*, ch. 54. For yet another example of similar advice, see the *Vita of Ioannikios by Peter*, ch. 8: "The father . . . knew that it would be unreasonable [to expect] someone not previously trained in ascetic struggles . . . to attain, at the very beginning, the loftiest [goal of] solitary contemplation."
16. (13) Ath. Typikon, ch. 40, *BMFD* 1:261.
17. Ibid., ch. 46, *BMFD* 1:262.
18. (30) Phoberos, ch. 58, *BMFD* 3:939–43.
19. See Talbot, "The Adolescent Monastic," 83–85.
20. Günter Prinzing, ed., *Demetrii Chomateni ponemata diaphora* (Berlin: De Gruyter, 2002), act no. 119.
21. *Vita of Euthymios the Patriarch*, ch. 2, pp. 8–11.
22. *Vita of Neilos of Rossano*, ch. 44.2.
23. Ibid., ch. 33.1.
24. *Vita of Ioannikios by Peter*, ch. 10–11.
25. *Vita of Cyril Phileotes*, ch. 52.6, 23.3.
26. See chapter 3, section "St. Maximos the Hutburner," 111, for another reference to this episode.

27. *Vita of Maximos by Theophanes*, ch. 16.2; the quotation is from Matthew 5:16.

28. *Vita of Maximos by Kochylas*, ch. 30, p. 545.

29. See chapter 3, section on "Food," 119–20, for fuller details.

30. (24) Christodoulos, ch. A23–24; *BMFD* 2:590–92.

31. *Vita of Sabas the Younger*, ch. 23.72–76. I have used the translation of Ivanov, *Holy Fools*, 229.

BIBLIOGRAPHY

PRIMARY SOURCES

Actes de Docheiariou	*Actes de Docheiariou*, ed. Nicolas Oikonomides (Paris: P. Lethielleux, 1984)
Actes de Kutlumus	*Actes de Kutlumus* (rev. ed.), ed. Paul Lemerle (Paris: P. Lethielleux, 1988)
Actes de Lavra	*Actes de Lavra*, ed. Paul Lemerle et al., 4 vols. (Paris: P. Lethielleux, 1970–1982)
Actes d'Iviron	*Actes d'Iviron*, ed. Jacques Lefort et al. (Paris: P. Lethielleux, 1985–)
Actes du Pantocrator	*Actes du Pantocrator*, ed. Vassiliki Kravari (Paris: P. Lethielleux, 1991)
Actes du Prôtaton	*Actes du Prôtaton*, ed. Denise Papachryssanthou (Paris: P. Lethielleux, 1975)
Actes de Vatopédi	*Actes de Vatopédi*, ed. Jacques Bompaire, Jacques Lefort, et al. (Paris: P. Lethielleux, 2001–)
Actes de Xéropotamou	*Actes de Xéropotamou*, ed. Jacques Bompaire (Paris: P. Lethielleux, 1964)
Athanasios I, *Correspondence*	*The Correspondence of Athanasius I, Patriarch of Constantinople*, ed. and trans. Alice-Mary Talbot (Washington, DC: Dumbarton Oaks, 1975)
Basil of Caesarea, *Long Rule*	Basil of Caesarea, *Regulae fusius tractatae*, PG 31:889–1052
BMFD	*Byzantine Monastic Foundation Documents*, ed. John P. Thomas and Angela C. Hero, 5 vols. (Washington, DC: Dumbarton Oaks, 2000)

Chomatenos	*Demetrii Chomateni ponemata diaphora*, ed. Günter Prinzing (Berlin: De Gruyter, 2002)
Chronicle of Sphrantzes	*The Fall of the Byzantine Empire: A Chronicle by George Sphrantzes, 1401–1477*, trans. Marios Philippides (Amherst: University of Massachusetts Press, 1980); Greek text, *Georgios Sphrantzes: Memorii*, ed. Vasile Grecu (Bucharest: Editura Academiei Republicii Socialiste România, 1966)
CIC	*Corpus iuris civilis*, ed. Paul Krueger, Theodor Mommsen, et al., 3 vols. (Berlin: Weidmann, 1928–1929)
Eustathios, "Ad stylitam"	Eustathios of Thessalonike, "Ad stylitam quendam Thessalonicensem," in *PG* 136:217–64, and in Eustathios, *Opuscula*, 182–96
Eustathios, *Opuscula*	*Eustathii metropolitae Thessalonicensis opuscula*, edited by T. L. F. Tafel (Frankfurt, 1832; reprint, Amsterdam, 1964)
Gregory of Tours, *History of the Franks*	Gregory of Tours, *History of the Franks*, trans. Ernest Brehaut (New York: Norton, 1969)
Laudatio of Plato of Sakkoudion	*PG* 99:804–50
Lenten Triodion	*The Lenten Triodion*, trans. Mother Mary and Archimandrite Kallistos Ware (London: Faber and Faber, 1978)
Leo the Deacon, *History*	*The History of Leo the Deacon: Byzantine Military Expansion in the Tenth Century*, trans. Alice-Mary Talbot and Denis F. Sullivan (Washington, DC: Dumbarton Oaks, 2005)
Meyer, *Die Haupturkunden*	*Die Haupturkunden für die Geschichte der Athosklöster*, ed. Philipp Meyer (Leipzig: Hinrich, 1894)
Neilos, *De octo spiritibus malitiae*	Neilos of Ankyra, *De octo spiritibus malitiae*, *PG* 79:1145–64

Bibliography 259

Philokalia	*The Philokalia: The Complete Text Compiled by St. Nikodimos of the Holy Mountain and St. Makarios of Corinth*, trans. G. E. H. Palmer, Philip Sherrard, and Kallistos Ware, 4 vols. (London: Faber and Faber, 1979–95)
Price, *Lives of the Monks of Palestine*	*Lives of the Monks of Palestine by Cyril of Scythopolis*, trans. Richard M. Price (Kalamazoo, MI: Cistercian Publications, 1991)
Ptochoprodromos	*Ptochoprodromos*, ed. and trans. Hans Eideneier (Cologne: Romiosini, 1991)
Rhalles-Potles, Σύνταγμα	Σύνταγμα τῶν θείων καὶ ἱερῶν κανόνων, 6 vols., ed. Georgios A. Rhalles and Michael Potles (Athens: G. Chartophylakos, 1852–1859)
Robert de Clari, *Conquête*, trans. Dufournet	*Robert de Clari: La conquête de Constantinople*, trans. Jean Dufournet (Paris: Honoré Champion, 2004)
Robert de Clari, *Conquête*, ed. Noble	*Robert de Clari: La conquête de Constantinople*, ed. and trans. Peter Noble (Edinburgh: Société Rencesvals British Branch, 2005)
Rule of Saint Benedict	*The Rule of Saint Benedict*, ed. and trans. Bruce L. Venarde (Cambridge, MA: Harvard University Press, 2011)
Symeon the New Theologian, *Catecheses*	*Syméon le Nouveau Théologien: Catéchèses*, ed. Basile Krivochéine, trans. Joseph Paramelle, 3 vols. (Paris: Editions du Cerf, 1963–65)
Talbot, *Byzantine Defenders of Images*	*Byzantine Defenders of Images: Eight Saints' Lives in English Translation*, ed. Alice-Mary Talbot (Washington, DC: Dombarton Oaks, 1996)
Talbot, *Holy Women*	*Holy Women of Byzantium: Ten Saints' Lives in English Translation*, ed. Alice-Mary Talbot (Washington, DC: Dumbarton Oaks, 1996)

Theodore of Stoudios, *Great Catechesis*	*Théodore Stoudite: Les grandes catéchèses* [*Livre 1*], trans. Florence de Montleau (Bégrolles-en-Mauges: Abbaye de Bellefontaine, 2002)
Theodore of Stoudios, *Letters*	*Theodori Studitae epistulae*, ed. Georgios Fatouros, 2 vols. (Berlin: De Gruyter, 1991)
Theoleptos, *Monastic Discourses*	*Theoleptos of Philadelpheia: The Monastic Discourses*, ed. and trans. Robert Sinkewicz (Toronto: Pontifical Institute of Mediaeval Studies, 1992)
Theophylact of Ohrid, *In Defense of Eunuchs*	*Théophylacte d'Achrida: Discours, traités, poésies*, ed. and trans. Paul Gautier (Thessalonike: Association de recherches byzantines, 1980), 289–331
Vita of Andrew the Fool	*The Life of Saint Andrew the Fool*, ed. and trans. Lennart Rydén, 2 vols. (Uppsala: Uppsala University, 1995)
Vita of Anna/Euphemianos	"The Life of St. Anna/Euphemianos," trans. Vasileios Marinis, *Journal of Modern Hellenism* [= *Byzantium: Essays in Honor of Angela Constantinides Hero*], 27 (2009–10): 53–69; Greek text: *SynaxCP* 174–78
Vita of Anthony of Egypt	*The Life of Antony and the Letter to Marcellinus*, trans. Robert C. Gregg (New York: Paulist, 1980); Greek text: *PG* 26:837–976
Vita of Anthony the Younger	*Life of Anthony*, ed. Athanasios Papadopoulos-Kerameus, *Sylloge Pravoslavnij Palestinskij Sbornik* 19, no. 3 (1907): 186–216
Vita of Anthousa of Mantineon	"Life of St. Anthousa of Mantineon," trans. Alice-Mary Talbot, in Talbot, *Byzantine Defenders of Images*, 13–19; Greek text, *SynaxCP* 848–52
Vita of Athanasia of Aegina	"Life of St. Athanasia of Aegina," trans. Lee F. Sherry, in Talbot, *Holy Women of*

Byzantium, 142–58; Greek text, "Vie de sainte Athanasie d'Egine," ed. François Halkin, in *Six inédits d'hagiographie byzantine* (Brussels: Société des Bollandistes, 1987), 179–95

Vita B of Athanasios of Athos — "Life of Athanasios of Athos, Version B," ed. and trans. Alice-Mary Talbot, in Greenfield and Talbot, *Holy Men of Mount Athos*, 127–367

Vita of Athanasios of Meteora — Nikos A. Bees, "Συμβολὴ εἰς τὴν ἱστορίαν τῶν μονῶν τῶν Μετεώρων," *Byzantis* 1 (1909): 237–70

Vita of Athanasios, patriarch of Constantinople — "Žitija dvuh' Vselenskih' patriarhov' XIV vv., svv. Afanasija I i Isidora I," ed. Athanasios Papadopoulos-Kerameus, *Zapiski istoriko-filologičeskago fakul'teta Imperatorskago S.-Peterburgskago Universiteta* 76 (1905): 1–51

Vita of Basil the Younger — *The Life of Saint Basil the Younger*, ed. and trans. Denis F. Sullivan, Alice-Mary Talbot, and Stamatina McGrath (Washington, DC: Dumbarton Oaks, 2014)

Vita of Blasios of Amorion — *AASS* Nov. 4:657–69

Vita of Cyril Phileotes — *La Vie de Sainte Cyrille le Philéote, moine byzantin (†1110)*, ed. and trans. Etienne Sargologos (Brussels: Société des Bollandistes, 1964)

Vita of David, Symeon and George — "Life of Sts. David, Symeon and George of Lesbos," trans. Dorothy Abrahamse and Douglas Domingo-Foraste, in Talbot, *Byzantine Defenders of Images*, 143–241; Greek text: "Acta graeca ss. Davidis, Symeonis et Georgii Mitylenae in insula Lesbo," ed. Joseph van den Gheyn, *Analecta Bollandiana* 18 (1899): 209–59

Vita of Euphrosyne the Younger — "De s. Euphrosyna Iuniore," *AASS* Nov. 3:858–77

Vita of Euthymios the Patriarch	*Vita Euthymii patriarchae CP*, ed. and trans. Patricia Karlin-Hayter (Brussels: Editions de Byzantion, 1970)
Vita of Euthymios the Younger	"Life of Euthymios the Younger," ed. Alexander Alexakis, trans. Alice-Mary Talbot, in Greenfield and Talbot, *Holy Men of Mount Athos*, 1–125
Vita of Evaristos	"La Vie de s. Evariste, higoumène à Constantinople," ed. Charles van de Vorst, *Analecta Bollandiana* 41 (1923): 288–326
Vita of George of Mytilene	Οἱ ἅγιοι Γεώργιοι, ἀρχιεπίσκοποι Μυτιλήνης [= Λεσβιακὸν Ἑορτολόγιον, 1], ed. Ioannes Phountoules (Athens, 1959), 33–43
Vita of Germanos Maroules	Φιλοθέου Κωνσταντινουπόλεως τοῦ Κοκκίνου ἁγιολογικὰ ἔργα, vol. Α΄, Θεσσαλονικεῖς ἅγιοι, ed. Demetrios G. Tsames (Thessalonike: Kentron Vyzantinon Ereunon, 1985), 110–71
Vita of Gregentios	*Life and Works of Saint Gregentios, Archbishop of Tafar*, ed. and trans. Albrecht Berger (Berlin: De Gruyter, 2006)
Vita of Ioannikios by Peter	"Life of St. Ioannikios," trans. Denis F. Sullivan, in Talbot, *Byzantine Defenders of Images*, 243–351; Greek text: *AASS* Nov. 2.1:384–435
Vita of Ioannikios by Sabas	*AASS*, Nov. 2.1:332–83
Vita of Irene of Chrysobalanton	*The Life of St. Irene, Abbess of Chrysobalanton*, ed. and trans. Jan Olof Rosenqvist (Uppsala: Uppsala University, 1986)
Vita of Joseph the Hymnographer	*Life of Joseph by Theophanes*, ed. Athanasios Papadopoulos-Kerameus, in *Sbornik grečeskich i latinskich pamjatnikov, kasajuščichsja Fotija patriarcha* [= *Monumenta graeca et latina ad*

	historiam Photii patriarchae pertinentia] (St. Petersburg: Tip. V. Kirshbauma, 1901), 2:1–14
Vita of Lazaros of Galesion	*The Life of Lazaros of Mt. Galesion: An Eleventh-Century Pillar Saint*, trans. Richard P. H. Greenfield (Washington, DC: Dumbarton Oaks, 2000); Greek text: *AASS* Nov. 3: 508–88
Vita of Leo Luke of Corleone	*AASS* Mar. 1:99–102
Vita of Leontios of Jerusalem	*The Life of Leontios, Patriarch of Jerusalem*, ed. and trans. Demetrios Tsougarakis (Leiden: Brill, 1993)
Vita of Luke of Steiris	*The Life and Miracles of St. Luke*, ed. and trans. Carolyn L. and W. Robert Connor (Brookline, MA: Hellenic College Press, 1987)
Vita of Luke the Stylite	*Les saints stylites*, ed. Hippolyte Delehaye (Brussels: Société des Bollandistes, 1923), 195–237
Vita of Makrina	"A Letter from Gregory, Bishop of Nyssa, on the Life of Saint Macrina," in *Handmaids of the Lord: Contemporary Descriptions of Feminine Asceticism in the First Six Christian Centuries*, trans. Joan M. Petersen (Kalamazoo, MI: Cistercian Publications, 1996), 51–86
Vita of Mary/Marinos	"Life of St. Mary/Marinos," trans. Nicholas Constas, in Talbot, *Holy Women of Byzantium*, 1–12; Greek text: "La Vie Ancienne de Sainte Marie surnommée Marinos," in *Corona Gratiarum. Miscellanea patristica, historica et liturgica Eligio Dekkers O.S.B. XII Lustra complenti oblata*, vol. 1 (Brugge: Sint Pietersabdij, 1975), 83–94
Vita of Mary the Younger	"Life of St. Mary the Younger," trans. Angeliki E. Laiou, in Talbot, *Holy*

	Women of Byzantium, 239–89; Greek text: *AASS* Nov. 4:692–705
Vita of Matrona of Perge	"Life of St. Matrona of Perge," trans. Jeffrey Featherstone and Cyril Mango, in Talbot, *Holy Women of Byzantium*, 13–64; Greek text: *AASS* Nov. 3: 790–813
Vita of Maximos by Kochylas	Patapios Kausokalyvites, "'Ιερομονάχου Ἰωαννικίου Κόχιλα, Βίος ὁσίου Μαξίμου τοῦ Καυσοκαλύβη [14ος αἰ.]," *Γρηγόριος ὁ Παλαμᾶς* 819 (2007): 513–77
Vita of Maximos by Niphon	"Life of Maximos the Hutburner by Niphon," ed. and trans. Richard P. H. Greenfield, in Greenfield and Talbot, *Holy Men of Mount Athos*, 369–439
Vita of Maximos by Theophanes	"Life of Maximos the Hutburner by Theophanes," ed. and trans. Richard P. H. Greenfield and Alice-Mary Talbot, in Greenfield and Talbot, *Holy Men of Mount Athos*, 441–567
Vita of Meletios of Myoupolis by Nicholas of Methone	Νικολάου ἐπισκόπου Μεθώνης βίος Μελετίου τοῦ Νέου, ed. B. Vasilievskij, *Pravoslavnij Palestinskij Sbornik* VI, 2 (1886): 1–39
Vita of Michael Maleinos	"Vie de s. Michel Maleinos," ed. Louis Petit, *Revue de l'Orient Chrétien* 7 (1902): 543–94
Vita of Neilos of Rossano	*Life of Saint Neilos of Rossano*, ed. and trans. Raymond L. Capra, Ines A. Murzaku, and Douglas Milewski (Cambridge, MA: Harvard University Press, 2017)
Vita of Nikephoros, patriarch	"Life of the Patriarch Nikephoros I of Constantinople," trans. Elizabeth A. Fisher, in Talbot, *Byzantine Defenders of Images*, 25–142; Greek text: *Nicephori archiepıscopi Constantinopolitani opuscula historica*, ed. Charles de Boor (Leipzig, 1880), 139–217

Vita of Nikephoros of Miletos	"Vita sancti Nicephori episcopi Milesii saeculo X," ed. Hippolyte Delehaye, *Analecta Bollandiana* 14 (1895): 129–66; reprinted in Theodor Wiegand, *Milet 3.1. Der Latmos* (Berlin: Staatliche Museen der Berlin, 1913), 157–71
Vita of Nikodemos of Thessalonike	"Nikodemos, a Holy Fool in Late Byzantine Thessalonike," trans. Alice-Mary Talbot, in *ΔΩΡΟΝ ΡΟΔΟΠΟΙΚΙΛΟΝ: Studies in Honour of Jan Olof Rosenqvist*, ed. Denis Searby and Johan Heldt (Uppsala: Uppsala University, 2012), 223–32; Greek text, Φιλοθέου Κωνσταντινουπόλεως τοῦ Κοκκίνου ἁγιολογικὰ ἔργα, Vol. Α΄, Θεσσαλονικεῖς ἅγιοι, ed. Demetrios G. Tsames (Thessalonike: Kentron Vyzantinon Ereunon, 1985), 83–93
Vita of Nikon	*The Life of Saint Nikon*, ed. and trans. Denis Sullivan (Brookline, MA: Hellenic College Press, 1987)
Vita of Niphon	"Life of Niphon of Athos," ed. and trans. Richard P. H. Greenfield, in Greenfield and Talbot, *Holy Men of Mount Athos*, 569–611
Vita of Paul of Latros	"Vita s. Pauli Iunioris in Monte Latro," ed. Hippolyte Delehaye, in Theodor Wiegand, *Milet. 3.1. Der Latmos* (Berlin: Staatliche Museen der Berlin, 1913), 105–57
Vita of Peter of Atroa	*La Vie merveilleuse de saint Pierre d'Atroa (†837)*, ed. and trans. Vitalien Laurent (Brussels: Société des Bollandistes, 1956)
Vita of Philotheos	"Life of Philotheos of Athos," ed. and trans. Stamatina McGrath, in Greenfield and Talbot, *Holy Men of Mount Athos*, 613–39

Vita of Romanos the Neomartyr	Latin translation by Paul Peeters, "S. Romain le néomartyr (†1 mai 780) d'après un document géorgien," *Analecta Bollandiana* 30 (1911): 393–427
Vita of Romylos of Vidin	"Days and Deeds of a Hesychast Saint: A Translation of the Greek Life of Saint Romylos," trans. Mark Bartusis, Khalifa ben Nasser, and Angeliki E. Laiou, *Byzantine Studies/Etudes byzantines* 9, no. 1 (1982): 24–47; Greek text: "Un ermite des Balkans au XIVe siècle: La vie grecque inédite de Saint Romylos," ed. François Halkin, *Byzantion* 31 (1961): 111–47
Vita of Sabas the Younger	Φιλοθέου Κωνσταντινουπόλεως τοῦ Κοκκίνου ἁγιολογικὰ ἔργα, Vol. Aʹ, Θεσσαλονικεῖς ἅγιοι, ed. Demetrios G. Tsames (Thessalonike: Kentron Vyzantinon Ereunon, 1985), 161–325; modern Greek tr., Ἁγίου Φιλοθέου Κοκκίνου Βίος Ἁγίου Σάββα τοῦ Βατοπεδινοῦ (Hagion Oros: Hiera Megiste Mone Vatopaidiou, 2000)
Vita of Stephen the Sabaite	*AASS* Jul. 3:504–84
Vita of Stephen the Younger	*La Vie d'Etienne le Jeune par Etienne le Diacre*, ed. and trans. Marie-France Auzépy (Aldershot: Ashgate, 1997)
Vita of Symeon the Fool	"The Life of Symeon the Fool," trans. Derek Krueger, in Krueger, *Symeon the Holy Fool*, 131–71; Greek text: ed. Lennart Rydén, in *Vie de Syméon le Fou, et Vie de Jean de Chypre*, ed. André-Jean Festugière (Paris: P. Geuthner, 1974), 55–104
Vita of Symeon the New Theologian	*The Life of Saint Symeon the New Theologian*, ed. and trans. Richard P. H. Greenfield (Cambridge, MA: Harvard University Press, 2013)
Vita of Theodora of Thessalonike	"Life of St. Theodora of Thessalonike," trans. Alice-Mary Talbot, in Talbot, *Holy Women of Byzantium*, 159–237; Greek

	text, Ὁ βίος τῆς ὁσιομυροβλύτιδος Θεοδώρας τῆς ἐν Θεσσαλονίκῃ. Διήγηση περὶ τῆς μεταθέσεως τοῦ τιμίου λειψάνου τῆς ὁσίας Θεοδώρας, ed. and trans. Symeon Paschalides (Thessalonike: Holy Metropolis of Thessalonike, Center for Hagiological Studies, 1991)
Vita of Theodora the Empress	"Life of St. Theodora the Empress," trans. Martha P. Vinson, in Talbot, *Byzantine Defenders of Images*, 353–82; Greek text: "Βίος τῆς αὐτοκρατείρας Θεοδώρας (BHG 1731)," ed. Athanasios Markopoulos, *Symmeikta* 5 (1983): 249–85
Vita of Theodore of Edessa	*Žitie iže vo sv. otca našego Feodora archepiskopa Edesskogo*, ed. Ivan V. Pomjalovskij (St. Petersburg, 1892)
Vita of Theodore of Kythera	"Ὁ βίος τοῦ ἁγίου Θεοδώρου Κυθήρων (10ος αἰ.)," ed. Nikolaos Oikonomides, *Πρακτικὰ Τρίτου Πανιονίου Συνεδρίου* (Athens, 1967), 1:264–91
Vita of Theodore of Stoudios by Michael	PG 99:233–328
Vita of Theoktiste of Lesbos	"Life of St. Theoktiste of Lesbos," trans. Angela Hero, in Talbot, *Holy Women of Byzantium*, 101–16; Greek text: *AASS* Nov. 4:224–33
Vitae of Theophanes the Confessor and Theodore	"Lives of Theophanes and Theodore," ed. Athanasios Papadopoulos-Kerameus, *Ἀνάλεκτα Ἱεροσολυμιτικῆς Σταχυολογίας* (St. Petersburg: V. Kirsvaoum, 1897; reprint, Brussels, 1963), 4:185–223, and (St. Petersburg: V. Kirsvaoum, 1898; reprint, Brussels, 1963), 5:397–99
Vita of Thomaïs of Lesbos	"Life of St. Thomaïs of Lesbos," trans. Paul Halsall, in Talbot, *Holy Women of Byzantium*, 297–322; Greek text: *AASS* Nov. 4:234–42

SECONDARY LITERATURE

Abrahamse, Dorothy. "Women's Monasticism in the Middle Byzantine Period: Problems and Prospects." *Byzantinische Forschungen* 9 (1985): 35–58.

Acheimastou-Potamianou, Myrtale. "The Basilissa Anna Palaiologina of Arta and the Monastery of Vlacherna." In *Les femmes et le monachisme byzantin/Women and Byzantine Monasticism: Actes du Symposium d'Athènes, 1988*, edited by Jacques Y. Perreault, 43–49. Athens: Institut canadien d'archéologie à Athénes, 1991.

Αγιολογία Ύστερης Βυζαντινής Περιόδου (1204–1453). http://byzhadb.eie.gr/.

Alexakis, Alexander. "A Meeting of Hypatia of Alexandria with St. Febronia of Nisibis in the Life of St. David, Symeon and George of Lesbos." In *Byzantine Religious Culture: Studies in Honor of Alice-Mary Talbot*, edited by Denis Sullivan, Elizabeth Fisher, and Stratis Papaioannou, 19–30. Leiden: Brill, 2012.

Ball, Jennifer. "Decoding the Habit of the Byzantine Nun." *Journal of Modern Hellenism* 27 (2009–2010) [= *Byzantium: Essays in Honor of Angela Constantinides Hero*. New York: Hellenic College Press, 2009], 25–52.

Beck, Hans-Georg. *Das byzantinische Jahrtausend*. Munich: Beck, 1978.

Belke, Klaus. "Heilige Berge Bithyniens." In *Heilige Berge und Wüsten: Byzanz und sein Umfeld. Referate auf dem 21. Internationalen Kongress für Byzantinistik. London, 21.–26. August 2006*, edited by Peter Soustal, 15–24. Vienna: Österreichische Akademie der Wissenschaften, 2009.

Boojamra, John L. *Church Reform in the Late Byzantine Empire: A Study for the Patriarchate of Athanasios of Constantinople*. Thessalonike: Patriarchikon Hidryma Paterikon Meleton, 1982.

"Boskoi: The Grazing Hermits." https://citydesert.wordpress.com/2014/01/04/boskoi-the-grazing-hermits/.

Brakke, David. "The Problematization of Nocturnal Emissions in Early Christian Syria, Egypt, and Gaul." *Journal of Early Christian Studies* 3 (1995): 419–60.

Bryer, Anthony. "The Late Byzantine Monastery in Town and Countryside." *Studies in Church History* 16 (1979): 219–41.

Bryer, Anthony, and Mary Cunningham, eds. *Mount Athos and Byzantine Monasticism*. Aldershot: Ashgate, 1996.

Caner, Daniel. *Wandering, Begging Monks: Spiritual Authority and the Promotion of Monasticism in Late Antiquity*. Berkeley: University of California Press, 2002.

Carr, Annemarie W. "Women as Artists in the Middle Ages: 'The Dark Is Light Enough.'" In *Dictionary of Women Artists*, edited by Delia Gaze, 1:14–17. London: Fitzroy Dearborn, 1997.

Charanis, Peter. "The Monk as an Element of Byzantine Society." *Dumbarton Oaks Papers* 25 (1971): 63–84.

Congourdeau, Marie-Hélène. "La terre sainte au XIVe siècle: La *Vie de Sabas de Vatopédi* par Philothée Kokkinos." In *Pèlerinages et lieux saints dans l'Antiquité et le Moyen Âge*, edited by Béatrice Caseau, Jean-Claude Cheynet, et al., 121–33. Paris: Association des Amis du Centre d'Histoire et Civilisation de Byzance, 2006.

Connor, Carolyn L. *Women of Byzantium*. New Haven, CT: Yale University Press, 2004.

Constable, Giles. Introduction to *Apologiae duae: Gozechini epistola ad Walcherum. Burchardi, ut videtur, abbatis Bellevallis apologia de Barbis*, edited by R. B. C. Huygens [= *Corpus Christianorum, Continuatio Medievalis*, 62], 114–30. Turnhout: Brepols, 1985.

Corrigan, Kevin. *The Life of Saint Macrina by Gregory, Bishop of Nyssa*. Toronto: Peregrina, 1989.

Ćurčić, Slobodan. "Monastic Cells in Medieval Serbian Church Towers: Survival of an Early Byzantine Monastic Concept and Its Meaning." In *ΣΟΦΙΑ: Sbornik statei po iskusstvu Vizantii i Drevnei Rusi v chest' A. I. Komecha*, edited by A. L. Batalov et al., 491–514. Moscow: Severnyi palomnik, 2006.

Cutler, Anthony, and Paul Magdalino. "Some Precisions on the Lincoln College Typikon." *Cahiers archéologiques* 27 (1978): 179–98.

Dafis, Spyros. *Treasures of Mount Athos: Nature and Natural Environment in Mount Athos*. Athos: Holy Community of Agion Oros, 1997. http://pemptousia.com/2012/09/nature-and-the-natural-environment-of-mount-athos/.

Dagron, Gilbert. "Les moines et la ville: Le monachisme à Constantinople jusqu'au concile de Chalcédoine (451)." *Travaux et Mémoires* 4 (1970): 229–76.

Darrouzès, Jean. "Notice sur Grégoire Antiochos (1160 à 1196)." *Revue des études byzantines* 20 (1962): 83–92.

Delehaye, Hippolyte, ed. *Deux typica byzantins de l'époque des Paléologues*. Brussels: M. Lamertin, 1921.

———. "Les femmes stylites." *Analecta Bollandiana* 27 (1908): 391–92.

———. *Les saints stylites*. Brussels: Société des Bollandistes, 1923.

Delierneux, Nathalie. "Anne-Euphémianos, l'épouse devenue eunuque: Continuité et évolution d'un modèle hagiographique." *Byzantion* 72 (2002): 105–40.

———. "Les moniales à Byzance, entre clôture et vie publique (VIIIe–début XIIe siècle)." In *Le saint, le moine et le paysan: Mélanges d'histoire byzantine offerts à Michel Kaplan*, edited by Olivier Delouis, Sophie Métivier, and Paule Pagès, 101–17. Paris: Publications de la Sorbonne, 2016.

Della Dora, Veronica. *Landscape, Nature, and the Sacred in Byzantium*. Cambridge: Cambridge University Press, 2016.

Delouis, Olivier. "Le *Testament* de Théodore Stoudite, est-il de Théodore?" *Revue des études byzantines* 66 (2008): 173–90.

———. "Le Testament de Théodore Stoudite: Édition critique et traduction." *Revue des études byzantines* 67 (2009): 77–109.

———. "Portée et limites de l'archéologie monastique dans les Balkans et en Asie Mineure jusqu'au Xe siècle." In Delouis and Mossakowska-Gaubert, *La vie quotidienne des moines en Orient et en Occident*, 1:251–74.

———. *Saint-Jean-Baptiste de Stoudios à Constantinople: La contribution d'un monastère à l'histoire de l'Empire byzantin*, 2 vols. Université Paris I/Panthéon-Sorbonne, 2005.

Delouis, Olivier, and Maria Mossakowska-Gaubert, eds. *La vie quotidienne des moines en Orient et en Occident, IVe–Xe siècle. I. L'état des sources*. Cairo: Institut français d'archéologie orientale; Athens: École française d'Athènes, 2015.

Dembińska, Maria. "Diet: A Comparison of Food Consumption between Some Eastern and Western Monasteries in the 4th–12th Centuries." *Byzantion* 55 (1985): 431–62.

Dennis, George. "Elias the Monk, a Friend of Psellos." In *Byzantine Authors: Literary Activities and Preoccupations: Texts and Translations Dedicated to the Memory of Nicolas Oikonomides*, edited by John W. Nesbitt, 43–62. Leiden: Brill, 2003.

Déroche, Vincent. "La vie des moines: Les sources pour l'Asie Mineure et les Balkans, ca. 300–1000 apr. J.C." In Delouis and Mossakowska-Gaubert, *La vie quotidienne des moines en Orient et en Occident, IVe–Xe siècle. I. L'état des sources*, 275–87.

Dietz, Maribel. *Wandering Monks, Virgins and Pilgrims: Ascetic Travel in the Mediterranean World, A.D. 300–800*. University Park: Pennsylvania State University Press, 2005.

Doran, Robert. *The Lives of Symeon Stylites*. Kalamazoo, MI: Cistercian Publications, 1992.

Dumbarton Oaks Hagiography Database. https://www.doaks.org/research/byzantine/resources/hagiography-database.

Elm, Susanna. *"Virgins of God": The Making of Asceticism in Late Antiquity*. Oxford: Clarendon, 1994.

Festugière, André-Jean. "Etude sur la vie de s. Sabas le Jeune qui simulait la folie." In *Vie de Syméon le Fou et Vie de Jean de Chypre*, edited by Lennart Rydén and André-Jean Festugière, 223–52. Paris: P. Geuthner, 1974.

Galatariotou, Catia. "Byzantine Women's Monastic Communities: The Evidence of the Typika." *Jahrbuch der Österreichischen Byzantinistik* 38 (1988): 262–90.

———. *The Making of a Saint: The Life, Times and Sanctification of Neophytos the Recluse*. Cambridge: Cambridge University Press, 1991.

Garland, Lynda. *Byzantine Empresses: Women and Power in Byzantium, 527–1204*. London: Routledge, 1999.

Gaul, Niels. "Eunuchs in the Late Byzantine Empire, c. 1250–1400." In *Eunuchs in Antiquity and Beyond*, edited by Shaun Tougher, 199–219. London: Classical Press of Wales and Duckworth, 2002.

———. "Writing 'with Joyful and Leaping Soul': Sacralization, Scribal Hands, and Ceremonial in the Lincoln College Typikon." *Dumbarton Oaks Papers* 69 (2015): 243–71.

Gerstel, Sharon. "Painted Sources for Female Piety in Medieval Byzantium." *Dumbarton Oaks Papers* 52 (1998): 89–111.

———. *Rural Lives and Landscapes in Late Byzantium: Art, Archaeology and Ethnography*. Cambridge: Cambridge University Press, 2015.

Gerstel, Sharon E. J., and Alice-Mary Talbot. "Nuns in the Byzantine Countryside." *Deltion tes Christianikes Archaiologikes Hetaireias* 27 (2006): 481–90.

Goldfus, Haim. "Urban Monasticism and Monasteries of Early Byzantine Palestine: Preliminary Observations." *ARAM Periodical* 15 (2003): 71–79.

Greenfield, Richard P. H., and Alice-Mary Talbot, eds. and trans. *Holy Men of Mount Athos*. Cambridge, MA: Harvard University Press, 2016.

Griffith, Sidney. "Asceticism in the Church of Syria: The Hermeneutics of Early Syrian Monasticism." In *Asceticism*, edited by Vincent L. Wimbush and Richard Valantasis, 220–45. New York: Oxford University Press, 1995.

Halkin, François. "Éloge de Ste Euphrosyne la Jeune par Constantin Akropolite." *Byzantion* 57 (1987): 56–65.

Handbook for Travellers in Greece. 2 vols. London: John Murray, 1884.

Harvey, Susan A. "The Stylite's Liturgy: Ritual and Religious Identity in Late Antiquity." *Journal of Early Christian Studies* 6, no. 3 (1998): 523–39.

Hasenfratz, Eovert. *Ancrene Wisse: Introduction*. http://d.lib.rochester.edu/teams/text/hasenfratz-ancrene-wisse-introduction.

Hatlie, Peter. *The Monks and Monasteries of Constantinople, ca. 350–850*. Cambridge: Cambridge University Press, 2007.

Hero, Angela C. "Irene-Eulogia Choumnaina Palaiologina, Abbess of the Convent of Philanthropos Soter in Constantinople." *Byzantinische Forschungen* 9 (1985): 119–47.

———. *A Woman's Quest for Spiritual Guidance: The Correspondence of Princess Irene Eulogia Choumnaina Palaiologina*. Brookline, MA: Hellenic College Press, 1986.

Hutter, Irmgard. *Corpus der byzantinischen Miniaturhandschriften: Oxford College Libraries*, 5.1 (text) and 5.2 (plates). Stuttgart: Hiersemann, 1997.

———. "Die Geschichte des Lincoln College Typikons." *Jahrbuch der Österreichischen Byzantinistik* 45 (1995): 79–114.

Ivanov, Sergei. *Holy Fools in Byzantium and Beyond*. Oxford: Oxford University Press, 2006.

Joannou, Périclès-Pierre, ed. *Discipline générale antique, I.1, Les conciles oecuméniques (IIe–IXe siècles)*. Grottaferrata: Tipographia Italo-Orientale "S. Nilo," 1962.

Jordan, Robert H., and Rosemary Morris, eds. *The Hypotyposis of the Monastery of the Theotokos Evergetis, Constantinople (11th–12th Centuries)*. Farnham: Ashgate, 2012.

Kaplan, Michel. "La vie de Théodora de Thessalonique: Un écrit familial." In *Approaches to the Byzantine Family*, edited by Leslie Brubaker and Shaun Tougher, 285–301. Farnham: Ashgate, 2013.

Kaplan, Michel, and Eleonora Kountoura-Galake. "Economy and Society in Byzantine Hagiography: Realia and Methodological Questions." In *The Ashgate Research Companion to Byzantine Hagiography*, edited by Stephanos Efthymiadis, 2:389–418. Farnham: Ashgate, 2014.

Karlin-Hayter, Patricia. "Notes sur les archives de Patmos comme source pour la démographie et l'économie de l'île." *Byzantinische Forschungen* 5 (1977): 189–215.

Kavvadias, Georgios. *Pasteurs-nomades méditerranéens: Les Saracatsans de Grèce*. Paris: Gauthier-Villars, 1965.

Kazhdan, Alexander. "Hagiographical Notes." *Byzantinische Zeitschrift* 78 (1985): 49–55.

———. "Hermitic, Cenobitic and Secular Ideals in Byzantine Hagiography of the Ninth through the Twelfth Centuries." *Greek Orthodox Theological Review* 30 (1985): 473–87.

Kazhdan, Alexander, and Giles Constable. *People and Power in Byzantium: An Introduction to Modern Byzantine Studies*. Washington, DC: Dumbarton Oaks, 1982.

Krausmüller, Dirk. "An Ascetic Founder: The Lost First Life of Athanasius the Athonite." In *Founders and Refounders of Byzantine Monasteries*, edited by Margaret Mullett, 63–86. Belfast: Belfast Byzantine Enterprises, Institute of Byzantine Studies, Queen's University of Belfast, 2007.

Krueger, Derek. *Symeon the Holy Fool: Leontius' Life and the Late Antique City*. Berkeley: University of California Press, 1996.

Külzer, Andreas. *Ostthrakien (Europe)*. Vienna: Verlag der Österreichischen Akademie der Wissenschaften, 2008.

Laiou, Angeliki. "Observations on the Life and Ideology of Byzantine Women." *Byzantinischen Forschungen* 9 (1985): 59–102.

———. "Sex, Consent, and Coercion in Byzantium." In *Consent and Coercion to Sex and Marriage in Ancient and Medieval Societies*, edited by Angeliki Laiou, 109–221. Washington, DC: Dumbarton Oaks, 1993.

Lampropoulou, Anna. "Εἰδήσεις γύρω ἀπὸ τὸ γυναικεῖο στυλιτισμὸ στὸ Βυζάντιο." *Theologia* 61 (1990): 187–99.

Lampros, Spyridon. *Catalogue of the Greek Manuscripts on Mount Athos*. 2 vols. Cambridge: Cambridge University Press, 1895–1900.

Laurent, Vitalien. "La direction spirituelle à Byzance: La correspondance d'Irène-Eulogie Choumnaina Paléologine avec son second directeur." *Revue des études byzantines* 14 (1956): 48–86.

———. "La direction spirituelle des grandes dames à Byzance: La correspondance inédite d'un métropolite de Chalcédoine." *Revue des études byzantines* 8 (1950): 63–84.

Leroy, Jules. "La conversion de saint Athanase l'Athonite à l'idéal cénobitique et l'influence stoudite." In *Le millénaire du Mont Athos, 963–1963: Études et mélanges*, 1:101–20. Chevetogne: Editions de Chevetogne, 1963.

———. "La vie quotidienne du moine stoudite." *Irénikon* 27 (1954): 21–50.

Licence, Tom. *Hermits and Recluses in English Society, 950–1200*. Oxford: Oxford University Press, 2011.

Luibheid, Colm, and Norman Russell. *John Climacus: The Ladder of Divine Ascent*. New York: Paulist Press, 1982.

Magdalino, Paul. "The Byzantine Holy Man in the Twelfth Century." In *The Byzantine Saint: University of Birmingham Fourteenth Spring Symposium of Byzantine Studies*, edited by Sergei Hackel, 51–66. London: Fellowship of St. Alban and St. Sergius, 1981.

———. "Paphlagonians in Byzantine High Society." In *Η βυζαντινή Μικρά Ασία*, edited by Stelios Lampakes, 141–50. Athens: Ethniko Hidryma Ereunon, Institouto Vyzantinon Ereunon, 1998.

Malamut, Elisabeth. *Sur la route des saints byzantins*. Paris: CNRS, 1993.

Mango, Cyril. *Byzantium: The Empire of New Rome*. New York: Weidenfeld and Nicolson, 1980.

Marinis, Vasileios. *Architecture and Ritual in the Churches of Constantinople, Ninth to Fifteenth Centuries*. New York: Cambridge University Press, 2014.

———. "Tombs and Burials in the Monastery *tou Libos* in Constantinople." *Dumbarton Oaks Papers* 63 (2009): 147–66.

Mathews, Thomas F. *The Byzantine Churches of Istanbul: A Photographic Survey*. University Park: Pennsylvania State University Press, 1976.

———. *The Early Churches of Constantinople: Architecture and Liturgy*. University Park: Pennsylvania State University Press, 1971.

McNeal, Edgar H. *The Conquest of Constantinople*. New York: Columbia University Press, 1936.

Messis, Charis. *Les eunuques à Byzance, entre réalité et imaginaire*. Paris: De Boccard, 2014.

Meyer, Philipp. "Bruchstücke zweier *typika ktetorika.*" *Byzantinische Zeitschrift* 4 (1895): 45–58.
Miller, Timothy S., and John Thomas. "The Monastic Rule of Patriarch Athanasios I." *Orientalia Christiana Periodica* 62 (1996): 353–71.
Mitsakis, Kariophilis. "Symeon Metropolitan of Euchaita and the Ascetic Ideal in the Eleventh Century." *Byzantina* 2 (1970): 301–34.
Mitsiou, Ekaterini. "Das Doppelkloster des Patriarchen Athanasios I. in Konstantinopel: Historisch-prosopographische und wirtschaftliche Beobachtungen." *Jahrbuch der Österreichischen Byzantinistik* 58 (2008): 87–106.

———. "Frauen als Gründerinnen von Doppelklostern im byzantinischen Reich." In Theis, Mullett, and Grünbart, *Female Founders in Byzantium and Beyond,* 333–43.

———. "Late Byzantine Female Monasticism from the Point of View of the Register of the Patriarchate of Constantinople." In *The Register of the Patriarchate of Constantinople: An Essential Source for the History and Church of Late Byzantium,* edited by Christian Gastgeber et al., 161–73. Vienna: Österreichische Akademie der Wissenschaften, 2013.

"Monastic Schools." In *New Catholic Encyclopedia.* https://www.encyclopedia.com/religion/encyclopedias-almanacs-transcripts-and-maps/monastic-schools.
Morris, Rosemary. *Monks and Laymen in Byzantium, 843–1118.* Cambridge: Cambridge University Press, 1995.

———. "The Origins of Athos." In Bryer and Cunningham, *Mount Athos and Byzantine Monasticism,* 37–46.

———. "Reciprocal Gifts on Mount Athos in the Tenth and Eleventh Centuries." In *The Languages of Gift in the Early Middle Ages,* edited by Wendy Davies and Paul Fouracre, 171–92. Cambridge: Cambridge University Press, 2010.

———. "Symeon the Sanctified and the Re-Foundation of Xenophon." *Byzantine and Modern Greek Studies* 33 (2009): 133–47.
Mullett, Margaret. "Theophylact of Ohrid's *In Defense of Eunuchs.*" In Tougher, *Eunuchs in Antiquity and Beyond,* 177–98.
Mylonas, Paul. *Pictorial Dictionary of the Holy Mountain Athos.* Tübingen: Wasmuth, 2000.
Nicol, Donald. *The Byzantine Lady: Ten Portraits, 1250–1500.* Cambridge: Cambridge University Press, 1994.

———. "*Instabilitas loci*: The Wanderlust of Late Byzantine Monks." *Studies in Church History* 22 (1985): 193–202.
Orlandos, Anastasios. *Μοναστηριακὴ Ἀρχιτεκτονική: κείμενον καὶ σχέδια*. Athens: Hestia, 1958.
Papachrysanthou, Denise. *Ὁ Ἀθωνικὸς μοναχισμός: ἀρχὲς καὶ ὀργάνωση*. Athens: Morphotiko Hidryma Ethnikes Trapezes, 1992.
———. "La vie monastique dans les campagnes byzantines du VIIIe au XIe siècles: Ermitages, groupes, communautés." *Byzantion* 43 (1973): 158–80.
Papadakis, Aristeides. "Byzantine Monasticism Reconsidered." *Byzantinoslavica* 47 (1986): 34–46.
Papadopoulos, S. A. *Ormylia: The Coenobium of the Annunciation*. Athens: Interamerican, 1992.
Papadopoulos-Kerameus, Athanasios. "Συνοδικὰ γράμματα Ἰωάννου τοῦ Ἀποκαύκου, μητροπολίτου Ναυπάκτου." *Byzantis* 1 (1909): 3–30.
Patlagean, Evelyne. "L'histoire de la femme déguisée en moine et l'évolution de la sainteté féminine à Byzance." *Studi Medievali*, ser. 3, 17 (1976): 597–623.
Patrich, Joseph. *Sabas, Leader of Palestinian Monasticism: A Comparative Study in Eastern Monasticism, Fourth to Seventh Centuries*. Washington, DC: Dumbarton Oaks, 1995.
Perreault, Jacques Y., ed. *Les femmes et le monachisme byzantin/Women and Byzantine Monasticism: Actes du Symposium d'Athènes, 1988*. Athens: Institut canadien d'archéologie à Athénes, 1991.
Peters-Custot, Annick. *Les grecs de l'Italie méridionale post-byzantine (IXe–XIVe siècle): Une acculturation en douceur*. Rome: École française de Rome, 2009.
Philippidis-Braat, Anna. "La captivité de Palamas chez les Turcs: Dossier et commentaire." *Travaux et Mémoires* 7 (1979): 109–221.
Power, Eileen. *Medieval English Nunneries, c. 1275–1535*. Cambridge: Cambridge University Press, 1922.
Pratsch, Thomas. *Der hagiographische Topos: Griechische Heiligenviten in mittelbyzantinischer Zeit*. Berlin: De Gruyter, 2005.
———. *Theodoros Studites: Zwischen Dogma und Pragma*. Frankfurt: P. Lang, 1998.
Quasten, Johannes. *Patrology*. 3 vols. Westminster, MD: Newman Press, 1960.

Ragia, Ephe. *Λάτρος: Ένα άγνωστο μοναστικό κέντρο στη δυτική Μικρά Ασία, με λεπτομερή σχολιασμό των εγγράφων του αρχείου της μονής Θεοτόκου του Στύλου.* Thessalonike: Ekdotikos Oikos Antone Stamoule, 2008.

Rapp, Claudia. "Figures of Female Sanctity: Edifying Manuscripts and Their Audience." *Dumbarton Oaks Papers* 50 (1996): 313–44.

Riehle, Alexander. "Theodora Raulaina als Stifterin und Patronin." In Theis, Mullett, and Grünbart, *Female Founders in Byzantium and Beyond*, 299–315.

Ringrose, Kathryn. *The Perfect Servant: Eunuchs and the Social Construction of Gender in Byzantium.* Chicago: University of Chicago Press, 2003.

Rochow, Ilse. "Die Vita der Euphrosyne der Jüngeren, das späteste Beispiel des Motivs der weiblichen Transvestitentums (*monachoparthenia*) in der byzantinischen Hagiographie." In *Mir Aleksandra Kazhdana: K 80-lettiiu so dnia rozhdenniia*, edited by Aleksandra A. Chekalova, 259–71. St. Petersburg: Aleteiia, 2003.

Rodley, Lyn. "Evergetis, Where It Was and What It Looked Like." In *The Theotokos Evergetis and Eleventh-Century Monasticism*, edited by Margaret Mullett and Anthony Kirby, 17–29. Belfast: Belfast Byzantine Enterprises, School of Greek, Roman and Semitic Studies, the Queen's University of Belfast, 1994.

Rubin, Rehav. "The *Melagria*: On Anchorites and Edible Roots in Judaean Desert." *Liber Annuus* 52 (2002): 347–52.

Safran, Linda. *The Medieval Salento: Art and Identity in Southern Italy.* Philadelphia: University of Pennsylvania Press, 2014.

Soustal, Peter, ed. *Heilige Berge und Wüsten: Byzanz und sein Umfeld. Referate auf dem 21. Internationalen Kongress für Byzantinistik. London, 21.–26. August 2006.* Vienna: Österreichische Akademie der Wissenschaften, 2009.

Speake, Graham. *Mount Athos: Renewal in Paradise.* New Haven, CT: Yale University Press, 2002.

Stramara, Daniel F. "Double Monasticism in the Greek East, Fourth through Eighth Centuries." *Journal of Early Christian Studies* 6, no. 2 (1998): 269–312.

Sullivan, Denis. "The Versions of the Vita Niconis." *Dumbarton Oaks Papers* 32 (1978): 159–73.

Taft, Robert F. *A History of the Liturgy of St. John Chrysostom*. Vol. 6, *The Communion, Thanksgiving, and Concluding Rites*. Rome: Pontificio istituto orientale, 2008.

Talbot, Alice-Mary. "The Adolescent Monastic in Middle and Late Byzantium." In *Coming of Age in Byzantium: Adolescence and Society*, edited by Despoina Ariantzi, 83–97. Berlin: De Gruyter, 2018.

———. "Affirmative Action in the 13th Century: An Act of John Apokaukos concerning the Blachernitissa Monastery in Arta." In *Philellen: In Honour of Robert Browning*, edited by Costas Constantinidis et al., 399–409. Venice: Istituto ellenico di studi bizantini e postbyzantini di Venezia, 1996.

———. "Agricultural Properties in Palaiologan Constantinople." In *Koinotaton Doron: Das späte Byzanz zwischen Machtlösigkeit und kultureller Blüte (1204–1461)*, edited by Albrecht Berger et al., 185–95. Berlin: De Gruyter, 2016.

———. "Bluestocking Nuns: Intellectual Life in the Convents of Late Byzantium." In *Okeanos: Essays Presented to Ihor Ševčenko on His Sixtieth Birthday by His Colleagues and Students [= Harvard Ukrainian Studies 7 (1983)]*, edited by Cyril Mango and Omeljan Pritsak, 604–18. Cambridge, MA: Ukrainian Research Institute, Harvard University, 1983.

———. "Building Activity in Constantinople under Andronikos II: The Role of Women Patrons in the Construction and Restoration of Monasteries." In *Byzantine Constantinople: Monuments, Topography and Everyday Life*, edited by Nevra Necipoğlu, 329–43. Leiden: Brill, 2001.

———. "The Byzantine Family and the Monastery." *Dumbarton Oaks Papers* 44 (1990): 119–29.

———. "Byzantine Women, Saints' Lives, and Social Welfare." In *Through the Eye of a Needle: Judeo-Christian Roots of Social Welfare*, edited by Emily A. Hanawalt and Carter Lindberg, 105–22. Kirksville, MO: The Thomas Jefferson University Press, 1994; reprinted in Talbot, *Women and Religious Life in Byzantium*, essay II.

———. "Caves, Demons and Holy Men." In *Le saint, le moine et le paysan: Mélanges d'histoire byzantine offerts à Michel Kaplan*, edited by Olivier Delouis, Sophie Métivier, and Paule Pagès, 707–18. Paris: Publications de la Sorbonne, 2016.

---. "Children, Healing Miracles, Holy Fools: Highlights from the Hagiographical Works of Philotheos Kokkinos (1300–ca. 1379)." *Bulletin of the Bysantinska Sällskapet* 24 (2006): 48–64.

---. "A Comparison of the Monastic Experience of Byzantine Men and Women." *Greek Orthodox Theological Review* 30 (1985): 1–20.

---. "The Compositional Methods of a Palaiologan Hagiographer: Intertextuality in the Works of Theoktistos the Stoudite." In *Imitatio—Aemulatio—Variatio: Akten des internationalen wissenschaftlichen Symposions zur byzantinischen Sprache und Literatur (Wien, 22.–25. Oktober 2008)*, edited by Andreas Rhoby and Elisabeth Schiffer, 253–59. Vienna: Österreichische Akademie der Wissenschaften, 2010.

---. "The Conversion of Byzantine Monasteries from Male to Female and Vice-Versa." In *ΠΟΛΥΠΛΕΥΡΟΣ ΝΟΥΣ: Miscellanea für Peter Schreiner zu seinem 60. Geburtstag*, edited by Cordula Scholz and Georgios Makris, 360–64. Munich: Saur, 2000.

---. "Empress Theodora Palaiologina, Wife of Michael VIII." *Dumbarton Oaks Papers* 46 (1992): 295–303.

---. "Fact and Fiction in the *Vita* of the Patriarch Athanasios I of Constantinople by Theoktistos the Stoudite." In *Les Vies des saints à Byzance: Genre littéraire ou biographie historique? Actes du IIe colloque international philologique. Paris, 6-7-8 juin 2002*, edited by Paolo Odorico and Panagiotis Agapitos, 87–101. Paris: Centre d'études byzantines, néo-helléniques et sud-est européennes, 2004.

---. *Faith Healing in Late Byzantium: The Posthumous Miracles of the Patriarch Athanasios I of Constantinople by Theoktistos the Stoudite*. Brookline, MA: Hellenic College Press, 1983.

---. "Family Cults in Byzantium: The Case of Theodora of Thessalonike." In *ΛΕΙΜΩΝ: Studies Presented to Lennart Rydén on His Sixty-Fifth Birthday*, edited by Jan Olof Rosenqvist, 49–69. Uppsala: Uppsala University, 1996.

---. "Female Patronage in the Palaiologan Era: Icons, Minor Arts and Manuscripts." In Theis, Mullett, and Grünbart, *Female Founders in Byzantium and Beyond*, 259–74.

---. "Female Pilgrimage in Late Antiquity and the Byzantine Era." *Acta Byzantina Fennica*, n.s., 1 (2002): 73–88.

---. "Late Byzantine Nuns: By Choice or Necessity?" *Byzantinische Forschungen* 9 (1985): 103–17.

---. "Personal Poverty in Byzantine Monasticism: Ideals and Reality." In *Mélanges Cécile Morrisson* [= *Travaux et Mémoires*, 16], 829–41. Paris: Association des Amis du Centre d'Histoire et Civilisation de Byzance, 2010.

---. "Une riche veuve de la fin du XIe siècle: Le testament de Kalè Pakourianè." In *Impératrices, princesses, aristocrates et saintes souveraines*, edited by Elisabeth Malamut and Andreas Nicolaïdès, 201–15. Aix-en-Provence: Presses universitaires de Provence, 2014.

---. "Les saintes montagnes à Byzance." In *Le sacré et son inscription dans l'espace à Byzance et en Occident*, edited by Michel Kaplan, 263–75. Paris: Publications de la Sorbonne, 2001.

---. "Two Accounts of Miracles at the Pege Shrine in Constantinople." In *Mélanges Gilbert Dagron* [= *Travaux et Mémoires* 14], edited by Vincent Deroche, Denis Feissel, et al., 605–15. Paris: Association des Amis du Centre d'Histoire et Civilisation de Byzance, 2002.

---. *Women and Religious Life in Byzantium*. Aldershot: Ashgate, 2001.

Tanner, Norman P., ed. *Decrees of the Ecumenical Councils*. 2 vols. London: Sheed and Ward, 1990.

Theis, Lioba, Margaret Mullett, and Michael Grünbart, eds. *Female Founders in Byzantium and Beyond* [= *Wiener Jahrbuch für Kunstgeschichte*, 60/61]. Vienna: Böhlau Verlag, 2011/12.

Theocharides, Georgios, ed. *Μία διαθήκη καὶ μία δίκη βυζαντινή: ἀνέκδοτα βυζαντινὰ ἔγγραφα τοῦ ΙΔ΄ αἰῶνος περὶ τῆς Μονῆς Προδρόμου Βεροίας*. Thessalonike: Hetaireia Makedonikon Spoudon, 1962.

Thomas, John. *Private Religious Foundations in the Byzantine Empire*. Washington, DC: Dumbarton Oaks, 1987.

Tougher, Shaun. "The Angelic Life: Monasteries for Eunuchs." In *Byzantine Style, Religion and Civilisation, in Honour of Sir Steven Runciman*, edited by Elizabeth Jeffreys, 238–51. Cambridge: Cambridge University Press, 2006.

---. *The Eunuch in Byzantine History and Society*. London: Routledge, 2008.

---. *Eunuchs in Antiquity and Beyond*. London: Classical Press of Wales and Duckworth, 2002.

Trone, Robert. "A Constantinopolitan Double Monastery of the Fourteenth Century: The Philanthropic Savior." *Byzantine Studies/Etudes byzantines* 10 (1983): 81–87.

Warren, Ann K. *Anchorites and Their Patrons in Medieval England.* Berkeley: University of California Press, 1985.
Wilson, Nigel. *Scholars of Byzantium.* Rev. ed. London: Duckworth, 1996.
Wortley, John. "Grazers (βοσκοί) in the Judaean Desert." In *The Sabaite Heritage in the Orthodox Church from the Fifth Century to the Present,* edited by Joseph Patrich, 37–48. Leuven: Uitgeveij Peeters en Departement Oosterse Studies, 2000.
Zekos, Nikos. *Παπίκιον Ορος: αρχαιολογικός οδηγός.* Makedonia: Synolo/ Ekdoses Periphereia An. Makedonias-Thrakes, 2001.

INDEX

abaton, principle of, 79–82
abbesses, 84, 90, 100
Abrahamse, Dorothy, 59, 73
acorns, as food for hermits, 108, 111, 116, 118–19
adelphaton (food allowance), 120, 177
akedia (depression), 29, 124, 132, 187
Anastasia Patrikia, nun disguised as monk, 169
anchoresses. *See* recluses
anchoritism, 2
Ancrene Wisse (*Guide for Anchoresses*), 135
Andrew in Krisei, St., convent of (CP), 88, 91
Andrew the Fool, St., 11, 165
animals, female domestic, banned at Stoudios, 19–20
Anna, abbess of convent of St. Stephen (Thessalonike), 56
Anna-Euphemianos, St., nun disguised as monk, 169–71
Anthony IV, patriarch of CP, 42
Anthony the Great, St., 2, 102
Anthony the Younger, St., 139
Anthousa of Mantineon, St., double monastery of, 87, 94

Antonios, recluse in Peloponnesos, 139
Apokaukos, John, metropolitan of Naupaktos, 77–78
archaeology, as source for monasticism, 13–14
Areia, monastery of, 40
Arsenios, superior of St. Mamas monastery, 45
Arsenios Autoreianos, patriarch of CP, 94
Arsenios the Great, St., *vita* of, 90
Aspietissa, Pheronike, unaffiliated nun, 179
Athanasia of Aegina, St., 217n9
Athanasios I, patriarch of CP, 89
monastery of (on Xerolophos, in CP), 89, 94–96
Nea Mone, double monastery on Mount Ganos, 94–95
typikon of, 229n183
vita of, 11
as wandering monk, 162–63
Athanasios of Athos, St., 25–38, 104–5
biography of, 26–37
conversion to cenobitic ideal, 34
as copyist of manuscripts, 238n106

283

Athanasios of Athos, St. (*continued*)
  image of, 27 fig. 3
  nun as foster mother, 176–77
  vitae of, 11, 193
Athanasios of Meteora, St., 121
Athos, Mount, 4, 105–7, 109–11
  archaeological evidence from, 13–14
  archives of, 6, 12
  ascent of, 122, 127
  biodiversity of, 118
  early monasticism on, 28–29
  geography of, 25–26
Attaleiates, Michael, 46–47
Auxentios, Mount St., 3, 103, 115, 136
Auxentios, St., Syrian monk, 3, 136

Bačkovo, monastery of, prohibition of eunuch monks, 45
Balsamon, Theodore, canonist, 53, 72, 100, 167, 191, 192
Basil, St., convent of (CP), 89
Basil of Caesarea, St., rules of, 2, 5, 157
Basil the Younger, St., 11, 166, 183–85
"Basilian Order," 5
beards for monks (in West), 50
Bebaia Elpis, convent of (CP). *See* Sure Hope (*Bebaia Elpis*), convent of
Beck, Hans-Georg, 50, 133
bell towers, rooms reserved for recluses, 144

Benedict of Nursia, St., 4
Benedictine Rule, 4, 48
Benedictines, monastic order, 4
Blachernitissa, monastery of (Arta), 77–78
  fresco at, 72
Blasios of Amorion, St., 117, 127
Boreine, monastery of. *See* Skoteine [Boreine], monastery of
boskoi, "grazers," 106–7, 119
Bryer, Anthony, 8

candles, manufacture of, 88
Carthage, Council of, 53
Cassian, John, 4
caves as hermitages, 107–9, 111, 112
cenobitism
  advantages of, 104, 189, 191–93, 194
  disadvantages of, 194
Chalcedon, Council of (451), 3
Charanis, Peter, 8
charitable activities, 37, 189
  of nunneries, 59, 99
  of pious matrons, 188
  superiority to asceticism, 195
Chariton, superior of Koutloumousiou monastery, 42
Charsianeites, monastery of (CP), 41, 192
choir monitor (*taxiarches*), 23
choir sisters, 83–84
Chomatenos, Demetrios, 194

Chonai, church of St. Michael, 160, 161, 187
Choumnaina, Irene-Eulogia, abbess, 81, 96–97
  spiritual director of, 186
Christ Panoiktirmon, monastery of (CP), 46
Christ Philanthropos, convent of (CP)
  cenobitic ideals, 67–68
  as double monastery, 96–97, 217n7
Christ the Savior, monastery of (Mount Galesion), 47, 52
Christodoulos, monastery of (Patmos), 45, 113, 124, 197
Cistercians, monastic order, 4
cisterns, 121–22
Constable, Giles, 48, 50
Constantine V Kopronymos, emperor, 137
Constantine IX Monomachos, emperor, *typikon* of, 44
Constantinou, Stavroula, 11
convents. *See* nunneries
conversion of male to female monasteries (and vice versa), 76–78
conversion of Muslims, 159
cowherds (on Athos), 117
Crete, 29, 30
Cyril of Skythopolis, 193
Cyril Phileotes, St., monk, 124, 186–88, 196
  criticism of wandering monks, 158–59

Damilas, convent of (Crete), 87, 88, 92
Damilas, Neilos, monastic founder, 89–90, 92
Daniel, unaffiliated hieromonk, 185
David of Lesbos, St., hermit, 127–28, 234n32
Dembińska, Maria, 50
Demetrios, hermit on Mount Latros, 108
Demetrios Hephaistos, eunuch, 47
Diabatene, Xene, nun, 175
disciples of elderly hermit, 112, 120–21
  abuse of, 120–21
Docheiariou, Athonite monastery, 42
Dominicans, monastic order, 4
dormitories, communal
  in Byzantium, 49–50, 56, 71–72
  in West, 21, 49, 67
Dumbarton Oaks Hagiography Database, 12

edible wild plants, 118–19
Egypt, early monasticism in, 2
ekklesiarchissa, 70, 85, 86
Elias, eleventh-century mendicant monk, 162
enclosure, rule of, 79–81, 135
  stricter rule for nuns, 80
endemousa synodos (standing synod), 225n126
Epitimia (Penances) of Theodore of Stoudios, 22–24

eremitism, 2
  eremitic lifestyle, 113–29
  spiritual advantages of, 131, 190, 195
  spiritual disadvantages, 125, 131–32, 189, 196, 197
  varieties of, 111–13
  See also hermits
Eucharist, hermits' access to, 125–128, 130, 153
Eulogia, Palaiologan nun, 224n98
eulogiai (tokens of spiritual blessing), 124, 237n73
eunuchs, 43–47
  acceptance of eunuch monks, 43–46
  decline of, in Palaiologan era, 213n125
  monasteries restricted to eunuchs, 46–47
  prohibition of eunuch monks, 43–45
  as staff at nunneries, 47, 82–83
Euphemia, ninth-century recluse, 145
Euphrosyne the Younger, St., 130–31
  as nun disguised as monk, 169, 171–72
  as recluse, 145–46
  vita by Nikephoros Kallistos Xanthopoulos, 241n146
Eustathios, recluse in village of Tzoullos, 241n5
Eustathios of Thessalonike, 155–56
Euthymios, patriarch of CP, 138–39, 195

Euthymios the Great, St., 232n14
Euthymios the Younger, St., 94, 105–8, 112, 197
  on Athos, 105–7
  founder of double monastery, 94
  as recluse, 137
  as stylite in Thessalonike, 107
Evaristos, St., 185
  as recluse, 138
Evergetis, monastery of. *See* Theotokos Evergetis, monastery of

family ties in monasteries, 65–66, 176, 187
fires for cooking, 122–23
fishing, 119, 120, 124, 152
flintstone, 122–23, 124
Franciscans, monastic order, 4

Galesion, Mount, 4, 131
  eunuchs on, 47
  hermitess on, 131
  idiorrhythmia at, 40
  stylites on, 152–55
Ganos, Mount, 94, 109, 163
gatekeeper (*pyloros*), 85, 86
Gennadios, monk in CP, 181
George, bishop of Mytilene, St., 233n16
Gerbenites, Nephon, pedophile monk, 194
geron (monastic elder), 36, 105, 106, 120, 121, 132
goat-hair tunics, 123
great habit (*megaloschemos*), 161

Great Lavra, Athonite monastery, 15–16, 25–38
  becomes idiorrhythmic, 42
  commercial activity at, 35
  foundation of, 29–33
  prohibition of eunuchs, 44
  size of, 31, 34, 37
  Stoudite influence on, 32–33, 34
  transformation to cenobitic monastery, 32, 34
  typikon of (ca. 973–75), 34, 35
Gregory, disciple of Romylos of Vidin, 120, 125
Gregory, *geron* of Athanasios of Meteora, 121
Gregory II of Cyprus, patriarch of CP, 91
Gregory of Akritas, St., 138
Gregory of Sinai, St., hesychast monk, 111, 126, 196

hagiography, as source on monasticism, 10–12, 54
handwork (*ergocheiron*), 87–89
hardtack/rusks (*paxamatia*), 108, 116, 121
hermitesses, 130–31
hermits, 101–32
  affiliated with *lavra*, 120
  asceticism of, 102
  clothing, 123
  criticism of, 193
  food, 116–21
  material possessions, 123–24
  pairs of, 106–7, 108–9, 112, 132
  relationship with nature, 128–29
  shelter, 113–16
  spiritual life, 125–28
  water supply, 121–22
  See also eremitism
hesychasm, 126–27
hieromonk, 48, 182, 185, 194
Hierotheos, hieromonk and holy fool, 166
Hilaria of Lesbos, recluse, 145
holy fools, 163, 165–69
  criticism of, 166–67
Holy Mountain. *See* Athos, Mount
holy mountains, 3–4, 103
  restrictions on women, 76
  See also Athos, Mount; Auxentios, Mount St.; Galesion, Mount; Ganos, Mount; Kyminas, Mount; Latros, Mount; Olympos, Mount; Papikion, Mount
homosexuality, 194
honey, wild, 119
hood, monastic (*koukoulion*), 73, 123
Hosios Loukas, monastery of, 51
house nunneries, 173–76
hunters, 116, 130, 211n84
Hypatia-Febronia, nun in house nunnery (CP), 174
hyperpyra, coins, 42

iconoclasm, 18
Ignatios, patriarch of CP, 43
Ignatios Theologites, monk in CP, 97–98
individualism in Byzantium, 51, 133, 190–91, 211–12n96, 255n11

Ioacheim of Zichna, monastic founder, 9
Ioannikios, hieromonk of Peribleptos monastery (CP), 182
Ioannikios of Bithynia, St., 112, 129, 196, 231n6
  as recluse, 137–38
Irene, empress, 16
Irene, nun on Mount Galesion, 131
Irene Doukaina, empress, 66
  typikon for Kecharitomene convent, 55
Irene of Chrysobalanton, St., abbess, 81, 83, 90, 230n198
Isaiah, recluse in tower of Nikomedeia, 241n3
Isaiah of Nineveh, 158
Isbes, Gregory, Athonite monk, 42
Ivanov, Sergei, 165

Janin, Raymond, 8
Jerusalem *typikon* of St. Sabas, 20
John, hermit on Mount St. Auxentios
  as *geron* of Stephen the Younger, 121
  as recluse, 136
John I Tzimiskes, emperor, 36
  typikon of (*Tragos*), 29, 36–37, 44, 157
John of the Ladder, monastic writer, 115
John Prodromos, St., monastery of (Mount Menoikeion), 9
John the Theologian, St., monastery of (Patmos)
  prohibition of eunuch monks, 45
  rules for *kelliotai*, 113, 124, 197
Joseph, Athonite hermit, 106–7
Joseph the Hymnographer, St., as recluse, 242n20
Judean Desert, 40, 106, 119, 130, 159

Kaloeidina, Hypomone, unaffiliated nun, 180
Kalothetina, Hypomone, unaffiliated nun, 179
Kanabina, Martha, unaffiliated nun, 180–81
Kantakouzene, Theodosia, foundress of hospice, 181
Kappadokes, unaffiliated monk, 185
Karya, monastery of (Mount Latros), 108
Karyes, Athonite monastery, 28–29
katholikon, monastic church, 6
Kaukanina, Hypomone Chrysokephalina, unaffiliated nun, 180
Kazhdan, Alexander, xii, 133, 191
Kecharitomene, convent of (CP)
  burial at, 224n103
  communal dormitory, 67
  female staff, 85
  privileges of imperial relatives, 67
  rule on visitation of relatives, 79–81
Kellibara, *lavra* of (Mount Latros), 108
kellion (cell, hut), 106

kelliotai (groups of hermits), 37, 41, 53, 106–9, 113, 193, 197, 240n131
  criticism of, 193
Kerykos, stylite on Mount Galesion, 154–55
Kleraina, convent of (CP), 79, 89, 226–27n142
Komnene, Anna, historian, 91, 220n41
Komnenos, Isaak, founder of Kosmosoteira monastery, 45
Kosmosoteira, monastery of, 45
  prohibition of eunuch monks, 45
Koutloumousiou, Athonite monastery, 42
Kyminas, Mount, 4, 28, 104

Latros, Mount, 4
lavra, 3, 28, 113, 116
Lazaros, St., monastery of (CP), 46
Lazaros of Galesion, St.
  foundation of monasteries on Mount Galesion, 152–54
  as stylite, 152–55
  as wandering monk, 160–62
Leo, bishop of Argos, 77
Leo Luke of Corleone, Italo-Greek monk, 158
library
  at convent of Damilas, 90
  at Stoudios, 23–24
Lincoln College Typikon, 60–62, 66. *See also* Sure Hope (*Bebaia Elpis*), convent of
Lips, convent of (CP), 56–59
  hospice at, 59
  image of, 57 fig. 4
  as mausoleum for Palaiologoi, 58
  typikon of, 57–59
literacy of nuns, 226n130
liturgical books, 125, 175
liturgical vessels, 175
liturgy, celebration of
  for cenobitic monks, 1, 9, 20, 38, 103
  for hermits, 127–28, 131
  at *lavrai*, 3, 105, 113, 116, 127
Luke of Steiris, St., 122, 124, 128, 129, 148, 235n46
  spiritual devotions, 126
  vita of, 11
Luke the Stylite, St., 148, 150–52
  image, 151 fig. 10
  as recluse, 150
  as stylite, 150–52
Lyon, Council of, 58

Makrina, nun in CP, 97–98
Makrina, sister of Gregory of Nyssa, 11, 173–74
Makrosina (near Hierissos), 117
male and female monasteries,
  comparison of, 69–72
  difference in iconographic programs, 72
  difference in locations, 73–76
  similarities in rules, 69–71
  similarity in physical structure, 71–72
Maleinos, Michael, St., abbot of Kyminas, 28, 104
Mamas, St., monastery of (CP), 45

manual labor
　in convents, 86–89
　at Great Lavra, 35–36, 88
　for hermits and their disciples, 124–25
　at Stoudios, 19–20, 24
Manuel II Palaiologos, emperor, *typikon* of, 42
manuscripts, copying of, 1, 19, 24, 29, 34, 91, 124, 126, 136
Marina, unaffiliated nun, 179
Markelos, monk at Xeropotamou monastery, 177
Maroules, Germanos, Athonite monk, 124–25
Maroules, monastery in CP, 72
Martha, unaffiliated nun in CP, 181
Martha Syriana, nun in CP, 78
Mary-Marinos, St., nun disguised as monk, 169
Mary of Egypt, St., 11, 130
Mary the Younger, St., 188
Matrona of Perge, St., nun disguised as monk, 169, 241n150
Matthew, hermit on Mount Latros, 108
Matthew I, patriarch of CP, 41, 192
Maximos, founder of Boreine monastery, 191–92
Maximos the Hutburner, St., Athonite hermit, 104, 109–11, 115, 126–27, 193
　as holy fool, 168
　image, 110 fig. 7
　as wandering monk, 160

meat, consumption of, 50
melagria (asphodel), 119
Melana (on Athos), 29, 31
Merkourios, stylite on Mount Galesion, 154
metanoiai (prostrations), 22
Methodios, unaffiliated monk in CP, 186
metochia (satellite monasteries), 49, 51, 211n82
Michael VIII Palaiologos, emperor, 58–59
Mighty Savior (*Soter Krataios*), convent of (CP), 90
millet, 117, 119
minuscule script, 24
Mitsiou, Ekaterini, 253n183
monasteries
　cenobitic, 2, 15–52
　double, 93–98, 173
　idiorrhythmic, 39–43, 49
　imperial, 7
　location of, 76–78
　numbers of, 7–8, 73–76
　patriarchal, 7
　private, 7
　size of, 7
monastic diet, 50
monastic habit (*schema*), 72–73
monastic orders, absent in Byzantium, 50–51, 52. *See also* "Basilian Order"
monastic stability (*stabilitas loci*), 48, 78–79, 129, 135
　in convents, 158, 164
　rejection of, 156–57
monastic vocations, involuntary, 64–65

monasticism
  Eastern and Western, comparison of, 4, 48–52
  origins of, 2–5
monks, unaffiliated, 183–86
Monte Cassino, 4
Morris, Rosemary, 51
Mylopotamos, *metochion* of Great Lavra, 35

Naukratios, monk of Stoudios monastery, 6, 18
Nea Mone, double monastery on Mount Ganos, 94–95
Neilos I Kerameus, patriarch of CP, and division of double monastery of Athanasios I, 96
Neilos of Ankyra, 157
Neilos of Rossano, Italo-Greek monk, 40, 63, 123, 126, 129, 195
  as copyist of manuscripts, 238n106
Neoi, island of (near Athos), 35, 49
Neophytos the Recluse, St., 141–43
Nicholas the Stoudite, scribe, 24, 138
Nikephoros, bishop of Miletos, as eunuch monk, 46
Nikephoros I, patriarch of CP, 17, 93
Nikephoros II Phokas, emperor, 30–32
Nikephoros the Naked, monk, 36
Nikodemos of Thessalonike, St., holy fool, 168–69

Nikon, stylite on Mount Galesion, 154
Nikon of the Black Mountain, 41
Nikon the Metanoeite, St., 11
Niphon of Athos, St., 11, 119, 128, 196–97
nocturnal emissions, 47
nunneries, 53–100
  artistic production at, 91–92
  female staff, 83–86
  idiorrhythmic, 92–93
  literary production at, 90–91
  male staff, 81–83
  poverty of, 88–89
nuns, 53–100
  disguised as monks, 169–72
  dissolute, 182–83
  as donors to village churches, 76, 177
  rural, 76, 78, 177
Nymphodora, nun from Siderokausia, 177
  as donor to Xeropotamou, 177

octopus, 111, 119
Olympos, Mount, 3–4, 170
onion and bread soup, 111
Ormylia, convent of (Chalkidike), 87

Pachomios, St., 2
Pakouriane, Kale-Maria, nun in private house in CP, 174–76
Pakourianos, Gregory, founder of Bačkovo monastery, 45
Palamas, Gregory, St., 11, 176
Palestine, early monasticism in, 2, 4

Pantokrator, Athonite monastery, 42
Pantokrator, monastery of (CP), 51
Paphnoutios, hermit on Mount Galesion, 112, 119, 121, 134
Papikion, Mount, 14, 109
Paraskeve the Younger, St., 230–31n198
patriarchate of Constantinople, acts of, 10, 12–13, 80, 185
Paul, founder of Evergetis monastery (CP), 203n33
Paul of Atroa, 147
Paul of Corinth, holy fool, 165
Paul of Latros, St., 108–9, 112, 119, 122
  monastery of, 46
  as stylite, 150
Paul the First Hermit, 2
Pausoslype, convent of (CP), 78
Peristerai, double monastery at, 94, 107
Peter, abbot of Karya monastery (Mount Latros), 108
Peter, Athonite hermit, St., 193
Peter, brother of Gregory of Nyssa, 173
Petra, rock pillar on Mount Galesion, 154–55
Petraleiphina, Euphrosyne, unaffiliated nun in CP, 178
Phantinos, St., 36
Phialitissa, Zenobia, unaffiliated nun, 181
Philotheos, Athonite monk, 98
Philotheos, recluse in CP, 140

Philotheos Kokkinos, patriarch of CP, 125
Phoberos, monastery of, 194
pilgrimage, 32, 37, 48, 141, 143, 159, 160–61, 163, 164, 166, 187
  female, 80, 81, 164
pirates
  as threats to Athos, 29, 77
  as threats to nuns, 77
pita bread, 111, 119, 122
Plato of Sakkoudion, St., 138
Pouzoulou, Kallone, unaffiliated nun in CP, 181
poverty, monastic, 49, 178
Power, Eileen, 54
"prayer of the heart," 126–27
precentor (*kanonarches*), 20, 23

Raoulaina, Theodora, erudite nun, 91
recluses (*enkleistoi*), 107, 109, 112, 134–47
  compared with Western anchoresses/anchorites, 135–36
  female, 145–47
Resurrection, monastery of (Mount Galesion), 40
Robert de Clari, 156
Roidion, monastery of, 40–41
Romanos II, emperor, 31
Romylos of Vidin, St., hermit, 120, 122

Sabas, St., *lavra* of (Mar Saba), 3, 131, 161
  idiorrhythmia at, 40

Sabas the Younger, St., 125, 129, 197, 233n23
   as holy fool, 163, 167–68
   as recluse, 143–44, 163
   as wandering monk, 159, 163
sacristan (*skeuophylakissa*), 85
Sakkoudion, monastery of, 16, 18
Sarakatsanoi, nomadic shepherds, 115
Sarantenos, Theodore, will of, 227n151
scapular (*analabos, epomis*), 73, 123
schools, monastic, 48–49
scribes, 24
self-sufficiency, economic
   of convents, 86–89
   of Stoudios, 5, 19–20
shelter for hermits
   caves, 113–15
   huts made of grasses and twigs, 115
   huts made of stone, 116
   image, 114 fig. 8
Shenoute, abbot, 2
Skepe, monastery of (CP), 171
Skoteine [Boreine], monastery of, 41, 191, 212n104
slaves, banned at Stoudios, 19
sleepless monks (*akoimetoi*) at Stoudios, 20
springs, 122
Stephen, St., convent of (Thessalonike), 55–56
Stephen Neolampes, St., recluse in CP, 147
Stephen the Younger, St., 3, 115
   cell, 115
   clothing, 123
   as disciple of *geron* John, 121, 122
   as recluse, 136–37
steward (*oikonomos*)
   at convents, 44, 47, 50, 80–86 passim, 225n117
   at male monasteries, 7, 20, 51, 142, 238n107
Stoudios, monastery of, 15–25
   clothing, 20–21
   dietary regimen, 21–22
   economic self-sufficiency of, 19–20
   emphasis on manual labor, 19–20, 24
   forms of punishment, 22–24
   liturgy at, 20
   as model for Great Lavra, 19
   scriptorium, 23–24
   sleeping arrangements, 21
   typikon of, 18–19
Stoudite federation, 18, 19, 51
Strategopoulina, Anna Komnene Raoulaina, patroness, 90
stylite, female, 155
stylites (pillar saints), 2–3, 107, 147–56
   absence in West, 147
   in CP in thirteenth century, 156
   criticism of, 155–56
   in Syria, 149
Stylos, monastery of (Mount Latros), 50
Sure Hope (*Bebaia Elpis*), convent of, 9, 60–63
   cenobitic ideals, 67

Sure Hope (*Bebaia Elpis*) (*continued*)
  egalitarian regimen, 67
  female staff, 85–86
Symeon, metropolitan of Euchaita, 155
Symeon Eulabes, elder at Stoudios monastery, 21, 45–46
Symeon of Emesa, St., holy fool, 165, 233n21
Symeon of Lesbos, St., stylite, 149
Symeon the New Theologian, St., 21, 140, 166
  as eunuch monk, 45
Symeon the Sanctified, eunuch monk, 44–45
Symeon the Stylite the Elder, St., 2–3, 149
Symeon the Stylite the Younger, St., 149, 161
Synadene, Euphrosyne, nun in CP, 60, 64
  image, 62 fig. 6
Synadene, Theodora, foundress of Sure Hope convent, 9, 60–65, 66
  image, 62 fig. 6
  typikon for Sure Hope convent, 55
  See also Lincoln College Typikon
Synaxis, monastery of, 205n48
Syria, early monasticism in, 2–3

textile production, 87–89
Theodora of Thessalonike, St., 55–56, 64, 65–66, 68
Theodora Palaiologina, empress, 56–59, 64, 66
  typikon for Lips convent, 55
Theodore, bishop of Edessa, 149
Theodore, spiritual father of Euthymios the Younger, 117
Theodore of Kythera, St., 139
Theodore of Stoudios, St., 5, 6
  biography of, 16–18
  image of, 17 fig. 1
  rules for Stoudios, 5, 16, 18–25
  testament of, 6, 18
  vitae of, 11
Theodotos, monastic patron, 65
Theoktiste of Lesbos, St., 11, 130, 223n83
Theoleptos of Philadelphia, 97
Theophylact, archbishop of Ohrid, 47
Theopiste, abbess of convent of St. Stephen (Thessalonike), 56, 64–65
Theopiste, nun in Thessalonike, 64–65
Theotokos Evergetis, monastery of, 38–39
  typikon of, 9–10, 19, 38–39
Theotokos of the Pege, monastery of (CP), 145, 172
Thiniatissa, dissolute nun in CP, 182
Thomaïs, abbess of Pausolype convent (CP), 85
Thomaïs, godmother of George Sphrantzes, 79
Thomaïs of Lesbos, St., 188
Thomas, John, 5, 28, 32, 48, 51

Timothy, second founder of Evergetis monastery, 203n33
ton Abramiton, monastery of (CP), 171
transvestite nuns. *See* nuns: disguised as monks
Trichinarea, convent of (Mount St. Auxentios), 222n82, 242n10
typika (monastic rules), 5, 6–7
　intertextual borrowings, 51
　ktetorika, 8–9
　as sources for monasticism, 8–10, 54–55
Typika (selected psalms), 128
Tzouroulene, Theodoule, unaffiliated nun in CP, 180
Tzymypinissa, Elaiodora Sarantene, unaffiliated nun in Thessalonike, 179

vegetable garden, 117
veil, monastic (*maphorion*), 73
vinedresser, 83, 111
Virgin, double monastery of, in Neapolis (Kavalla), 98
Virgin Hodegetria, icon of, 72
Virgin of Sure Hope, icon of, 63
Vlachs, 115
　as shepherds on Athos, 42

wandering monks (*gyreutai, kykleutai*), 156–64
　charity toward, 159–60, 161–62
　criticism of, 157
　as fraudulent ascetics, 162
　motivations for wandering lifestyle, 159, 163–64
　prohibition of, 157
　sexual temptation of, 161
wandering nuns, rarity of, 164
water supply for hermits, 121–22
White Monastery (near Sohag, Egypt), 2
widows, 63–64
wild animals, taming of, 129
Wolflaicus, French stylite, 147

Xenophon, Athonite monastery, 44
xerophagia (punitive dietary regimen), 22
Xeropotamou, Athonite monastery, 28, 177

Zoe, nun in Thessaly, 63–64
Zygos, Athonite monastery, 29, 205n48

ALICE-MARY TALBOT is the editor of the Byzantine Greek series of the Dumbarton Oaks Medieval Library and director emerita of Byzantine Studies at Dumbarton Oaks. She is the author and editor of a number of books, including service as the executive editor of the three-volume *Oxford Dictionary of Byzantium*.

www.ingramcontent.com/pod-product-compliance
Lightning Source LLC
Chambersburg PA
CBHW061430300426
44114CB00014B/1624